The Structure of Investment Arbitration

Although a State's treatment of foreign investors has long been regulated by international law, it is only recently that international investment law has emerged as an independent discipline in its own right. In recent decades, the practical success of investment arbitration has allowed international investment law to develop both its own cadre of academic and professional specialists and its own legal doctrines. This book analyses the structure of international investment law, as it has developed through the practice of investment arbitration in order to see how a variety of international investment law doctrines should be understood and applied. The book demonstrates how a structural analysis can shed light on several major controversies within investment law and also examines what an 'investment' actually is. The book offers an original interpretative approach to the resolution of problems in international investment law, and so is one of the few books within the field to attempt to give investment law a solid theoretical basis. It also focuses on only a select number of problems, rather than attempting to deliver the universal coverage currently popular for investment law books. As a result, those issues that are addressed get a detailed discussion rarely available in competing texts.

Tony Cole is Senior Lecturer at Brunel Law School and Director of the Brunel Centre for the study of Arbitration and Cross-Border Investment. He works primarily in international arbitration and international investment law, and authors the blog, A Canon for Arbitration and Investment Law.

The Structure of Investment Arbitration

Tony Cole

Routledge
Taylor & Francis Group
LONDON AND NEW YORK

First published 2013
by Routledge
4 Park Square, Milton Park, Abingdon, Oxon OX14 4RN
605 Third Avenue, New York, NY 10017

Routledge is an imprint of the Taylor & Francis Group, an informa business

British Library Cataloguing in Publication Data
A catalogue record for this book is available from the British Library

Library of Congress Cataloguing in Publication Data
A catalog record for this book has been requested.

ISBN 978-0-415-57985-8 (hbk)
ISBN 978-0-203-75875-5 (ebk)

Typeset in Garamond
by Taylor & Francis Books

Contents

Detailed contents

Acknowledgements

Throughout this book are elements of the following previous publications:

Cole, T. & Kumar Vaksha, A. 2011 "Power-Conferring Treaties: The Meaning of 'Investment' in the ICSID Convention" 24(2) *Leiden Journal of International Law* 355.
– Reproduced with the kind permission of Cambridge University Press

Cole, T. 2012 "Non-Binding Documents and Literature", from International Investment Law: The Sources of Rights and Obligations (Eric De Brabandere and Tarcisio Gazzini eds.).
– Reproduced with the kind permission of Martinus Nijhoff Publishers

Cole, T. 2012 "The Boundaries of Most Favored Nation Treatment in International Investment Law", 33(3) *Michigan Journal of International Law* 537.
– Reproduced with the kind permission of the Michigan Journal of International Law

Cole, T. 2012 "ICS v. Argentina", 27(2) *ICSID Review – Foreign Investment Law Journal* 268.
– Reproduced with the kind permission of Oxford University Press

Introduction

International investment law is a very young discipline, with the length of its existence appropriately measured in years, rather than decades, let alone centuries. This being said, it is also the case that cross-border investment has been regulated by governments since the first ambitious trader moved to a foreign city to set up his own shop, rather than continuing to sell his goods to local traders, who would in turn sell them directly to customers. Understanding how these statements can simultaneously be true is essential for understanding the approach to analysing investment law that is adopted in this book.

The key is that while law regulating the conduct of cross-border investment has indeed existed for centuries, 'international investment law' existed until very recently only as a topic within public international law. It included the rules governing a particular factual context in which States interacted, but those rules were merely context-specific applications of the traditional rules governing State-State interaction more generally. Similarly, while the significant increase in cross-border investment that occurred in the twentieth century resulted in the production of the first specialised works on the regulation of international investment, those works were uniformly produced by specialists in public international law and reflected the traditional approach of studying international investment law as merely the context-specific application of the generally-applicable principles of public international law.

A fundamental change occurred, however, with the arrival of investment arbitration as the dominant mechanism for the resolution of cross-border investment disputes. Instances of investor-State arbitration had, of course, occurred throughout the twentieth century, and the adoption in 1966 of the Convention on the Settlement of Investment Disputes between States and Nationals of Other States ('ICSID Convention') had made investor-State arbitration both an acknowledged and even encouraged mechanism for the resolution of cross-border investment disputes. Nonetheless, despite this public endorsement by States of investor-State arbitration, the rarity with which such arbitrations took place prior to the 1990s, along with the consistent use of public international law specialists as arbitrators in investor-State disputes, meant that in reality arbitration had little real impact on the substantive development of international investment law.

In the final decade of the twentieth century, however, what could legitimately be called a 'revolution' occurred in international investment law, driven primarily by a sharp increase in the number of cross-border investment disputes resolved through investor-State arbitration. Arbitration tribunals, of course, do not bind other tribunals in their interpretations of the law, and so the mere fact that the direct involvement of private investors in arbitral proceedings allowed non-State entities to influence arbitrators' interpretations of the law could not in itself significantly alter the nature of international investment law. More important, then, was the development because of this increase in rates of investor-State arbitration of investment arbitration as a field of legal practice. For the first time, that is, a community of arbitrators, practitioners and commentators began to develop whose primary interest was in the development and application of the principles of international investment law *per se*, rather than in the application of public international law in the cross-border investment context. Public international law was certainly not ignored, of course, but it was for the first time approached as an external field that was applicable only when the rules of international investment law itself said public international law applied.

As a substantive field of law, then, contemporary international investment law had a fundamentally practical beginning. This beginning, however, is the direct source of one of the primary problems currently besetting the field. One of the unavoidable consequences of the emergence of any new field is that in its early days it has no solid theoretical grounding. A new field, after all, by definition can't simply invoke the same theoretical justifications that were used to justify the field or fields from which it developed, as any new field's existence as an independent topic of study and practice requires that it be substantively distinguishable from those older and more established fields. Moreover, while any new field of law will have some dedicated specialists working on the theoretical development of its foundations, any such efforts will unavoidably be handicapped by the fact that new fields do not emerge 'fully formed' from their parent disciplines, but begin their existence in a rapidly-changing and inherently-uncertain state. As a result, even the most dedicated commentator will be reduced to merely proposing an interpretation of the field's future form, rather than identifying with any precision the form it currently has.

This is the situation international investment law currently finds itself in. Moreover, the lack of development of international investment law at the moment of its 'birth' was magnified by the fact that it did not achieve its separation from public international law because of any recognition of its fundamental theoretical distinctness, but rather because of the development of investment arbitration as a field of legal practice. As a result, international investment law developed a life of its own long before the intellectual work necessary to give it any significant degree of coherence had been performed.

It is for this reason that the present book, while certainly directed by an overriding theoretical conception, is not intended to present a fully-formed theory of contemporary international investment law. Investment arbitration, quite simply, has not yet developed to a point at which any conclusive argument can be made for any particular theoretical interpretation. The field itself is simply too undeveloped and unpredictable. As a result, while the field certainly benefits from the work currently being done by the relatively small number of theoretically-informed commentators, all such work needs to be recognised as the provisional work that it is, rather than adopted, even by its most ardent proponents, as a justified interpretation of the field.

This being said, it nonetheless remains true that commentary unguided by any theoretical stance is ultimately blind. Consequently, while it may be impossible at the moment to present a truly justified theory of investment arbitration, any commentary should, at the very least, be clear about the theoretical foundations on which its analysis has been built. Honesty about this underlying theoretical stance will, after all, remove the veil of objectivity that would otherwise exist, and allow readers to evaluate the arguments being made with a full awareness of the background views on which they ultimately depend.

This book, then, is premised on the notion that the adoption in 1966 of the ICSID Convention has important implications for the substance of contemporary international investment law, despite the Convention's silence on questions of substantive law. In short, the adoption of the Convention constituted a form of 'constitutionalisation' of international investment law. However, whereas constitutionalisation is traditionally understood as involving the adoption of certain fundamental substantive laws, the adoption of the ICSID Convention constituted a purely procedural constitutionalisation: a dispute resolution procedure was adopted, but nothing was agreed about the substantive rules that tribunals operating as part of that dispute resolution system should apply. Nonetheless, the existence of the Convention requires a fundamental change in the method of analysis appropriate to questions in international investment law, even when the Convention itself is not directly implicated, and gives considerations of structure an importance that they do not normally have in more substantive constitutional regimes.

The Convention, that is, while clearly itself a treaty governed by the rules of public international law, was nonetheless not an attempt to provide a dispute resolution mechanism for the substantive rules of public international law. Instead, the adoption of the Convention was fundamentally premised on a recognition of public international law's failure to provide a workable system of international investment law. It included a procedure for the resolution of international investment disputes but entirely avoided mandating what law should or should not be applied in those disputes. The Convention, indeed, embodied a rejection of the very notion of a unitary regime of substantive international investment law, and endorsed instead what can be called a system of 'bounded anarchy'.

It is, of course, quite conventional to refer to public international law as an 'anarchic' system, characterised as it is by the lack of both a governing legislative body and an institution with the legitimate power to enforce those laws that exist.[1] The 'bounded' nature of the anarchy being attributed here to international investment law, then, is important to emphasise. In contrast to the genuine anarchy that characterises public international law, the incorporation of international arbitration into international investment law has created a legal system that includes enforceable restrictions on the freedom of States to act in whatever way they judge to be appropriate. Consent, of course, retains a central role in the application of those boundaries, as investment arbitration only takes place when both the investor and the State have agreed to arbitrate. Nonetheless, when investor-State arbitration moved from being merely a possible option for the resolution of international investment disputes to the accepted dispute resolution mechanism for the field, a structure was created in which the jurisprudence of arbitral tribunals is now the central means by which investment law is now developed.

The essential difference between the straightforward anarchy of public international law, then, and the bounded anarchy of international investment law, is the combination in the latter of a predesigned procedural structure and a substantive anarchy that exists within the boundaries set by that structure. However, the interrelation between these two aspects of international investment law must be stressed. The procedural structure of international investment law was not adopted in isolation from the substantive anarchy that it contains. As noted above, the ICSID Convention did not merely provide States and investors with a mechanism for resolving international investment disputes, it also reflected a particular stance on how international investment should be substantively regulated.

International arbitration, that is, was seen as a desirable mechanism for the resolution of international investment disputes precisely because it was clear that too much diversity existed amongst States on the substantive rules applicable to foreign investment for any regime of universally binding substantive law to be adopted. Adopting international arbitration as a dispute resolution mechanism, however, created a procedural structure that delivered effective enforcement but avoided the development of any universally binding substantive law. International arbitration, then, combined substantive anarchy and procedural enforceability in a way no other available dispute resolution mechanism could.

What matters for present purposes, however, is not the fact of international investment law's two-tiered structure, but the impact of that structure on the content of international investment law. In any anarchic system, after all, the social relations between participants achieve a central importance, as the lack of any coercive legal institutions means that only voluntary recognition of social obligations can generate binding legal rules. This 'social' approach to the generation of legal rules can be seen clearly in the traditionally anarchic system of public international law, in which universally-binding rules only develop through the recognition by States that certain behaviour is obligatory. When an anarchy is bounded, however, the importance of these socially derived rules is affected by the parallel importance of the structure within which those rules are permitted to develop. The constraining structure of the system both creates limits on the substantive rules that the participants are allowed to develop, and influences the interpretation that any rules developed must be given.

The chapters of this book, then, although addressing questions of substantive law, place particular emphasis on arguments concerning the procedural and other structures within which that law exists. Not every issue of substantive international investment law, of course, can be resolved by appealing to the structures within which that law exists, and no attempt is made here to provide a purely structure-focused analysis. However, ignoring issues of structure in a legal system designed to operate as a bounded anarchy results only in conclusions that are fundamentally unfaithful to the law, and unfair to those who must act within it.

In short, then, this is ultimately a modest book. It is not intended to deliver a fully realised theory of international investment law, and is also not intended to address every major area of contention within investment law. It is, instead, merely an exploration of a particular approach to the analysis of problems within international investment law, undertaken through the close examination of certain specific topics. The goal of the book, that is, is merely to demonstrate the usefulness of structural reasoning within international investment law, and it is not offered with the intention or expectation that it will fundamentally revolutionise the study of international investment law. It is, however, indicative of a much more ambitious project, of which this book merely forms the first exploratory step. Hopefully it is at least a helpful step, and will suffice until the next, more substantial, step is taken.

1 The meaning of 'investment' in the ICSID Convention[1]

1 Introduction

The preceding Introduction has developed an argument for attending to structural concerns when analysing issues within international investment arbitration, but no real evidence has yet been presented that doing so will actually yield important results. The current chapter is intended to provide an initial step towards producing this evidence, through a demonstration that attending to structure can provide significant insights into one of the most intractable problems in contemporary investment arbitration. Moreover, it will demonstrate that focusing on structure can produce important insights even when the only structures under consideration are those of a treaty, for the purpose of interpreting that treaty's terms.

The current chapter, that is, while intended to demonstrate the usefulness of structural analysis, is not an attempt to demonstrate every conceivable way in which attention to structure might influence the understanding that should be given to issues in international investment arbitration. It is instead a more modest analysis, undertaken within the confines of traditional treaty interpretation, and intended to show that attending to structure can yield important results even if the broader theoretical stance outlined in the Introduction is rejected.

As is well known, Article 25 of the ICSID Convention, which provides the jurisdictional boundaries of arbitration at the International Centre for Settlement of Investment Disputes (ICSID), restricts the use of ICSID's facilities to the resolution of 'legal dispute[s] arising directly out of an investment'.[2] Nowhere in the ICSID Convention, however, is any attempt made to clarify what the term 'investment' should be understood to mean, despite the role that the existence of an 'investment' plays as a precondition for an arbitration to be held at ICSID.

Attempts to address this topic, and thereby give some semblance of discernible meaning to the boundaries of the ICSID Convention, have taken widely divergent paths.[3] Some commentators and tribunals have turned to the *travaux préparatoires* of the Convention in the hope of determining what the Contracting States to the Convention may have understood the term 'investment' to mean at the time the Convention was adopted.[4] Others have proposed the adoption for the purposes of the Convention of a particular definition of 'investment' that is commonly used in some other context, on the ground that this definition is either likely to be what the Contracting States themselves originally had in mind, or is otherwise in some way just a desirable definition of the term.[5] Yet others have argued that the Contracting States deliberately avoided giving the term 'investment' any particular meaning, with the intention that the meaning of the term should be created anew for each dispute by a combination of arbitral tribunals and the parties participating in the arbitration.[6]

Of course, given the wide variety of divergent analyses that have been provided of this topic, some attention has certainly been paid to the structure of the ICSID Convention, and to how this structure might influence the proper understanding of the meaning of 'investment'. The goal of the current chapter, however, is to demonstrate that a more serious consideration of structure can provide greater insight into this question than has so far been gained through other methods. Specifically, it will argue that while commentators have been correct in focusing on the deliberate decision of the Contracting States not to adopt any specific understanding of the term 'investment' for the purposes of Article 25(1), they have not followed this insight far enough, as this recognition alone cannot provide the answer to how the term 'investment' should be interpreted.

This is because the decision not to imbue 'investment' with a specific meaning merely eliminates the need for arguments about what meaning the term was intended to have. This is a purely negative consequence. Further analysis is still required to determine the positive meaning the term should be understood to possess. Moreover, close attention to the structure of the ICSID Convention will more reliably provide insight into this positive meaning than will a focus on broad, generalising statements about the intentions of the Contracting States.

Central to the analysis being undertaken in this chapter is the notion that the ICSID Convention is properly understood as what can be called a 'power-conferring' treaty. That is, a treaty in which the Contracting States did not simply agree on a set of rules intended to govern their future interactions, but instead created a legal framework designed to allow entities other than the Contracting States themselves to exert significant control over the legal effects that the Convention will have. Once this aspect of the Convention is fully acknowledged, the essential question in interpreting the Convention becomes not what the 'intentions' of the Contracting States were with respect to any particular issue, but rather what the structural features of the Convention indicate about which entities were to have control over which aspects of the Convention, and precisely how much control they were delegated.

A power-conferring treaty, that is, by its nature is designed to operate to a significant degree beyond the control of the States that have created it. It is, in short, to some degree an autonomous creation, designed to develop in ways determined by its own internal structure, rather than in accordance with the specific intentions of the States that originally put it in motion. Because of this semi-autonomous nature of a power-conferring treaty, the intentions of the Contracting States to such a treaty are less significant in interpreting that treaty's terms than is the linguistic and legal structure within which those terms are designed to operate.[7]

The remainder of this chapter proceeds in three stages. Sections 2 and 3 will develop in more detail the idea of a power-conferring treaty, and the context in which the decision was taken to make the ICSID Convention a power-conferring treaty. Section 4 will then introduce the controversy that has developed regarding the interpretation of the term 'investment' in Article 25(1). Finally, the remainder of the chapter will then focus on specific aspects of the Convention, in order to determine what the Convention's structure dictates about how the term 'investment' in Article 25(1) should be understood.

2 Interpretation of power-conferring treaties

It is, of course, already standard in contemporary international law commentary to note that the latter part of the twentieth century has seen a move away from the traditional understanding of international law as solely based on the consent of States.[8] As just two examples, human rights obligations are now often recognised as binding even States that have signed no treaty acknowledging the existence of those obligations, and customary international law has in some contexts become more influential than treaties,[9] despite its ability to bind even States that have never agreed to the custom in question.[10]

Treaties, too, are recognised as having changed. They remain, of course, an agreement between States,[11] and as with any agreement the consent of the parties is determinative of both a treaty's existence and its content.[12] However, States have recently demonstrated an increasing willingness to place their treaty-making powers in the hands of other actors.[13] That is, while States have long used treaties as a means of promoting the interests of non-State entities judged to be of particular national importance,[14] contemporary treaty-making practice often allows non-State entities a more active role in the creation and even implementation of treaties than would previously have been viewed as acceptable.[15]

Nonetheless, despite these large-scale changes in the relevance of non-State entities to the treaty process, no significant change has occurred in how treaties are interpreted. Instead, no matter how central a role non-State entities may have played in both the creation and implementation of a treaty, any tribunal interpreting a treaty will apply the same set of rules, developed at a time that State control over the treaty process remained pervasive, and designed for a far more State-centred form of treaty than the tribunal is actually interpreting.[16]

Tribunals may, of course, adopt a teleological approach to the interpretation of treaty language if a treaty is seen as intended by the Contracting States to achieve certain goals not easily captured by precise language.[17] However, even a teleological approach to treaty interpretation remains fundamentally focused on the Contracting States, and so is simply unable to capture accurately the reality of a treaty in which non-State entities play a significant role. The tribunal, after all, merely understands the Contracting States as having granted it the authority to fashion its own rules to achieve the treaty's goals, rather than viewing the treaty as designed to operate in accordance with some standard other than the 'object and purpose' of the Contracting States.[18]

Power-conferring treaties, however, do not merely entrust tribunals with the power to fashion the means by which the treaty's goals should be achieved. Rather, the semi-autonomous manner in which a power-conferring treaty is designed to function entails that the intentions of the Contracting States are relevant only with respect to ascertaining the structure through which the treaty is designed to operate. Those intentions are not determinative of the specific legal rules that the treaty contains. As a result, an emphasis in treaty interpretation on the 'object and purpose' of a power-conferring treaty, despite being dictated by the rules of the Vienna Convention on the Law of Treaties (VCLT),[19] will actually generate an interpretation inconsistent with the treaty as it should properly be understood.

This does not, of course, mean that considerations such as the 'object and purpose' of the Contracting States are irrelevant when interpreting a power-conferring treaty. Power-conferring treaties remain treaties, and hence their interpretation is governed by the rules of customary international law reflected in the VCLT.[20] However, the relevance of the traditional rules captured in the VCLT is restricted to determining the structure of the treaty, including the determination of which elements of the treaty are power-conferring, and which powers are and are not conferred. They cannot then be used to determine substantive questions of the meaning of the treaty, without at least being subjected to the moderating effect of the treaty's power-conferring nature.

A power-conferring treaty, after all, by its nature has a different relationship to any possible goals of the Contracting States than does a normal treaty. Indeed, one of its primary purposes is to facilitate the actions of third parties, thereby allowing those third parties to achieve their own goals through the mechanisms put into place by the treaty. Because of this, close attention must be paid when interpreting a power-conferring treaty to determining precisely which powers have been conferred on which parties, in order to ensure that the interpretation derived achieves the correct balance between adherence to the intentions of the Contracting States, and adherence to the substantive choices of those entities on whom powers have been conferred.

At the most basic level, then, recognition that a treaty is power-conferring entails that some aspects of the treaty that would ordinarily have been given an interpretation designed to achieve the goals of the Contracting States when entering into the treaty, must instead be given an interpretation that will effectively implement the decisions taken by one or more non-parties to the treaty. Moreover, this must be done even when the decisions in question will generate a result seemingly inconsistent with the goals of the Contracting States. By creating a power-conferring treaty, the Contracting States have created a semi-autonomous legal structure, and have thereby given away at least part of their control over the results that the structure generates.

With respect to the ICSID Convention, for example, the object and purpose of the Convention has often been described in terms such as 'to promote the flow of private investment to contracting countries by provision of a mechanism which, by enabling international settlement of disputes, conduces to the security of such investment'.[21] Applying the rules of the VCLT in accordance with this understanding of the Convention's object and purpose would seem to justify giving an expansive interpretation to the Convention's vague jurisdictional provisions. After all, the Convention cannot help promote the security of private investment if ICSID tribunals only accept jurisdiction over a small range of cases that meet a narrow definition of 'investment'.

If the ICSID Convention is recognised as power-conferring, however, this description of its object and purpose becomes less clearly relevant to the interpretation of all of its provisions. Promoting the private flow of investment may have been a goal of the Contracting States in entering into the Convention, but if, for example, powers to constrain ICSID jurisdiction have been conferred on entities other than the Contracting States, that goal clearly cannot be a useful guide in interpreting the Convention's jurisdictional provisions. Those non-parties have, after all, been given the power to constrain ICSID jurisdiction in ways that may limit the promotion of the flow of private investment, even though increasing that flow was precisely what motivated the Contracting States to enter into the Convention in the first place.

An accurate interpretation of the ICSID Convention's jurisdictional provisions, instead, must focus on ascertaining clearly the nature of the framework within which those third parties have been permitted to exercise power. The mere existence of the Convention in itself only indicates that the Contracting States believed that conferring power on third parties within the framework of the Convention would achieve the States' goal of promoting the flow of private investment. By choosing to pursue this goal through the framework of a semi-autonomous legal structure, however, the States created the risk that the powers they conferred would be used in ways inconsistent with the goals they were pursuing. As a result, only if the Convention can be shown to have created a framework that is itself structurally designed to favour the promotion of the flow of private investment can that goal be used in interpreting those provisions of the Convention with respect to which powers have been conferred on third parties.

The following section will, therefore, take an initial look at the large-scale structure of the ICSID Convention, in order to determine whether it can reasonably be concluded that the Convention is structurally designed to favour the promotion of private investment.

3 The balance between power-conferral and retention of sovereignty in the ICSID Convention

The ability of legal rules to confer powers, rather than just regulate behaviour, has come to have particular importance for international investment law since the middle of the twentieth century. Traditionally, investors in a foreign State who believed they had been mistreated by that State were generally required to pursue their claim in the State's own domestic courts.[22] If this failed to generate adequate compensation, the investor was then forced to turn to its Home State[23] and ask its government to undertake 'diplomatic protection' efforts on its behalf.[24] If the investor's plea was successful, the Home State government would enter into negotiations with the government of the Host State[25] as a means of settling the investor's claim. Potentially, the two governments might both consent to submit the dispute to arbitration.[26]

Diplomatic protection, however, has significant weaknesses as a means of resolving international investment disputes.[27] First, the Home State has no obligation to pursue the investor's claim at all.[28] It may, for example, conclude that pursuing the investor's claim would be incompatible with its own foreign-policy objectives with respect to the Host State. Second, even if the Home State does pursue the investor's claim, the investor has no control over how this is done.[29] Consequently, the investor may find that its claim has been settled for far less than it believes it is actually worth. Alternatively, if arbitration is commenced, it is the Home State and not the investor that controls the arbitration, and the investor only participates to the extent permitted by the Home State.[30]

While diplomatic protection arguably functioned adequately for hundreds of years, the globalisation of business in the twentieth century brought out clearly its significant limitations.[31] Increasing amounts of foreign investment were being made into an increasing diversity of countries, which, in turn, led to an increasing number of investment-related disputes.[32] As a result, States found themselves petitioned more and more often to intervene on behalf of a citizen or domestic corporation that had invested abroad. Similarly, States that were recipients of foreign investments found their domestic activities more frequently challenged by other States, whose investors had been affected by the measures in question. Finally, investors were forced to avoid potentially profitable investments due to concerns that they would not receive adequate compensation if mistreated by the Host State.

It was in this context that, in the mid-twentieth century, States began collectively to examine methods for encouraging international investment that would both provide an alternative to diplomatic protection and minimise the involvement of the Home State in the resolution of investment-related disputes. ICSID was a primary embodiment of this goal.[33] Expressly designed as a forum in which investors and Host States could resolve disputes directly with one another, it was seen as a means of depoliticising investment disputes, allowing them to be resolved on a purely legal basis.[34] More importantly for present purposes, however, the creation of a standing forum for the resolution of investor-State disputes represented a grant of power to investors, who now had primary control over the prosecution of their own claims.

Nonetheless, when described in this way the truly revolutionary nature of the ICSID Convention is not apparent, as Host States had always possessed the ability to arbitrate directly with foreign investors, rather than waiting for the investor's Home State to exert diplomatic protection on the investor's behalf.[35] What was truly revolutionary about the Convention, then, was not that it created a standing forum for the arbitration of disputes between investors and Host States, but that it simultaneously deprived the Home State of any right to intervene in the arbitral process.[36]

The ICSID Convention, that is, could have conferred only minimal powers on investors, granting them the right to bring and control their own claims, but nonetheless retaining for the Home State the right to intervene whenever it believed that larger political interests were at stake. If created along these lines, ICSID would still have been a revolutionary forum for the resolution of investor-State disputes through arbitration, but it would have undertaken its activities under the strong control of traditional diplomatic protection.

The desire to insulate ICSID arbitration from political disputes, however, resulted in the creation of a very different structure for ICSID arbitration, and a very strong grant of power to investors. Home States, that is, not only do not participate in the ICSID arbitral process, they are also precluded by the ICSID Convention from undertaking any diplomatic protection efforts once a claim has been brought to ICSID.[37] However, given international law's long-standing doctrine that the purpose of diplomatic protection is to redress an injury received by the Home State, rather than the injury received by the investor, precluding the Home State from pursuing diplomatic protection constitutes a very significant privileging of the interests of the investor above those of the Home State.[38]

Moreover, in investment treaty arbitration, in which the investor's claim is derived from obligations the Host State has undertaken in a treaty with the investor's Home State, allowing the investor to pursue its own claim in arbitration means that it is the investor, and not the Home State that is actually a party to the treaty, that decides which arguments will be advanced regarding the interpretation of the treaty obligations in question.[39] Consequently, the incorporation of investor-State arbitration into contemporary bilateral investment treaties (BITs) actually grants investors the power to determine when the home State's own substantive rights should be protected, and even the interpretation that those rights should be given.[40]

Nonetheless, while the ICSID Convention clearly reflects a considerable conferral of power on investors, it cannot be said that the Convention created a framework that is, as a whole, structurally designed to favour the promotion of private investment. This is because although some elements of the Convention confer very significant powers upon investors, and thus encourage the flow of private investment, others significantly limit those powers.

Most prominently, for example, Host States can simply refuse to agree to ICSID arbitration. ICSID arbitration could, that is, have been mandatory whenever a claim was brought by an investor from one Contracting State against another Contracting State. Such a structure would have been consistent with the notion that the ICSID Convention was designed to encourage the flow of private international investment, as it would have ensured that all investors covered by the Convention could secure an independent arbitral resolution of any claims they wished to raise. Instead, however, a structure was chosen that allowed the Host State to determine which investors it was willing to arbitrate with, and thereby limit the degree to which it promoted the flow of private international investment into its territory.

Similarly, while the ICSID Convention provides a mechanism for the arbitration of investor-State disputes, and even provides for the enhanced enforcement of arbitral awards delivered in investor-State arbitrations, it expressly disclaims any attempt to overcome the traditional resistance to enforcement against States found in the doctrine of sovereign immunity.[41] Yet a Convention structured in a manner designed to promote the flow of private international investment would hardly include a provision significantly reducing the likelihood that investors will be able to gain compensation that the Host State owes but is unwilling to pay.

The ICSID Convention, then, while clearly including very significant conferrals of power upon investors, nonetheless does not create a legal structure designed solely to encourage the flow of private international investment. It reflects, rather, a balancing between the desire to remove Home States from the dispute resolution process, and thereby eliminate the problems entailed by the politicisation of investment disputes, and the desire on the part of States to retain traditional powers of sovereignty, as seen particularly in the efforts made by many developing States to limit the jurisdictional power of the Convention.

Because of this balancing, any question regarding interpretation of the ICSID Convention must be approached through a close examination of the precise ways in which it may be affected by the power-conferring aspects of the Convention, as well as a careful consideration of precisely how the powers in question have been structured. No over-arching interpretation of the Convention in terms of its alleged objects and purposes can capture the complexities that a power-conferring treaty unavoidably contains.

For this reason, the remainder of this chapter will be devoted to examining more closely both which provisions of the ICSID Convention should be understood as being power-conferring with respect to the meaning of 'investment' in Article 25(1), and how those powers which have been conferred should be understood as functioning.

4 The controversy regarding the meaning of 'investment' in the ICSID Convention

One of the most distinctive aspects of the power-conferring nature of the ICSID Convention, and the one that has given rise to the most controversy, is the incorporation into the jurisdictional constraints of ICSID that it is a centre for the settlement of 'investment' disputes, and not merely disputes between States and citizens of other States.[42] One of the foundational concepts of any form of arbitration is that parties are only obligated to arbitrate in accordance with the consent to arbitration that they have given.[43] That consent need take no particular form and may be merely formal, rather than considered and fully voluntary,[44] but, ultimately, arbitration is consensual and unless consent to the arbitration by both parties can be found, an arbitral tribunal has no jurisdiction.[45]

However, while parties may arbitrate any dispute they wish to arbitrate, arbitral institutions have no obligation to administer any arbitration that does not meet whatever standards they wish to impose. Consequently, when two parties agree to arbitrate under the auspices of a particular institution, they thereby also subject themselves to the additional possibility of a constraint based upon the nature of the parties to the dispute or the dispute itself, rather than just party consent. That is, a party can only be obligated to arbitrate in accordance with its consent to arbitration, and if it has agreed to arbitrate only at ICSID, but for some reason the arbitration does not meet the requirements of ICSID arbitration, the arbitration agreement will fail.

In accordance with this feature of institutional arbitration, one of the distinctive aspects of jurisdiction under the ICSID Convention is that the fact that an investor and a Host State have both agreed to arbitrate at ICSID does not suffice to ground the jurisdiction of an ICSID tribunal. Instead, the ICSID Convention explicitly restricts ICSID arbitration to disputes 'arising directly out of an investment'.[46] No dispute that fails to meet this standard can be arbitrated at ICSID, even if both the Host State and the investor wish to do so.[47]

Such a restriction is, of course, very important in the context of identifying the degree to which and ways in which the ICSID Convention can be understood as power-conferring, as on its face it expressly limits the power that has been granted to investors, the relevant non-parties to the Convention. Investors are given the right to attempt to gain compensation through ICSID, that is, but only for a limited subset of the injuries that an investor can potentially receive from a Host State.[48] The conferral of power upon investors, as a result, is balanced by a restriction that clearly reflects an interest of Member States of the Convention. Investors are only being given the power to pursue compensation because Host States have determined that cross-border investment is particularly desirable *to them*, and thus a carve-out is made from the still-applicable rule that injured citizens must seek compensation through the intervention of their Home State.

The complication with any such argument is that while potentially a fairly straightforward constraint, this aspect of the jurisdiction of ICSID tribunals ultimately has come to be one of the most controversial topics in ICSID arbitration, due to the way in which the constraint is written into the ICSID Convention.[49] Whilst Article 25(1) of the Convention explicitly restricts ICSID arbitration to disputes 'arising directly out of an investment', no indication is given anywhere in the Convention as to exactly what constitutes an 'investment' for the purposes of the jurisdiction of an ICSID tribunal.[50] As a result, it is not immediately clear the degree to which the incorporation of the term 'investment' into Article 25(1) is indeed supposed to act as a limit on the powers conferred on investors by the Convention. If 'investment' as used in the Convention has an expansive definition it will be a relatively insignificant constraint, while if it has a narrow definition it will be very restrictive. It is clear, that is, that the incorporation of the term 'investment' reflects a limitation on the degree to which the Convention is fully power-conferring, but it is unclear exactly what that limitation is.

The lack of clear textual indications as to the meaning of 'investment' in the ICSID Convention has meant that ICSID tribunals have been left with a difficult interpretative task when determining the boundaries of their own jurisdiction. While early ICSID arbitrations concerned paradigmatic cases of international investment, such that the existence of an investment under Article 25(1) was not challenged, the enormous growth since the mid-1990s in the number of disputes brought to ICSID has resulted in a number of arbitrations in which the existence of an investment was less clear.[51] As a result, in a series of recent cases States have argued that the requirement for the existence of an investment was not met and the tribunal was therefore obligated to decline jurisdiction.[52]

A variety of approaches have been proposed for how to deal with this problem, but they can very broadly be sorted into two categories: 'objective' and 'subjective'.

According to the 'objective' approach, the term 'investment' in Article 25(1) has a solid and discernible meaning, often described in accordance with what have come to be known as the *Salini* criteria.[53] As an inherent aspect of the meaning of 'investment' as it is used in the Convention, the constraints placed by this meaning cannot be removed by the parties to a dispute, any more than can constraints that also exist regarding the nationality of the parties. Consequently, even if both parties to a dispute have agreed that the transaction underlying the dispute constitutes an investment and both wish their arbitration to be held under the auspices of ICSID, a tribunal must decline jurisdiction where the objective requirements of an Article 25(1) 'investment' have not been met.[54]

Unquestionably the touchstone of all 'objective' proposals is that made by Christoph Schreuer in his 2001 commentary on the ICSID Convention.[55] Rather than attempting to determine autonomously what the term 'investment' should be taken to mean, Schreuer instead invoked ICSID's 'experience' as providing the proper testing ground for a definition.[56] That is, he analysed transactions that had been found by tribunals to constitute 'investments' under the ICSID Convention, and identified a set of characteristics they had in common, declaring these characteristics to be a strong guide to the existence of an 'investment' for the purposes of the Convention.[57]

While Schreuer himself provides no clear rationale for this approach, it must be understood as founded on the belief that the term 'investment' in

Article 25(1) was left deliberately vague when the Convention was agreed, in order to allow the details of that definition to be fleshed out by tribunals in subsequent cases. Only on such a rationale can it make sense to rely on the decisions of tribunals.

If this picture of the functioning of the ICSID Convention were accurate, the Convention would certainly not be unique, as other treaties and indeed much domestic legislation take a similar approach. Unfortunately, however, there is no clear support for such an interpretation in either the Convention itself or the *travaux préparatoires*. Indeed, the structure created by the Convention for the operation of tribunals argues strongly against such a conception. Not only is there no precedent in ICSID arbitration, a fact that undermines the notion that tribunals were expected to develop a coherent case law, but non-parties to the Convention, namely investors, have an active role in the selection of the individuals who serve on tribunals.[58] Such a structure of arbitral appointment and lack of precedent is simply inconsistent with the structures used by other legal systems in which one or more tribunals are expected over time to develop consistent understandings of vague terms. Tribunals in such systems are expected to co-ordinate their interpretations of the law in a way that reflects that they are all operating as part of a single legal structure. ICSID tribunals, by contrast, lack any similar systemic unity, and unsurprisingly have displayed little recognition of any obligation to reach rulings consistent with those of earlier tribunals.[59]

This lack of systemic unity among ICSID tribunals means that the only way Schreuer's emphasis on developing ICSID jurisprudence can be correct is if the Contracting Parties to the ICSID Convention left vague one of the Convention's central jurisdictional constraints, with the expectation that it would be given content by arbitrators whose sole qualification for their role was that they were appointed by one of two parties who just happened to be having a dispute. Contracting States and foreign investors whose disputes did not rise to the level of ICSID arbitration would have no role in developing the term's content, even though they might subsequently be bound by it. Moreover, not only would those parties involved in determining the content of the Convention's terms represent only a small minority of the States and investors with an interest in the determination reached, they would also have an incentive to appoint an arbitrator from the perspective of tactical advantage in their current dispute, rather than with an eye to any serious long-term development of Convention jurisprudence. There is, in short, no reason to attribute such a view to the Contracting States, and no evidence to support such an attribution.

Nonetheless, whatever questions there might be about the justification for Schreuer's suggestion, there is no question of its impact on investment arbitration jurisprudence. As has already been mentioned, Schreuer's work resulted directly in what has come to be known as the *Salini* criteria – five elements that have been adopted by some tribunals as an important guide to whether the transaction underlying the dispute they are adjudicating constitutes an 'investment' for the purposes of Article 25(1). As usually listed, the criteria are: (a) a certain duration; (b) a regularity of profit and return; (c) an assumption of risk by both parties; (d) a significant financial commitment by the investor; and (e) a contribution to the development of the Host State.[60]

While some critics of the use of the *Salini* criteria have accused its proponents of taking too rigid an approach to their application, and applying them as though they constituted a mandatory checklist for the existence of an 'investment' rather than just an indicative guide, there is little real evidence for such practice in arbitral awards.[61] Rather, proponents of the *Salini* criteria insist that they merely serve as an indicative list that can assist tribunals in determining whether an 'investment' exists for the purposes of Article 25(1).[62] The failure of a given transaction to meet one or more of the criteria does not in itself justify a conclusion that no 'investment' exists.[63]

Nonetheless, whether the *Salini* criteria are approached as a checklist or merely an indicative guide, many tribunals and commentators have rejected the formalisation embodied in the *Salini* criteria, and the 'objective' approach as a whole. Instead, proponents of what can be called the 'subjective' approach argue that while the use of the term 'investment' in Article 25(1) means that any dispute arbitrated at ICSID must indeed arise directly from an investment, the failure of the Convention to provide any definition of 'investment' results from a decision by the Contracting States to allow the parties to each dispute to determine the meaning of the term for themselves.[64] As a result, they argue, when both parties to a dispute have agreed that the transaction underlying their dispute constitutes an investment, an ICSID tribunal should not conduct any further analysis of the existence of the investment and merely hold Article 25(1)'s requirement of an investment to have been met.[65]

By contrast with the 'objective' approach, then, the 'subjective' approach adopts a view of ICSID that makes it fundamentally resemble a commercial arbitration facility, available to be used whenever two parties have agreed between themselves that it would be a desirable location for their arbitration. On a technical level, only disputes that arise directly out of an 'investment' may be brought to ICSID, but whether this criterion has been satisfied is a matter to be agreed between the parties, not determined independently through consideration of characteristics of the institution itself.

The difficulty inherent in the 'subjective' approach is clear, as allowing the parties to a dispute to decide for themselves whether an 'investment' under Article 25(1) exists eliminates the ability of Article 25(1) to constrain the jurisdiction of ICSID tribunals in any meaningful way. Nonetheless, as the following section of this chapter will make clear, there is solid evidence that some version of the 'subjective' approach was indeed adopted by the Contracting States during negotiations for the Convention, with the power to define 'investment' in Article 25(1) being delegated to the parties to each new ICSID arbitration.

The remainder of this chapter, therefore, will be dedicated to examining to precisely what extent the power to define 'investment' under Article 25(1) has indeed been conferred on the parties to ICSID arbitrations, and within what constraints they must nonetheless use that power. Moreover, it will also argue that while proponents of the 'subjective' approach are demonstrably correct in their overall understanding of the Convention, they are mistaken in viewing the parties to an arbitration as the only entities granted such a power. Consequently, while the parties to any individual arbitration do indeed have a central role in determining whether the transaction underlying the dispute constitutes an investment for the purposes of Article 25(1), they can only do so within the constraints of the similar powers granted to other entities.

5 The power of the parties to a dispute to define 'investment' under Article 25(1) of the ICSID Convention

The first step in establishing which entities have been conferred powers under the ICSID Convention to determine the meaning of 'investment' in Article 25 (1) must be to demonstrate that Article 25(1) is indeed power-conferring. After all, although the term 'investment' in Article 25(1) is entirely undefined and hence potentially subject to a wide variety of interpretations, this cannot by itself suffice to demonstrate that Article 25(1) is power-conferring. This vagueness may simply have resulted from poor drafting.

There is, though, clear evidence from the *travaux préparatoires* of the ICSID Convention that the vagueness of the term 'investment' in Article 25(1) not only was deliberate, but was adopted with the explicit intent that the content of the term would be filled by entities other than the Contracting States to the Convention. *Travaux préparatoires* must certainly be used carefully, not only because of the notoriously ambiguous nature of such documents, but also because the VCLT is uniformly recognised as embodying a primarily textual approach to treaty interpretation, in which the actual language incorporated into a treaty has priority over any unexpressed intentions that the Contracting States may have had when negotiating the treaty.[66] Consequently, the use of *travaux préparatoires* to interpret a treaty can be controversial.[67]

Moreover, while it is being argued in this chapter that the power-conferring nature of the ICSID Convention impacts upon the way that the Convention's provisions should be interpreted, it is not being argued that power-conferring treaties are somehow exempt from the application of the customary international law rules expressed in the VCLT's Articles on treaty interpretation. Consequently, a demonstration that the Convention is power-conferring with respect to the meaning of 'investment' can only rely on *travaux préparatoires* to the degree allowed by the rules of treaty interpretation codified in the VCLT.

Nonetheless, the VCLT's rules on treaty interpretation clearly allow that use of *travaux préparatoires* is acceptable when the meaning of a term is ambiguous or otherwise unclear.[68] Yet, if any treaty term has ever been ambiguous, it is 'investment' in Article 25(1) of the ICSID Convention.[69] Not only does the term have no uniformly accepted meaning outside the Convention, but no indication is given in the Convention itself as to what it should be understood as meaning. There has been little controversy, then, surrounding the repeated references that have been made in a variety of sources to the *travaux préparatoires* of the Convention, in attempts to understand the meaning of 'investment' in Article 25(1).[70]

Examination of the *travaux préparatoires* of the ICSID Convention, however, makes clear that neither the objective nor subjective views on the interpretation of 'investment' can be regarded as fully correct. Rather, while the meaning of 'investment' clearly involves a conferral of power by the Contracting States on the parties to each individual dispute, one of whom will not be a Contracting State, in line with the subjective approach, that conferral is clearly not absolute, and some limits are placed on that power, in line with the objective approach.

Clear evidence that the vagueness of Article 25(1) constitutes a grant of power to entities other than the Contracting States to the Convention can be found in a famous statement in the Report of the Executive Directors on the Convention on the Settlement of Investment Disputes between States and Nationals of Other States ('Report of the Executive Directors'), published alongside the Convention, that '[n]o attempt was made to define the term 'investment' given the essential requirement of consent by the parties'.[71] That is, neither States nor investors are required to bring investment disputes to ICSID, even if both the Home and Host States involved in the dispute are signatories to the Convention. Instead, the Convention requires an independent consent, from both the Host State and the investor, for any specific dispute to be brought before an ICSID tribunal.[72] As indicated by the above statement in the Report of the Executive Directors, however, the negotiating history of the Convention clearly illustrates that the requirement of this second consent played a primary role in convincing many Contracting States to accept the vagueness of the definition of 'investment' in Article 25(1). As each State retained the ability to decide for itself which disputes it was willing to consent to bring to ICSID, a precise definition of the term 'investment' was ultimately decided to be unnecessary, as each State could effectively define the term for itself. In this respect, then, the decision to incorporate into Article 25(1) only the term 'investment', with no clarifying language, constituted a conferral of powers upon the parties to any given dispute to define that term for themselves.

Nonetheless, this should not be understood as meaning that the parties to a dispute have unconstrained freedom with respect to the definition of 'investment'. After all, the Contracting States could have omitted the term 'investment' completely from Article 25(1), thereby giving parties to a dispute total freedom to determine for themselves which of their disputes should be brought before an ICSID tribunal. The deliberate retention of this constraint, then, indicates clearly that while parties to a dispute were to be largely free to define the term 'investment' however they wished, it must nonetheless accord with some broader, party-independent meaning of the term.

Indeed, the *travaux préparatoires* of the ICSID Convention make it clear that the statement quoted above from the Report of the Executive Directors, if taken at face value, is highly misleading, as it is simply not accurate to say that 'no attempt' was made to define 'investment'.[73] Rather, while a decision was indeed ultimately taken not to adopt a specific definition of 'investment', this decision followed a protracted series of disputes regarding the precise definition that the term should be given.[74]

While the Working Paper prepared to serve as an initial foundation for negotiation of the ICSID Convention and had completely omitted the term 'investment' from the jurisdictional constraints of ICSID, this approach was rejected by negotiators and a reference to 'investment' was included in all subsequent drafts.[75] In addition, once the term was incorporated within the jurisdictional constraints of ICSID tribunals, the States negotiating the Convention did not simply proceed to ignore it, accepting that it had no content in and of itself. Rather, the definition of 'investment' in Article 25(1) became a point of high contention, with many proposals being made as to the precise way that it should be defined.[76] It was only when it became clear that no agreement was going to be reached on the precise meaning of an Article 25(1) investment that a proposal was accepted that no definition be adopted at all, leaving the term 'investment' included within Article 25(1) but with no indication given as to its meaning.[77]

The *travaux préparatoires* of the ICSID Convention, then, certainly make it clear that the vagueness of 'investment' in Article 25(1) was deliberate and was intended to confer power upon the parties to a dispute to determine for themselves whether their transaction constituted an investment. Nonetheless, they are also clear that this conferral of power was not an unrestricted one, as the insistence of the Contracting States that the term 'investment' be added to the Convention, combined with the extensive efforts made during negotiations to reach an acceptable definition of the term, is simply inconsistent with such a claim.[78]

Expressly recognising the ICSID Convention as power-conferring, then, rather than merely invoking the idea of a 'subjective' definition, makes conceptual sense of the balance between freedom and constraint that is found in the definition of 'investment' in the Convention. That is, if 'investment' in Article 25(1) is indeed 'subjective' to the parties to a dispute, in any meaningful sense, then it is unclear how the 'objective' component of that definition is supposed to work. After all, when one says that the meaning of a given term is 'subjective', one surely thereby gives up the ability to reject the subjective definition chosen.

It is, of course, certainly possible to argue that the definition of 'investment' is subjective within certain boundaries, rather than absolutely subjective. However, using the term 'subjective' in such a situation requires the ability to draw a principled distinction between the objective aspect of the definition, and the subjective aspect that is open to control by the parties to a dispute. A principled distinction of this type, however, is simply impossible to draw in this case. The 'objective' limits on the power of the parties to a dispute to decide for themselves the meaning of 'investment' are simply limits imposed by entities other than the parties to the dispute.

It is not, that is, that the definition of 'investment' is a subjective determination of the parties to the dispute, but rather that they have been conferred the power to decide part of that definition. This distinction in terminology between 'subjective' and 'power-conferring' is important, as it can have significant effects. Describing the definition as 'subjective' serves as an invitation to tribunals to step back and let the parties define it as they wish. Describing it as involving the conferral of a power, on the other hand, emphasises the need to clearly delineate precisely what the limits of that power are, and thus precisely what freedom the parties to a dispute do indeed have to determine the definition of 'investment' for themselves.

Having established, then, that Article 25(1) of the ICSID Convention is best understood as involving the conferral of a definitional power upon the parties to a dispute, the next section of this chapter will focus on one of the ways that this power must be understood as being constrained by the Convention. It will argue that Article 64 of the Convention confers on any two or more Contracting States the power to agree between themselves a definition of 'investment' under Article 25(1), and that this definition will then serve as a boundary within which parties to certain disputes must use the power that has also been conferred on them to decide precisely the same definition.

6 The power of Home and Host States to define 'investment' in Article 25(1) of the ICSID Convention through mutual agreement under Article 64 of the ICSID Convention

This chapter has thus far focused on Article 25(1) of the ICSID Convention, the provision in the Convention that most directly addresses the meaning of 'investment' in so far as it operates as a jurisdictional constraint to ICSID arbitration. However, a complete understanding of the meaning of 'investment' in the Convention is not possible without considering a second Article of the Convention, even though this Article does not itself directly refer to 'investment'.

Article 64 of the ICSID Convention is the type of State-State dispute resolution clause found in many treaties, and there is no indication that during its adoption any consideration was given to the possibility that it might be used to define 'investment' under Article 25(1). Nonetheless, this section of the chapter will attempt to demonstrate that the specific wording used in Article 64, when combined with the power-conferring nature of Article 25(1), must be understood as allowing any group of two or more States to reach a mutually binding agreement on the meaning of the term 'investment' in Article 25(1).

As discussed earlier, prior to the creation of ICSID, investors with a legitimate claim against a foreign government were usually forced to rely upon often unsatisfactory diplomatic protection efforts by their Home State. Unhappiness with this system was the most important motivation behind the creation of ICSID.

Given this context, although the potential risks for a Host State of consenting to arbitrate with an investor at ICSID are clear, a Home State is itself not unaffected by its ratification of the ICSID Convention. A Home State that ratifies the Convention does not just risk having claims brought against it as a Host State. It also surrenders the traditional power it had to use its investors' claims against Host States for its larger political purposes. After all, there is no provision within the Convention that allows a Home State to prevent one of its investors bringing a claim against a Host State or even just allows it to intervene in an ICSID arbitration in order to express its own views on the dispute.[79] Ratification of the Convention, then, represents a significant loss of power even for States that expect predominantly to be Home States in disputes, rather than Host States.

However, although a Home State does not possess any power to intervene directly in an ICSID arbitration between one of its investors and a foreign State, Article 64 means that a State need not be entirely without influence in such a dispute. Under this Article, Contracting States are permitted to resolve any dispute regarding the interpretation of the Convention through negotiation, and if negotiations are not successful may institute a case at the International Court of Justice (ICJ).[80] While commentary on this Article has focused on its grant of adjudicatory power to the ICJ, the recognition of the power of ICSID Contracting States to resolve disputes through negotiation is more important in the present context.[81]

Although Article 64 has never been used, either as the foundation for a case at the ICJ or as the ground for a negotiated agreement, its language is nonetheless clear as to the power it grants to groups of ICSID Contracting States. While a provision acknowledging that the Contracting States to a treaty retain the power to agree on the interpretation of any element of that treaty might be unremarkable,[82] Article 64 expressly states that the power to negotiate agreed interpretations of Convention provisions is exercisable by limited groups of Contracting States and does not require the participation of all ICSID Contracting States.[83]

As a result, Article 64 confers on groups of two or more Contracting States the power to adopt an interpretation of the Convention that will be applicable between them, but that is potentially inconsistent with an interpretation adopted by one or more other groups of Contracting States. It is, therefore, a mechanism by which a single treaty can ultimately be transformed into what is effectively a variegated set of treaties, consistent in most provisions, but diverging in important ways on certain points.

It should be emphasised, however, that Article 64 only gives Contracting States the power to negotiate agreements regarding the 'interpretation or application' of the Convention.[84] Consequently, it cannot be a means of altering or terminating the Convention. The Convention, therefore, remains a single treaty, subject to a variety of interpretations, rather than actually constituting a linked set of bilateral treaties.

With respect to the definition of 'investment' in Article 25(1), then, Article 64 confers on groups of Contracting States the power to negotiate an agreed definition that will be applicable in any arbitration between any Contracting State party to that agreement and an investor from another Contracting State also party to the agreement.

Article 64 does not itself specify any formal requirements for such an agreement. Consequently, while an agreement to a particular interpretation of 'investment' in Article 25(1) may take the form of an independent document, explicitly referring to Article 64 of the Convention, nothing in Article 64 requires that this be so. Rather, so long as an agreement between the Home and Host States was reached through 'negotiation' or 'another method of settlement' agreed between the States concerned, Article 64 makes this agreement a binding interpretation of the Convention.

The lack of formal requirements for an Article 64 agreement is important because a significant majority of recent ICSID arbitrations have been based on BITs negotiated between States, rather than on agreements directly between the investor and the Host State.[85] In contrast to the ICSID Convention, however, these BITs often include very detailed definitions of what constitutes an 'investment' under the BIT. If, then, the definition of 'investment' in a BIT can be fairly characterised as an agreement on the meaning of 'investment' under the Convention, then through Article 64 the BIT definition of 'investment' also becomes an interpretation of Article 25(1) that is binding on the States concerned.

The definition of 'investment' in a BIT is, of course, not directly an agreement on the definition of 'investment' in Article 25(1) of the ICSID Convention. Consequently, it might initially seem that BIT definitions of 'investment' are simply irrelevant to Article 64, which only applies to agreements relating to the 'interpretation or application' of the Convention.[86]

There are, however, good reasons to reject such a conclusion, tied to the role that Article 25(1)'s definition of 'investment' plays in the ICSID Convention. As already discussed above, Article 25(1) is not a standard treaty provision, but rather a power-conferring provision, intended to be given content by the agreement of the parties to a dispute. In itself, this fact cannot serve to give two States, one of which is not a party to the dispute, the power to do the same thing. It clarifies, however, that 'investment' in Article 25(1) is ultimately not a substantive term, to be interpreted in accordance with any particular understanding of what is or is not truly an 'investment'. It is, rather, a functional term, that within certain limits represents solely the willingness of the two parties to the dispute to arbitrate at ICSID.

Once this notion of 'investment' in Article 25(1) as a functional term is accepted, however, a further possibility also exists, through the inclusion in the Convention of Article 64. Article 64, after all, allows any group of two or more Contracting States to agree on an 'interpretation' of the Convention.[87] By combining this power with the functional nature of 'investment' in

Article 25(1), it follows that where any group of two or more Contracting States have agreed on the types of disputes that should be arbitrable at ICSID, this constitutes an agreed interpretation of 'investment' in Article 25(1).

Consequently, when two States enter into an agreement that includes both consent to ICSID arbitration and a definition of investment that acts as a jurisdictional constraint to the States' consent to ICSID arbitration, they have thereby reached agreement upon precisely what constitutes the meaning of 'investment' under Article 25(1). They were, of course, likely not attempting to do so, as they were merely placing a jurisdictional constraint on their own consent to arbitration under the BIT. However, once it is recognised that 'investment' under Article 25(1) is a functional term relating to the willingness of States to arbitrate directly with investors, rather than a reference to a substantive type of transaction, then evidence of this willingness can provide content to the term no matter its source.

By way of parallel, although there is little controversy surrounding the idea that the parties to a dispute brought at ICSID have been delegated at least partial responsibility to define the term 'investment' under Article 25(1) through their agreement to arbitrate, there is little question that in entering into that agreement to arbitrate they would very rarely, if ever, have been attempting to define 'investment' under Article 25(1). Rather, they were simply specifying the conditions under which they would be willing to arbitrate their disputes at ICSID. It is only through the functional nature of 'investment' under Article 25(1) that their agreement has this uncontemplated effect.

Of course, even if it is accepted that Article 64 can have this effect, the question remains as to what happens when a conflict arises between the definition adopted by the Home and Host States under Article 64, and the definition agreed between the investor and the Host State under Article 25(1). The Article 25(1) agreement might, that is, include under the definition of 'investment' transactions that are excluded by the Article 64 agreement. Alternatively, the Article 64 agreement might be broader than the Article 25(1) agreement.

The answer must surely be that as both mechanisms have been incorporated into the ICSID Convention, both must be given effect. As described above, after all, the two mechanisms are in effect mirror provisions, each delegating power-conferring authority on certain individuals or entities, in the case of Article 25(1) with respect to a single term, and in the case of Article 64 with respect to any term in the Convention. Consequently, only transactions that meet both the definition of 'investment' under Article 25(1) and the definition of 'investment' under Article 64 can serve as the basis for an ICSID arbitration. If the Article 25(1) definition has not been met, then the parties to the dispute have not both consented to ICSID arbitration, and the consent prerequisite for any form of arbitration has not been met. On the other hand, if the Article 64 definition has not been met, then the two States whose consent to ICSID arbitration is a prerequisite for an investor from one of those States to be able to arbitrate at ICSID with the other State have not consented.

Consequently, where the consent to arbitration of a State and an investor is contained in an agreement directly between those two parties, but the transaction underlying the dispute does not qualify as an 'investment' under an applicable BIT between the Host and Home States, the definition of 'investment' in the BIT becomes incorporated into the ICSID Convention as an agreed refinement of the definition of 'investment' in Article 25(1), for any disputes involving one of the two States party to the BIT and an investor from the other. As a result, if the transaction underlying the agreement between the investor and the Host State does not fall within the definition included in the BIT, it thereby also does not fall within Article 25(1).[88]

That is, whenever a BIT includes both a consent to ICSID arbitration and a definition of 'investment' that serves as a jurisdictional limit on that consent, neither State party to the BIT may arbitrate a dispute at ICSID that arises out of a transaction that would not qualify as an 'investment' under the BIT, even though the arbitration is brought based on a consent in a separate agreement directly between the investor and the Host State.

7 The minimum content of the definition of 'investment' in Article 25(1) of the ICSID Convention

This chapter has been concerned with explaining the idea of the ICSID Convention as a power-conferring treaty, elucidating the entities that have been granted the power to define 'investment' under Article 25(1), and clarifying the means by which they can exercise that power. However, the history of the negotiations that resulted in Article 25(1) makes clear that these powers were not unconstrained. That is, while entities other than the Contracting States to the Convention have been granted the power to define 'investment' under Article 25(1), they have not been given complete freedom to do so. Such a claim would, after all, make nonsense of the insistence that the term 'investment' be included within Article 25(1), as it would eliminate the ability of the term to act as a constraint. There must, then, be some element of control over the definition of 'investment' that has been retained by the Contracting States to the Convention – some 'minimum content' that even those entities granted the power to define 'investment' do not have the power to eliminate. This concluding section of the chapter, will be dedicated to explaining the nature of this 'minimum content' and how it can be identified.

7.1 *The problem of interpretative subjectivity*

Before addressing directly the manner in which the minimum content of Article 25(1)'s definition of 'investment' should be analysed, it is important to note the unavoidable need for a tribunal-independent understanding of this minimum content.

That is, even proponents of the 'subjective' approach to the interpretation of Article 25(1) concede that there must be some outer limit to the meaning of 'investment', such that even party agreement to bring certain types of dispute to ICSID cannot suffice to ground a tribunal's jurisdiction.[89] However, it is clearly untenable to maintain that the decision not to incorporate a precise definition of 'investment' into Article 25(1) was taken because it was decided that the meaning of 'investment' was clear and no further specificity was required. Although the principle architect of the Convention, Aron Broches, did indeed suggest that one justification for omitting a detailed definition of 'investment' was precisely that the existence of an investment was readily recognisable, the inability of the negotiating States to reach a consensus on the definition despite extensive efforts indicates clearly that if any consensus existed on the definition of 'investment' in Article 25(1), it was at a very basic level.[90]

There is, then, simply no single clear definition of 'investment' to which tribunals attempting to interpret Article 25(1) can appeal. As a result, each tribunal has, of necessity, been forced to rely upon its own intuitive understanding of what is or is not 'obviously' not an investment.[91]

The difficulty this creates is that while the ICSID Convention clearly conferred upon the parties to dispute the power to define 'investment', it did not do the same for arbitral tribunals. Yet, any tribunal that bases an interpretation of Article 25(1) on the intuitions of its members regarding what does or does not constitute an investment has indeed exercised this power. That is, the tribunal has determined the meaning of 'investment' under Article 25(1), but not through interpretation of the Convention or identification of the views of the parties to the dispute. It has, rather, simply imposed the view that its own members prefer.

The problem this creates is apparent. The arbitrators have been selected by the parties through a procedure that allows them to be chosen because of certain substantive views they hold, including on the definition of 'investment' in Article 25(1).[92] However, when ruling on the outer boundaries of Article 25(1)'s definition of 'investment', tribunals are determining the minimum content of the term that was explicitly reserved from the definitional power conferred on the parties. Consequently, by appealing to their own intuitions when determining the 'minimum content', the tribunal allows the parties to take control of precisely that element of the definition of 'investment' that the Contracting States restricted from party control.

This situation causes a serious practical problem because, under Article 54 of the ICSID Convention, Contracting States, even though not themselves either the Host State or the Home State in a given dispute, undertake to enforce the pecuniary obligations of any ICSID award.[93] Consequently, unless there is a minimum content to the definition of 'investment' that is beyond the power of either the parties or the Home and Host States to define, other Contracting States will be obligated to enforce awards resulting from disputes concerning transactions that are plausibly an ICSID investment only because the parties to the dispute agreed that they wanted it to be. This approach entirely eviscerates the constraint that ICSID be a centre for the resolution of investment disputes, and only investment disputes.[94]

Despite the variety of ways already discussed in which the Host State, Home State and investors can give content to Article 25(1)'s definition of investment, then, it is clear that there must be a constraint on their freedom. Moreover, this constraint must be one objectively ascertainable and not merely confined to the discretion of the arbitrators in each dispute.

Nonetheless, this does not entail that the minimum content of 'investment' in Article 25(1) must be invariant. As the next subsection of this chapter will argue, the minimum content of an Article 25(1) 'investment' is best understood as being evolutionary in nature, changing over time to reflect changing understandings of the meaning of the term. As a result, the meaning of the term is to be determined through an examination of the contemporary practice of all Contracting States to the Convention, rather than by attempting to discern the meaning of 'investment' at the time the Convention was adopted, or by imposing any other form of invariant definition.

7.2 Determination of the minimum content of an 'investment' under Article 25(1) of the ICSID Convention

As argued above, the term 'investment' in the ICSID Convention has content beyond that provided by either party agreement or agreement between the Host and Home States. However, it is also indisputable that no single definition of the term was acceptable to all Contracting States when the Convention was negotiated. The best insight into the nature of the minimum content of an Article 25(1) investment comes, therefore, from considering when the Contracting States to the Convention would plausibly see the term 'investment' as providing a substantive jurisdictional constraint, even without the incorporation of a clear definition.

The inability to reach agreement on even the most basic elements of a definition preclude the notion that the term was simply intended to refer to some extra-Convention definition of 'investment', such as might be found in economics or some other branch of international economic law.[95] In addition, the willingness of the Contracting States to allow parties to disputes and Home and Host States to define 'investment' differently at different times and in different contexts is inconsistent with the idea that they simultaneously agreed to limit their own impact upon the definition of 'investment' to a single usage currently being made of the term at the time the ICSID Convention was concluded.

Rather, as has already been noted, the *travaux préparatoires* of the ICSID Convention show that the concern motivating the disputes over the definition of 'investment' in Article 25(1) focused on the obligation of States to enter into investor-State arbitration, not what does or does not actually constitute an investment. Recognising this fact, it is clear that a tribunal attempting to determine whether a transaction falls within the minimum content of the term 'investment' in Article 25(1) should similarly focus on identifying whether that transaction is a type of transaction that Contracting States to the Convention are currently willing to submit directly to investor-State arbitration. This can be done through examining whether the transaction would constitute an 'investment' under other agreements concluded by the Contracting States to the Convention that also include consent to investor-State arbitration.

Importantly, however, as the concern is not with the definition of 'investment', but with the willingness to submit to investor-State arbitration, the only agreements that are relevant to this determination are those that include consent to investor-State arbitration.[96] Where the term 'investment' is used in agreements that do not include consent to investor-State arbitration, even if they are also in some way related to international investment, such usages of 'investment' are not directly relevant for determining the meaning of the term under Article 25(1).

Of course, the practice of States in this respect changes constantly and has evolved considerably in the period since the ICSID Convention came into force.[97] The minimum content of 'investment' under Article 25(1), then, must be understood as evolutionary, reflecting at any given time the types of investments that States are willing to arbitrate directly with investors.[98]

The consequence of such a conclusion is that it is simply impossible to make any form of absolute statement regarding what is or is not an investment under Article 25(1) of the ICSID Convention. Rather, while a certain form of transaction may not currently constitute an Article 25(1) investment, changing practice may result in its becoming one in the future. Similarly, a type of transaction currently regarded as a paradigm form of investment may well lose its status in the future if practice begins to exclude it.

The question remains, however, how widespread the agreement to arbitrate a particular type of transaction must be before it is taken to have been incorporated into Article 25(1)'s definition of 'investment'. It is tentatively suggested here that the appropriate standard is that used to determine whether a rule of customary international law has developed. That is, if the inclusion of a particular type of transaction within the definition of 'investment' in relevant international agreements has not reached a level of uniformity and diversity that would support, in another context, a finding of the existence of a rule of customary international law, then the type of transaction in question should not be found to have been incorporated into Article 25(1)'s definition of 'investment'.[99] Only with such a standard can the consent of the large number of States bound by the ICSID Convention be respected.

8 Conclusion

This chapter has attempted both to lay out clearly the notion of a power-conferring treaty, and to clarify how understanding the ICSID Convention as power-conferring can help in resolving one of the most contentious issues in contemporary international investment arbitration. The larger goal, however, has been to provide an initial indication of the benefits that can be gained from attending to structural concerns when analysing problems in international investment arbitration.

The meaning of 'investment' under the ICSID Convention is a significant source of ongoing disagreement within the field, with identifiable 'camps' evolving based primarily on differing interpretations of the fundamental goals of ICSID arbitration and of the motivations that lay behind the creation of the Convention. This chapter has attempted to demonstrate that it is possible to make advances in resolving this issue without adopting any particular substantive viewpoint on these fundamentally contested issues. Rather, by recognising that the Convention is a power-conferring treaty, and thus creates a legal structure intended to operate semi-autonomously from the goals of those that created it, attention appropriately shifts to objective questions regarding the structure of the Convention, and away from larger political debates in which no agreement is likely to be achieved. This does not mean that these larger debates no longer have any relevance to the interpretation of the Convention, but through structural analysis it is at least possible to attempt to create a foundation on which all sides can agree, and that can either be objectively demonstrated to be false, or is only unacceptable because the foundation proposed does not serve pre-decided political objectives.

2 The legal impact of notifications under Article 25(4) of the ICSID Convention

1 Introduction

Chapter 1 has argued that the ongoing controversy over the meaning of the term 'investment' in Article 25(1) of the ICSID Convention can best be addressed, at least initially, through a focus on the internal structure of the Convention. In particular, it has been argued that the Convention was created as a power-conferring treaty, under which certain entities have been given the power to define the term 'investment', resulting in a different definition coming into effect from one dispute to another, and from one time to another.

No attention has yet been paid, however, to Article 25(4) of the ICSID Convention, one of the most distinctive and least well understood provisions of the Convention, even though Article 25(4) can be interpreted as itself conferring a power to define 'investment' in Article 25(1). Article 25(4), after all, grants Contracting States the power to 'notify the Centre of the class or classes of disputes which it would or would not consider submitting to the jurisdiction of the Centre'. While this provision makes no reference to either 'investment' or Article 25(1), Chapter 1 has argued that the term 'investment' in the Convention should be understood as having a functional definition, indicating the class of disputes a State is willing to arbitrate before an ICSID tribunal. This is, however, precisely the information that Article 25(4) allows States to 'notify' to the ICSID. Consequently, it might be argued that Article 25(4) merely provides a method by which States can exercise the power conferred on them with respect to the meaning of 'investment' in Article 25(1). As a result, any Article 25(4) notification will be binding in precisely the same way as either of the other methods of defining 'investment' discussed in Chapter 1.

The difficulty with such an argument is that each of the powers to define 'investment' examined in Chapter 1 was a shared power, expressing the agreement of two or more entities and applicable only to disputes with which both of those entities was connected.[1] The power granted by Article 25(4), by contrast, is a unilateral one, exercisable by a single Contracting State, and not subject to the moderating influence of any other entity. It represents, therefore, a fundamentally different type of power than those discussed in

Chapter 1. Even more importantly, however, if an Article 25(4) notification is held to contribute to the definition of 'investment' under Article 25(1), it will have the ability to preclude ICSID arbitration of disputes even when an applicable arbitration agreement exists between an investor and the State issuing the notification. That is, it would give Contracting States the power to undermine the very notion of agreement that is central to all arbitration.

It is concerns such as these that have resulted in the interpretative vacuum that now characterises Article 25(4). Indeed, not only is there no broadly agreed scholarly understanding of the effect of an Article 25(4) notification on the jurisdiction of an ICSID tribunal, but those few tribunals that have directly addressed Article 25(4) have consistently interpreted it as having no impact on the dispute before them, even while differing on the precise reason no impact existed.[2] Because of this interpretative vacuum, Article 25(4) has, in short, become spurious to the Convention.[3]

The goal of this chapter, however, is to demonstrate that when properly interpreted, Article 25(4) does indeed have a significant role to play in determining the jurisdiction of ICSID tribunals. Moreover, while the existence of an Article 25(4) notification will not always preclude ICSID jurisdiction, there are situations in which this will be the consequence of notification, even in situations in which a tribunal would normally hold that jurisdiction existed.

Section 2 will address the context in which Article 25(4) was added to the ICSID Convention, and the impact this context has on the interpretation that should be given to the role of Article 25(4) in the Convention's jurisdictional framework. Sections 3, 4 and 5 will then examine the three primary interpretations that Article 25(4) could be given on a traditional understanding of the Convention, explaining why each is ultimately inadequate. Lastly, section 6 will offer an interpretation of Article 25(4) derived from what has been argued here to be the power-conferring nature of the Convention.

2 The incorporation of Article 25(4) into the ICSID Convention

Although every treaty must to some degree impose obligations on the States that are party to it, Chapter 1 has examined two ways in which the ICSID Convention should be understood to be power-conferring, rather than purely obligation-imposing. The discussion in that chapter, however, concentrated on specific examples of particular powers given by the Convention to particular entities. The power-conferring nature of the Convention is, however, far more pervasive and fundamental than these examples of isolated powers might indicate.

The ICSID Convention, of course, certainly imposes some binding obligations on Contracting States, and these obligations are not trivial.[4] Nonetheless, its primary purpose as a treaty is actually to expand the opportunities available to Contracting States, rather than to obligate those States to use the opportunities provided. That is, although the Convention creates a mechanism for the arbitral resolution of international investment disputes, States may become parties to the Convention without ever using those facilities – even if they do indeed have investment disputes to resolve.[5] In the words of the Report of the Executive Directors, published alongside the Convention as an explanatory aid, 'Consent of the parties is the cornerstone of the jurisdiction of the Centre'.[6]

There is, of course, a level at which this statement is obvious, as the jurisdiction referred to by the Report of the Executive Directors is that of an arbitral institution, and arbitral jurisdiction is always based on consent. However, any such reading of this statement both understates the meaning of the Executive Directors, and misses the important role that statements of this type played in the Convention's negotiation. As is clear from the *travaux préparatoires* of the Convention, while the idea of a centre for the arbitral settlement of investment disputes had wide support from States of all varieties, there was significant resistance by developing States in particular to anything in the ICSID Convention that might obligate them to use those facilities.[7] As a result, the Convention was crafted in a way that created an institution at which Contracting States could resolve investment disputes through arbitration directly with investors, but that carefully avoided imposing any obligation on Contracting States to actually use ICSID's facilities.

For this reason, any proper analysis of the legal framework created by the ICSID Convention requires that attention be paid not only to the powers conferred by the Convention on various entities, and the opportunity the Convention creates for direct investor-State arbitration, but also to the restrictions that were deliberately placed on any perceived obligation of Contracting States to actually use those facilities. These restrictions, after all, were incorporated into the Convention as a direct expression of the unwillingness of many States to use ICSID's facilities, and thereby give up the traditional power they possessed to resolve investment disputes through their own domestic courts and through State-State negotiations.

The first significant restriction included in the ICSID Convention on the obligation of Contracting States to use the ICSID's facilities occurs in the requirement of Article 25 that consent to arbitrate any dispute at ICSID must be given 'in writing'. This provision might not in itself appear significant, as the requirement that an arbitration agreement be in writing was far from unusual at the time the Convention was adopted. Indeed, even the New York Convention, a treaty whose primary purpose is to facilitate the enforcement of arbitral agreements and arbitral awards, incorporates a requirement that arbitral agreements, if they are to be enforced under the treaty, must be in writing.[8] Moreover, although the ICSID Convention requires that agreements to arbitrate at ICISD be in writing, it does not impose any requirements at all on the particular form that the writing must take.[9] A writing must exist, but any writing will do.

Nonetheless, it is important not to underestimate the significance of the ICSID Convention's writing requirement, even while recognising its limitations.

The inclusion of a writing requirement, after all, means that even if there is indisputable evidence that a Host State promised to arbitrate at ICSID with an investor, and encouraged the investor to rely on that promise, it still has no obligation under the Convention to actually live up to its promise. The incorporation of a writing requirement into the Convention, that is, reflects a choice by the Contracting States to the Convention that it is preferable for some investors to be denied the arbitral dispute resolution they were indisputably promised, than for any State to be forced to arbitrate at ICSID if there is any question it has agreed to do so.

Of course, on its face a writing requirement is even-handed, and protects investors from being forced into ICSID arbitrations against their will as much as it does Host States. Such a reading of this provision, however, ignores that the standard alternative to arbitration of investment disputes is litigation against the Host State in the Host State's own courts.[10] There is little question, then, that the incorporation of a writing requirement into the Convention benefited Host States far more than it did investors.

This impression of a treaty consciously designed to avoid imposing any obligation on States to arbitrate at ICSID finds further expression in the requirement for a 'second consent' that was also incorporated into the ICSID Convention. The term 'second consent' has come to refer to the fact repeatedly emphasised throughout the course of the negotiations for the Convention that merely becoming an ICSID Contracting State does not obligate a State to arbitrate any disputes at ICSID.[11] Instead, a Contracting State is only obligated to arbitrate at ICSID if it has specifically agreed to ICSID arbitration of a particular dispute with a particular investor. This incorporation into the Convention of the requirement of a second consent played a central role in convincing developing States that they could join the Convention while still insulating themselves from what they perceived as the potential negative consequences of investor-State arbitration. They could, after all, merely refuse to agree to arbitrate any disputes at ICSID.

The *travaux préparatoires* of the ICSID Convention are clear, however, that even this incorporation of a second consent was not enough to eliminate all the concerns that developing States had about agreeing to an investor-State arbitration mechanism. Developing States were, that is, concerned that even though consent was the 'cornerstone' of the Convention, that consent could be pressured out of them by either developed States or powerful foreign investors. In such a situation, an ICSID tribunal would clearly have jurisdiction, as the formal requirements of the Convention would have been met, but the Host State would nonetheless have been forced into ICSID arbitration against its will.

It was in response to this concern that Article 25(4) was incorporated into the ICSID Convention. Developing States had attempted to address their concern through the incorporation of a specific definition of 'investment' into Article 25(1), as this would have precluded arbitration of disputes not meeting this definition, even if consent by the Host State otherwise existed.[12]

However, none of the detailed definitions of 'investment' proposed were able to achieve enough support from the body of negotiating States that they could be incorporated into the Convention.

In the face of an impasse, a proposal was made by the UK delegation, and accepted by the other negotiating States, that 'investment' in Article 25(1) would remain undefined, but that a provision would be inserted into Article 25 through which Contracting States could notify ICSID, and thereby the other Contracting States, of 'the class or classes of disputes which it would or would not consider submitting to the jurisdiction of the Centre'. Through such a notification, it was argued, States could protect themselves against having to arbitrate at ICSID classes of disputes that they did not wish to arbitrate. A State could, for example, submit a notification that it was unwilling to arbitrate at ICSID any disputes arising out of its domestic oil industry, thereby removing the necessity to make such a statement in every document including a consent to ICSID arbitration.

On its face, Article 25(4) seems to be a clear solution to the concerns expressed by developing States. It would allow a State to identify any particular category of disputes that it was unwilling to arbitrate at ICSID, and then even if it subsequently bowed to pressure from a developed State or foreign investor and agreed to arbitrate such a dispute at ICSID, it would nonetheless retain the ability to refuse to arbitrate, based on its Article 25(4) exclusion. Moreover, Article 25(4) would also address the problem faced by many developing States, in which low levels of internal governance can result in representatives of the State entering into agreements that are contrary to the central government's wishes. Under Article 25(4), interpreted in the way just described, the State in question could simply invoke its Article 25(4) exclusion and then refuse to arbitrate.

Both ICSID jurisprudence and the weight of scholarly commentary argue, however, that Article 25(4) does not have this type of preclusive effect on the jurisdiction of an ICSID tribunal.[13] Instead, a consensus has developed that even if a State has lodged an Article 25(4) notification that it would not arbitrate a particular type of dispute at ICSID, if it nonetheless consents to ICSID arbitration of a dispute of that type, an ICSID tribunal does have jurisdiction over the dispute.[14]

The following three sections of this chapter will examine the three main interpretations that have been offered of Article 25(4): (a) that a notification under Article 25(4) serves only as a communication to investors of the State's policies; (b) that a notification serves as an interpretative guide for future arbitration agreements; and (c) that a notification is totally ineffective when it contradicts a 'specific consent' to arbitration by the Host State. The final section of this chapter will then argue that understanding both the Convention generally and Article 25(4) specifically as power-conferring provides a more acceptable interpretation of the legal effect of an Article 25(4) notification.

3 Article 25(4) notifications as communications to investors

Perhaps the most straightforward interpretation of an Article 25(4) notification is that it is able to serve as a direct response to developing State concerns that they may face pressure to agree to ICSID arbitration even when they do not believe it is in their best interest. Article 25(4), that is, might be understood as simply providing States with a public mechanism through which they can advertise to future investors that they are unwilling to agree to ICSID arbitration in certain situations.[15] This would free them from the need to explain this situation during negotiations with foreign investors, and allow their negotiators to reference the announced restriction as a clear statement of the limits within which they are able to negotiate.

There is no question that an Article 25(4) notification can serve as a communication to investors regarding the types of dispute a State is willing to arbitrate at ICSID. It merely has to be communicated to a potential foreign investor. In such a case, an Article 25(4) notification functions no differently to any other non-contractual communication made between contractual partners, and only has any direct legal effect to the extent allowed by the applicable contract law.

An initial problem with this interpretation is that it simply does not accurately reflect the way that an Article 25(4) notification actually functions. An Article 25(4) notification, after all, is communicated by the Host State to ICSID and thereby to the other Contracting States.[16] Absolutely nothing in the ICSID Convention requires that it ever be communicated directly to investors. It is, therefore, not immediately obvious why such a notification should be characterised as a notification *to investors*.

One response to this point is to argue that investors are held to be 'constructively' aware of Article 25(4) notifications, whether or not they are actually aware.[17] The procedure by which Article 25(4) notifications are communicated to ICSID and to Contracting States, that is, rather than to investors themselves, is simply a recognition of the difficulty involved in notifying every potential investor in a State. The onus is therefore placed on investors to determine for themselves if an Article 25(4) notification has been made.

Ultimately, though, this response fails to address the most serious problem with the 'communications to investors' interpretation of Article 25(4), which is that under this interpretation Article 25(4) simply does not give States any power that they did not already possess prior to Article 25(4)'s adoption. Article 25(4), after all, was adopted as a means of pacifying States that were concerned that they might be pressured into agreeing to ICSID arbitration against their better judgement. Yet even before the incorporation of Article 25(4) into the Convention, States possessed the ability not just to 'constructively' notify investors of their unwillingness to arbitrate certain types of disputes at ICSID, but to give potential investors 'actual' notice. Foreign investors, after all, do not have an inherent right to invest in any State, and may need to secure State permission in order to do so.[18] Consequently, any

State wishing to notify potential foreign investors of its unwillingness to arbitrate at ICSID certain types of disputes could simply provide that information to all potential foreign investors during the investment approval process.

Moreover, as the 'communications to investors' interpretation of Article 25(4) attributes no direct legal effect to an Article 25(4) notification, the existence of a notification does not preclude ICSID arbitration if a State has otherwise consented to it. Under this interpretation of Article 25(4), then, States are still exposed to potential pressure to agree to ICSID arbitration, despite having previously notified investors of their unwillingness to do so.

On the 'communication to investors' interpretation, then, Article 25(4) notifications are singularly unable to resolve precisely the problem that they were adopted to resolve. States gain no new powers from Article 25(4) to notify investors of their policy choices, and they remain just as open to pressure from foreign States and powerful investors as was the case before Article 25(4) was adopted. It is, therefore, simply inconsistent with what is known about the reasons motivating the incorporation into the Convention of Article 25(4) notifications for them to be understood as merely communications to investors.

4 Article 25(4) notifications as interpretive aids

The second potential interpretation of Article 25(4) notifications is closely linked to the 'communication to investors' interpretation, and is without question the interpretation that has been most influential in both jurisprudence and commentary. On this interpretation, an Article 25(4) notification is not a mere advance warning to investors regarding a type of dispute that a State is or is not willing to submit to ICSID arbitration, but instead serves as an 'interpretative aid' to future tribunals tasked with interpreting the breadth of the State's consent to ICSID arbitration. That is, whereas on the 'communications to investors' interpretation an Article 25(4) exclusion equates to a pronouncement to investors that 'We will not even discuss ICSID arbitration of this type of dispute', on the 'interpretative aid' interpretation it equates to a pronouncement to future arbitrators that 'If any consent we give to ICSID arbitration is unclear, we did not mean to agree to arbitrate this type of dispute'.

The 'interpretative aid' understanding of Article 25(4) notifications has most famously been advanced by Christoph Schreuer, who has argued that 'notifications under Article 25(4) are for purposes of information only and are designed to avoid misunderstandings. They do not have any direct legal consequences'.[19] However, as Schreuer notes, on this interpretation

> notifications may have an indirect bearing on jurisdiction. A consent clause that is not entirely clear may be interpreted by reference to a prior notification of classes of disputes in respect of which the Host State has expressed its intentions. In the absence of contrary evidence, it may

> be assumed that a State intended to remain within the limits of its notification when entering into the consent agreement.[20]

The 'interpretative aid' understanding, then, extends beyond the 'communications to investors' understanding in that it recognises a clear relevance of Article 25(4) notifications to the question of whether a State has indeed consented to ICSID arbitration of a specific dispute. Importantly, however, this is not because such notifications are regarded as having any direct legal effect. Rather, the existence of the notification merely serves as evidence of the State's desire to avoid ICSID arbitration of certain types of disputes. To this extent, then, the 'interpretative aid' and 'communications to investors' interpretations are consistent.

What distinguishes the 'interpretative aid' interpretation is that it introduces a presumption that any State making an Article 25(4) notification retains its opposition to ICSID arbitration of disputes covered by the notification as long as the notification is in effect. Consequently, a presumption arises that any consent to ICSID arbitration negotiated after the lodging of an Article 25(4) notification was intended by the State in question to conform to the notification. Nothing prevents the State from negotiating an arbitration agreement that is inconsistent with an existing Article 25(4) notification, but it will be presumed not to have done so, and its decision to overrule the existing notification must be clear if consent to ICSID arbitration is to be found.

The primary advantage of the 'interpretative aid' interpretation over the 'communications to investors' interpretation is that it manages to provide a plausible explanation why developing States saw Article 25(4) as resolving some of their concerns about ICSID jurisdiction. The 'communications to investors' understanding, after all, left any State making an Article 25(4) notification open to the claim that although it had notified investors of its unwillingness to agree to ICSID arbitration of a particular type of dispute, during negotiations with a certain investor it had altered its policy position and agreed to ICSID arbitration. The investor in question could then introduce any evidence it could produce supporting such a claim, including evidence of other arbitration agreements the State had made that were also inconsistent with the notification in question, and the tribunal would be left to determine which side had the stronger case.

By contrast, because of the presumption incorporated into the 'interpretative aid' interpretation, circumstantial evidence of State intent, such as the willingness of the State to enter into other arbitration agreements inconsistent with its Article 25(4) notification, becomes irrelevant to interpreting the State's intent in any specific case. Instead, the language adopted in each individual arbitration agreement holds paramount importance, affected only by evidence specifically relating to the agreement being interpreted. Moreover, the interpretation to be made by the tribunal is not an even-handed evaluation of which of the two parties has the strongest evidence for its claim, but is instead weighted by a presumption that the State did not agree to arbitrate any claims covered by its Article 25(4) notification. Only clear evidence of a willingness on the State's part to override its notification can suffice to do so.

Nonetheless, while the 'interpretative aid' interpretation is for this reason clearly preferable to the 'communications to investors' interpretation, it cannot be correct as an interpretation of Article 25(4) of the ICSID Convention, as the language used in that Article is simply inconsistent with the 'interpretative aid' interpretation's image of a mechanism designed solely to guide future tribunals. Article 25(4), that is, does not give a Contracting State the power to 'notify the Centre of the class or classes of disputes which it is or is not willing to submit to the jurisdiction of the Centre', an even-handed provision that gives equal weight to both 'willing' and 'not willing'. Instead, it gives Contracting States the power to notify ICSID of the types of disputes that they 'would or would not consider' submitting to the jurisdiction of ICSID.

The impact of the word 'consider' on the meaning of Article 25(4) is important to recognise.[21] Even with respect to a positive notification that a State 'would consider' arbitrating certain types of disputes at ICSID, the inclusion of the word 'consider' makes this announcement significantly less supportive of ICSID jurisdiction than it would have been had it said that the State 'is willing' to arbitrate the class of disputes in question. Even though the notification is framed in positive language, the inclusion of the word 'consider' simultaneously expresses an opposition by the State to ICSID arbitration, without which it would have been unnecessary to publicise the fact that arbitration of the type of dispute covered by the notification is at least a possibility.

This negative slant to the language of Article 25(4) becomes even more pronounced when the Article 25(4) notification is a negative one, expressing that the State 'would not consider' ICSID arbitration of a particular type of dispute. Such a notification does not merely express the State's policy decision not to arbitrate the class of disputes in question at ICSID, as would have been captured by a notification that the State is 'not willing' to arbitrate such disputes. It is, rather, a statement of fundamental opposition to ICSID arbitration of the type of dispute covered by the notification. It affirms that the State is so opposed to arbitration of the class of disputes covered by the notification that the possibility of doing so is not even open for discussion.

Moreover, this interpretative weighting of Article 25(4) notifications does not find expression only in the language of Article 25(4) itself, but is also found in the commentary on Article 25(4) included in the Report of the Executive Directors. The Report, that is, while noting that 'a statement by a Contracting State that it would consider submitting a certain class of dispute to the Centre would serve *for purposes of information only*' makes no equivalent qualification with respect to statements that the State 'would not' consider submitting a given class of disputes to ICSID.[22] Instead, the only qualification made with respect to negative notifications is that they do not 'constitute a reservation to the Convention'.

The distinction contained in this section of the Report of the Executive Directors between the legal effect of positive and negative notifications under Article 25(4) matches precisely the impact just discussed of the incorporation into Article 25(4) of the word 'consider'. That is, a positive notification that a State 'would consider' arbitrating a certain type of dispute at ICSID imposes no binding legal obligation on the State to arbitrate anything, and indeed 'serve[s] *for purposes of information only*'. A negative statement, on the other hand, that a State 'would not consider' arbitrating a particular type of dispute at ICSID is not a mere provision of information, but instead has at least some impact on the jurisdiction of ICSID.

The Report of the Executive Directors does, of course, note that a negative notification does 'not constitute a reservation to the Convention', but this should not be understood as equivalent to a statement that such a notification has no legal effect. After all, if this was the information that the Report was attempting to convey, it could have done so by simply stating that *both* positive and negative notifications under Article 25(4) 'serve *for purposes of information only*'. That qualification, however, is restricted solely to positive notifications.

The reference to reservations in this section of the Report of the Executive Directors, then, is best understood as arising from the constant efforts made during negotiations for the ICSID Convention to avoid *any* reservations being made to the Convention.[23] It does not preclude that a negative Article 25(4) notification might have some form of direct legal effect, but rather only clarifies that whatever legal effect such a notification has, it is not the same effect as had by a reservation. As a result, the goal of avoiding all reservations to the Convention has been maintained.

Even if the interpretative weighting created by the language of both Article 25(4) and the Report of the Executive Directors is overlooked, however, a significant additional obstacle nonetheless remains to the acceptability of the 'interpretative aid' interpretation of Article 25(4). As already mentioned, the concern on the part of developing States that the incorporation into the Convention of Article 25(4) was alleged to have addressed was not merely that unclear arbitration agreements might be misinterpreted. It was also that weaker States might find themselves pressured by developed States and powerful investors to agree to ICSID arbitration even in areas for which they believed ICSID arbitration to be inappropriate. On the 'interpretative aid' interpretation, however, Article 25(4) does absolutely nothing to address this concern. So long as the agreement to arbitrate that a State was pressured to sign is clear, there is no question of interpretation to which any contrary Article 25(4) notification is relevant. Consequently, on the 'interpretative aid' interpretation, Article 25(4) does absolutely nothing to resolve one of the primary concerns that it was adopted to resolve.

The 'interpretative aid' interpretation of Article 25(4) notifications, then, while superficially plausible, ultimately fails to be consistent both with what is known of the negotiations underlying the adoption of Article 25(4) of the

ICSID Convention, and with the language included in both Article 25(4) itself and in the Report of the Executive Directors.

5 Conflicts between an Article 25(4) notification and a 'specific consent' to ICSID arbitration

One of the arguments that has given the strongest support to the 'interpretative aid' interpretation of Article 25(4) of the ICSID Convention invokes the fact that the *travaux préparatoires* of the Convention appear to contain clear recognition by the Contracting States that a 'specific consent' to arbitrate a dispute at ICSID will be given effect even if the dispute in question is covered by a negative Article 25(4) notification.[24] Proponents of the 'interpretative aid' interpretation have appealed to this aspect of the *travaux préparatoires* as supporting their argument that Article 25(4) notifications must be understood to serve informational purposes only. After all, if an Article 25(4) notification cannot override a contrary agreement to arbitrate, it is difficult to see what direct legal effect such a notification can be understood to have.

These arguments, however, have uniformly been based on a purely intuitive understanding of what the term 'specific consent' should be understood to mean, with no real attempt being made to determine what the term was actually understood to mean at the time that it was used during negotiations for the ICSID Convention. 'Specific consent' has, therefore, been understood as covering any type of agreement to arbitrate at ICSID, whether arising from an agreement directly between an investor and a Host State, or from the broad consent to ICSID arbitration contained in a BIT or domestic investment legislation.

Close attention to the discussion in the *travaux préparatoires* in which the reference to 'specific consent' occurs, however, makes questionable the broad interpretation that this term has been given. The phrase 'specific consent' is used with respect to Article 25(4) when the delegate from Spain asks the delegate from the United Kingdom, with respect to the UK's proposal for what ultimately became Article 25(4), what the result would be 'of a conflict between a specific consent and a notification to exclude the type of dispute covered by the specific agreement from those disputes which a State was willing to submit to the jurisdiction of the Centre?'[25] The delegate from the United Kingdom responded that '[s]ince the jurisdiction was based on consent the specific and particular consent would govern'.[26]

The difficulty in interpreting this exchange arises from the alternation that occurs in this section of the *travaux preparatoires* between the terms 'specific consent' and 'specific agreement', which are used interchangeably by the Spanish and UK delegates despite not being equivalent terms.[27] A 'consent' to arbitration, after all, can exist when only one party has expressed its willingness to arbitrate, even if the other party has not yet done so. The 'consent' in such a situation merely constitutes an offer to arbitrate, such as is now accepted as being made by many BITs. A 'specific agreement' to arbitrate, by contrast, cannot exist until both parties to the agreement have offered their consent. There can, therefore, be situations in which a 'specific consent' to ICSID arbitration exists, but a 'specific agreement' does not. The question becomes, therefore, why the delegates at the ICSID Convention found interchangeable these two terms that clearly have substantively different meanings.

The answer to this question can be found in an article published in 1966, the year in which the ICSID Convention came into force, by Aron Broches, General Counsel of the World Bank during the period in which the ICSID Convention was developed and chairman of the legal committee throughout the course of the negotiations.[28] Among the many issues addressed in the article, Broches spends some time discussing the different forms that consent to ICSID arbitration might take, and the impact that these different forms might have on the provision in Article 25(1) of the Convention that '[w]hen the parties have given their consent, no party may withdraw its consent unilaterally'.

While Broches does not see any particular difficulties arising with respect to consent to arbitration that is found in an agreement to arbitrate reached directly between a Host State and an investor, he argues that consent found in the Host State's domestic investment legislation presents a far more complex situation.[29] Broches identifies three distinct forms that domestic legislation expressing a Host State's consent to ICSID arbitration might take:

> In *Case I* the legislation provides that all disputes arising under it with respect to investments to which it is applicable 'shall be settled by arbitration in accordance with the provisions of the Convention, *provided the investor shall have consented to such arbitration in writing prior to the approval of the investment hereunder*' ... In *Case II* the language of the legislation omits the language in italics ... [In *Case III*], under the investment promotion legislation of the Host state the investor is given the right to ask for arbitration under the Convention if a dispute arises regarding the rights or privileges granted by such legislation.[30]

Broches concludes that *Case I* is unproblematic, as both the Host State and the investor will have expressed their consent to ICSID arbitration prior to the investment taking place, and as a result, under the clear terms of Article 25(1) of the ICSID Convention, neither party may subsequently unilaterally withdraw its consent.[31]

The important point for the present discussion, however, occurs with respect to Broches' comments on *Case II* and *Case III*. As Broches acknowledges, once a foreign investor has accepted the Host State's offer to arbitrate, and proffered its own consent, the situation is again simple, as a binding agreement to arbitrate exists, and so again the Host State may no longer withdraw its consent.[32] For Broches, however, a notably different situation exists prior to the investor accepting the State's offer to consent. At that point, Broches argues, it is simply unclear whether or not a Host State has the right to withdraw the consent it has offered, such as by amending its investment legislation to preclude ICSID arbitration.[33] As a result, noting that this involves 'troublesome questions',[34] Broches simply concludes that 'it would clearly be desirable from the point of view of the Host state as well as that of the investor to avoid ambiguity and to spell out clearly the terms of their mutual consent'.[35]

While the uncertainty that is at the core of Broches' discussion can hardly be taken to lend direct support for any particular interpretation of Article 25(4), it has important consequences for understanding the exchange in the *travaux préparatoires* under discussion here. The difficulty involved in interpreting that exchange, after all, was that the terms 'specific consent' and 'specific agreement' were used interchangeably even though they have substantively different meanings. This problem is resolved, however, if the exchange is understood as referring solely to the 'consent' contained in a concluded arbitration agreement. In such a situation, 'specific consent' and 'specific agreement', while nonetheless remaining substantively different, could be used interchangeably without difficulty. There would, after all, be no situation in which a 'specific consent' existed, but a 'specific agreement' did not.

The importance of Broches' comments, then, is that they make clear that this must indeed have been the understanding of those involved in the negotiations when the exchange in question took place. It was, after all, completely unresolved at that time whether or not a State retained the right to retract its consent to ICSID arbitration prior to that consent being accepted by an investor. It would, however, have made little sense for those involved in the negotiations to maintain that even though it was possible that a State might have an absolute power to withdraw its consent at any point prior to the investor reciprocating with its own consent, allowing it to do so through the mechanism of an Article 25(4) notification would be inconsistent with the principle that ICSID jurisdiction was based on consent.

Interpreting the exchange in the *travaux préparatoires* in accordance with this understanding of 'specific consent', then, makes clear that what was in question in the exchange was not the legal effect of an Article 25(4) notification, but the possibility of a conflict between Article 25(1) and Article 25(4) of the ICSID Convention. That is, the exchange was addressing whether a State that has entered into a mutually binding agreement to arbitrate with an investor, and cannot retract its consent under the explicit terms of Article 25(1), can nonetheless effectively retract that consent through an Article 25(4) notification. Unsurprisingly, it was agreed that Article 25(4) could not be used as a means of avoiding the restrictions incorporated into Article 25(1).

6 The direct legal effect of Article 25(4) notifications

The preceding discussion has attempted to demonstrate the problems involved in interpreting Article 25(4) as nothing more than a mechanism through which States can provide information on their policy choices about arbitration at ICSID. As has been argued, any interpretation of this type is inconsistent not only with the language of both Article 25(4) itself and the Report of the Executive Directors, but also with the role that Article 25(4) played in the negotiations over the jurisdictional provisions of the ICSID Convention, and with the evidence available from the *travaux préparatoires* of how Article 25(4) was understood during those negotiations.

Nonetheless, while it is clear that Article 25(4) notifications cannot fairly be viewed as having no direct legal effect on the jurisdiction of ICSID tribunals, it is also clear that they cannot be understood as imposing absolute jurisdictional restrictions, incapable of being overridden even by a specific consent to arbitration. The remainder of this chapter, therefore, examines closely the practical application of Article 25(4), as a means of elucidating a principled interpretation of that provision, which respects both its ability to limit ICSID jurisdiction, and its ability to be overridden by specific agreements to ICSID arbitration.

Central to this interpretation is the need to understand Article 25(4) as a power-conferring provision of the ICSID Convention. Article 25(4), that is, confers on States the unilateral power to control ICSID jurisdiction, even though this is not a power without limitation. Because of this, when faced with a conflict between an Article 25(4) notification and a specific agreement to arbitrate, the obligation of a tribunal is to determine whether giving effect to the Article 25(4) notification or to the conflicting arbitration agreement best reflects the Host State's limited power to define ICSID jurisdiction that it has been granted through Article 25(4).

The operation of Article 25(4) of the ICSID Convention, when understood as a power-conferring provision, can best be demonstrated through a close examination of five factual situations in which a conflict between an Article 25(4) notification and a specific consent to ICSID arbitration might arise.

6.1 Case I

State A provides a notification under Article 25(4) of the ICSID Convention that it would not consider arbitrating at ICSID any disputes arising out of oil concessions. However, it already has in place a concession contract with a concessionaire that includes an agreement by both sides to ICSID arbitration of any disputes arising out of the concession.

It is clear from the preceding discussion that the pre-existing arbitration agreement remains binding on State A despite State A's Article 25(4) notification. Article 25(4) does not, after all, override the provision in Article 25(1) that '[w]hen the parties have given their consent, no party may withdraw its consent unilaterally'. Limiting ICSID jurisdiction through an Article 25(4) notification might not technically constitute a withdrawal of consent, as the consent in the concession agreement remains effective, but allowing State A to preclude ICSID arbitration through an Article 25(4) notification would be tantamount to allowing it to retract its consent. Respect for the structure of Article 25, however, prevents allowing one element of it to so clearly undermine another. Moreover, as the previous discussion has made clear, the best interpretation of the *travaux préparatoires* is that this precise issue was addressed during negotiations, with it being understood that the arbitration agreement should be given effect.

6.2 Case II

State A provides a notification under Article 25(4) of the ICSID Convention that it would not consider arbitrating at ICSID any disputes arising out of oil concessions. However, 2 years later it enters into an oil concession contract with a foreign investor, which specifies ICSID arbitration as the forum for the resolution of any disputes arising under the contract.

Allowing the Article 25(4) notification to override the agreement to arbitrate would not in this instance violate Article 25(1). Because the notification preceded the agreement to arbitrate included in the concession contract, allowing it to override that agreement would mean that the agreement never became effective. As a result, State A was never under an obligation to arbitrate at ICSID, and so never needed to retract its consent in violation of Article 25(1).

This being said, however, it nonetheless remains the case that the best interpretation of Case II is that the agreement to arbitrate again overrides the Article 25(4) notification, and State A is obligated to arbitrate at ICSID. This is so, despite the ineffectiveness of Article 25(1), because of the power conferred on State A, through Article 25(4), to control its own consent to ICSID jurisdiction. The post-notification decision by State A to enter into the arbitration agreement with the concessionaire clearly manifests the State's judgment that ICSID arbitration was desirable with respect to that specific agreement. Upholding the Article 25(4) notification against the arbitration agreement would, therefore, actually reduce the power of the Host State to control its consent to ICSID jurisdiction, by preventing the State consenting to ICSID arbitration when it decides it is in its best interest to do so.

6.3 Case III

State A provides a notification under Article 25(4) of the ICSID Convention that it would not consider arbitrating at ICSID any disputes arising out of oil concessions. However, it already has in place a BIT with State B that includes a standing offer of ICSID arbitration for all disputes arising directly out of investments made by investors from State B, specifically including oil concessions. Prior to the Article 25(4) notification being issued, a concessionaire from State B files a request for arbitration at ICSID of a claim arising out of the operation of its concession, and invoking the standing consent to arbitration included in the BIT between State A and State B.

Although this situation involves a standing consent to arbitration included in a treaty, rather than an agreement to arbitrate reached directly between a

Host State and an investor, the same reasoning applies here as applied in Case I. A binding agreement to arbitrate is formed as soon as the investor accepts State A's standing offer to arbitrate. As a result, under the clear language of Article 25(1), State A cannot subsequently withdraw its consent to arbitration through an Article 25(4) notification.

6.4 Case IV

State A provides a notification under Article 25(4) of the ICSID Convention that it would not consider arbitrating at ICSID any disputes arising out of oil concessions. However, it already has in place a BIT with State B that includes a standing offer of ICSID arbitration for all disputes arising directly out of investments made by investors from State B, specifically including oil concessions. After the Article 25(4) notification is issued, but while the treaty between State A and State B remains in effect, a concessionaire from State B files a request for arbitration at ICSID of a claim arising out of the operation of its concession, invoking the standing consent to arbitration included in the BIT between State A and State B.

Although in the parallel situation discussed in Case II, involving a direct agreement between State A and the investor, the agreement to arbitrate was held to be binding, where the agreement to arbitrate arises from the acceptance by an investor of a standing offer to arbitrate included in a treaty or in domestic investment legislation the Article 25(4) notification should be understood as precluding the investor's claim from being arbitrated at ICSID.

Although entering into an agreement directly with an investor to arbitrate at ICSID manifests State A's decision that ICSID arbitration is desirable for that specific situation, State A is not involved in the investor's decision to accept its standing offer to arbitrate. Consequently, allowing the arbitration agreement to take precedence over the Article 25(4) notification cannot be portrayed as respecting the power granted to State A through Article 25(4) to control its own consent to ICSID jurisdiction.

Rather, the only times that State A has made an explicit decision about the arbitrability at ICSID of disputes arising out of oil concessions were when it entered into the treaty with State B, and when it issued its Article 25(4) notification. As the Article 25(4) notification was issued after the treaty with State B was negotiated, the notification must be taken as overriding the consent in the treaty. Only this conclusion respects the power that Article 25(4) grants to State A to control its own consent to ICSID jurisdiction.

Moreover, as the investor had not accepted State A's standing offer to arbitrate at the time the Article 25(4) notification was issued, Article 25(1) was not implicated. Consequently, at the time the investor attempted to commence ICSID arbitration, arbitration of disputes arising out of oil concessions was precluded by State A's Article 25(4) notification.

State A would, of course, likely be found to be in violation of its treaty with State B, as it is not fulfilling its obligation under that treaty to offer

ICSID arbitration to investors from State B. However, this is a determination that would have to be made in some other forum than ICSID.

6.5 Case V

State A provides a notification under Article 25(4) of the ICSID Convention that it would not consider arbitrating at ICSID any disputes arising out of oil concessions. However, it already has in place a BIT with State B that includes a standing offer of consent to ICSID arbitration for certain disputes arising directly out of investments made by investors from State B, and a direct agreement with a concessionaire from State C to arbitrate at ICSID certain disputes arising out of the concession. However, in both instances it is unclear whether the consent to ICSID arbitration covers the claim brought by the investor.

In both instances the Article 25(4) notification should be understood to preclude ICSID arbitration, due to the vagueness of the arbitration agreements. Importantly, however, this is not because the Article 25(4) notification functions as an 'interpretative aid' for the tribunal, but because only this holding respects the power granted to State A under Article 25(4) of the ICSID Convention to control its own consent to ICSID jurisdiction.

Preventing the investor relying on an unclear consent to ICSID arbitration does not, after all, prevent ICSID arbitration. It merely allows State A to reach a decision on whether ICSID arbitration of this particular dispute, despite the existence of the Article 25(4) notification, is in its best interest. This is a decision that has been allocated to State A by Article 25(4) of the ICSID Convention. If State A decides it does wish to arbitrate at ICSID with the investor, it can simply enter into a new agreement to do so, and the arbitration can take place.

By contrast, allowing the tribunal to determine, as a matter of interpretation of the arbitration agreement, whether State A must arbitrate at ICSID creates the risk that State A will be forced to arbitrate in some situations in which it legitimately did not believe that the arbitration agreement covered oil concessions. In such situations, State A would effectively have been deprived of the power granted it under Article 25(4) of the ICSID Convention to control its own consent to ICSID jurisdiction.

7 Conclusion

Article 25(4) of the ICSID Convention played a central role in convincing developing States to accept the vague jurisdictional provisions of the Convention, but it has nonetheless consistently been interpreted in a way that deprives it of any direct legal effect. It has been argued in this chapter that these interpretations have relied on misunderstandings of both the language of the Convention and of the discussions of Article 25(4) that are found in the *travaux préparatoires*.

Article 25(4) is an important aspect of the power-conferring structure of the Convention, a fact that is reflected both in the language of the Article itself, and in the role that adoption of the Article played in allaying the concerns of developing States. Only an interpretation that reflects the grant of power contained in Article 25(4) can serve as a faithful interpretation of the Convention.

3 The role of an investment arbitrator and the use of non-binding documents and literature in investment arbitration

1 Introduction

Law is not advice.[1] It can certainly play important roles in guiding behaviour or establishing standards, and it need not be generated in particular ways or by certain bodies. However, while the formal structures within which law is created and implemented can vary significantly from one legal system to another, one essential characteristic that all law must possess is that it is binding on those to whom it is directed.[2]

This, at least, is the conception of law that has long been dominant in international law, and that is reflected in the classical statement of the sources of international law, Article 38 of the Statute of the International Court of Justice (ICJ Statute).[3] Article 38 only identifies three types of instrument that can legitimately serve as sources of international law, and all three unquestionably generate norms that are intended to have binding force.[4] As a result, while an instrument that is not binding can be useful as a source of information on the content of international law, it cannot be a source of that law.[5] It cannot, that is, create binding legal obligations or alter any legal obligations already in effect.

While this conception of the legitimate sources of international law remains dominant, it has been increasingly challenged in recent years, with even the ICJ allowing non-binding instruments to influence its decisions.[6] The arguments in favour of acknowledging the relevance of non-binding instruments to international law are varied, but socio-legal scholarship in particular has been influential, with writers arguing that the conception of law embodied in Article 38 of the ICJ Statute is unrealistically narrow.[7] In addition, some writers have argued that this conception is particularly problematic in the context of international law, as it results in the interests and attitudes of developed States being privileged over those of developing States.[8]

This chapter will not directly address this debate, but will instead take as given that the classical statement of the sources of international law, as found in Article 38 of the ICJ Statute, is indeed correct. It will argue, though, that in the context of international investment law it is inappropriate to concentrate solely on correctly identifying and understanding the sources of international law. Such an approach ignores an equally important question, namely the nature of an international investment arbitrator's role.[9]

As a substantive area of law, international investment law originally developed from public international law, and so the content of public international law is unquestionably relevant to any attempt to determine the content of international investment law.[10] Nonetheless, while at a substantive level the two fields of law are clearly closely tied, they have come to be implemented through fundamentally different mechanisms. Public international law is dominated by a permanent court, populated by judges with long-term appointments, while international investment law is dominated by arbitration tribunals, composed of individuals selected by the parties to the dispute being heard, and with no ongoing role beyond that single appointment. International investment arbitration arbitrators, that is, are simply performing a different institutional role than ICJ judges, for whom Article 38 of the ICJ Statute was developed.

Section 2 of this chapter will offer a structural analysis of investment arbitration, arguing that the manner in which investment arbitration tribunals are appointed and operate undercuts any argument that they are bound by the constraints of Article 38 of the ICJ Statute. Consequently, the rules that should guide investment arbitration tribunals in their use of non-binding documents and literature cannot be derived from Article 38, but must instead be determined through an analysis specific to international investment arbitration.

The remainder of this chapter is divided into two sections, corresponding to what are argued to be the two different types of non-binding instrument. Section 3 addresses 'authoritative instruments', which are those relied upon by investment arbitration tribunals as authoritative guides to the content of international investment law. It will be argued that although investment arbitration tribunals can legitimately rely upon soft law instruments as a means of understanding the obligations existing between two or more States, the highly contested nature of international investment law precludes any other instrument serving as an authoritative guide to the content of international investment law.

Section 4 will then address 'persuasive instruments', which are those relied upon by tribunals as sources of arguments regarding the content or interpretation of international investment law. Although such writings are already used significantly more often by investment arbitration tribunals than is standard in public international law, it will be argued that they are nonetheless used less often than is required by the structure of international investment arbitration.

2 The use of non-binding instruments in investment arbitration

The classical approach to the sources of international law, as enunciated in Article 38 of the ICJ Statute, is deliberately restrictive in terms of the sources on which tribunals can rely in determining the content of international law. This was, after all, a system devised by States, for the resolution of State-State disputes. There was, then, little support for any approach to the sources of international law that would detract from the high level of control States had always possessed over the content of that law.[11]

As a result, Article 38 of the ICJ Statute explicitly recognises as sources of international law only three things, each of which incorporates a requirement that States have acknowledged its contents to be legally binding.[12] By contrast, while some recognition of the relevance of non-binding instruments was ultimately included in Article 38, it was very limited, and extended only to 'the teachings of the most highly qualified publicists'.[13] Moreover, even these 'teachings' were acknowledged to be relevant only as a 'subsidiary means' for determining which rules of international law existed, not as actual sources of international law. That is, under Article 38, non-binding instruments cannot themselves give rise to international law, but can provide confirmation that a rule of law has developed by means of one of the three acknowledged binding sources.[14]

While criticism has been made of Article 38's restrictive approach to the sources of international law, particularly in recent years, it nonetheless remains the accepted statement of the sources of international law, not only for the ICJ itself, but for international tribunals generally.[15]

What is important for the present chapter, however, is not the applicability of Article 38 of the ICJ Statute to public international law tribunals generally, but the potential impact of its application in the international investment law context. After all, if IIA tribunals are bound by Article 38, then they cannot legitimately rely on any non-binding instrument other than 'the teachings of the most highly qualified publicists' when determining international law. Other non-binding instruments might be relevant as context to the interpretation of an applicable treaty, but they can play no role in the tribunal's efforts to determine the content of international investment law.

Unlike most public international law treaties, however, which detail with some precision the rights and obligations of the States party to the treaty, international investment treaties are characterised by their inclusion of generalised references to international norms. Thus, for example, rather than detailing precisely which actions States party to a treaty may and may not take with respect to investors, investment treaties will commonly include a simple reference to an obligation to provide 'fair and equitable treatment', thereby incorporating an international standard in place of an explicit agreement between the parties.[16]

If, however, investment arbitration tribunals are understood to be bound by Article 38 of the ICJ Statute, then the parties' inclusion of an international law norm into their treaty has major consequences for the instruments upon which the tribunal may rely in interpreting the treaty. That is, if 'fair and equitable treatment' were merely a treaty term then the tribunal could legitimately rely upon any instrument that would clarify the parties' understanding of the term. However, since 'fair and equitable treatment' is an international law standard, Article 38 requires that the only non-binding instruments that can be used in its interpretation are 'the teachings of the most highly qualified publicists'.

The combination, then, of the inclusion of international legal standards in investment treaties and the application of Article 38 of the ICJ Statute to investment arbitration tribunals, stands to impact significantly upon the work of investment arbitration tribunals. It will restrict their use of non-binding instruments not only with respect to the determination of the content of international law, but even with respect to their interpretation of certain treaty provisions.

The remainder of this section of the chapter will, however, attempt to demonstrate that any concerns of this type are unfounded. It will be argued that even if it is accepted that Article 38 of the ICJ Statute is binding for all international tribunals determining the content of international law, Article 38 is nonetheless not binding on investment arbitration tribunals. Investment arbitration tribunals, that is, are not part of the judicial structure of international law, and consequently are simply not engaged in the same enterprise as those tribunals bound by Article 38.

This is perhaps a counterintuitive claim, given the role that investment arbitration tribunals unquestionably have in enforcing and interpreting international investment law. However, a close examination of the structure of international investment dispute adjudication, and specifically of the role of arbitrators within that structure, makes clear that an investment arbitrator simply cannot be understood as a judge, objectively interpreting and applying law that is independent of the parties. Instead, he or she is best understood as involved in the resolution of a dispute, even though the nature of the dispute requires that international law be used as a reference point.

Two primary structural differences are essential to recognising the important difference between ICJ judges and investment arbitrators with respect to the instruments upon which they can legitimately rely. The first relates to the differing structures of dispute resolution used in public international law and international investment law, while the second relates to the different ways in which ICJ judges and IIA arbitrators are appointed to their posts.

Traditionally, of course, disputes in international investment law and public international law were resolved through precisely the same mechanisms. Some would be resolved through negotiation, some through resort to domestic courts, and a small minority would be addressed through arbitration.[17] An important change occurred at the beginning of the twentieth century, however, with the institutionalisation of public international law as a result of the creation of the Permanent Court of International Justice (PCIJ), and then the ICJ.[18] While neither court was ever the exclusive forum for the resolution of public international law disputes, the prominence of both courts and the high degree of international consensus that lay behind their creation, meant that both the PCIJ and the ICJ assumed a position as final arbiter on the content of international law.[19]

In the current structure of public international law, that is, the ICJ serves as a norm-adopting institution, fixing the substance of the rules of public international law through its decisions.[20] Other tribunals are not formally bound by the decisions of the ICJ, but the authority of the ICJ as a permanent court created by States to resolve disputes over the content of the international law that they themselves have created, ensures the deference of other tribunals to its decisions. If the ICJ says that a certain rule of international law exists, then it exists, and it exists because the ICJ says that it does.[21]

International investment law, however, has taken a fundamentally different path. The resolution of international investment law disputes remained closely entwined with the resolution of public international law disputes for most of the twentieth century.[22] However, this changed fundamentally in the 1990s with the rise of BIT arbitration, and today international investment arbitration is unquestionably the central dispute resolution mechanism for international investment disputes.[23] Consequently, while the ICJ has become the authoritative centre of public international law, to the extent that role exists in international investment law it is played by a network of investment arbitration tribunals, which routinely cite one another's decisions when attempting to establish the content of international investment law.

While the ICJ and investment arbitration tribunals have parallel central roles in their respective fields, however, they operate in importantly different institutional contexts. Neither has the capacity to deliver interpretations of the law that are binding on other tribunals. However, the ICJ is an ongoing institution established through the almost-universal agreement of States,[24] while investment arbitration tribunals are temporary bodies established to hear a single case and constituted solely by the parties to the dispute.[25] Investment arbitration tribunals, that is, simply lack the institutional context that gives the ICJ its status as an authoritative interpreter of the law.

This, though, is not the only important structural difference between ICJ judges and investment arbitrators. The ICJ's ability to act as a norm-adopting authority for public international law is importantly tied to the fact that ICJ judges hold long-term appointments, and are selected through a process that operates independently of any individual case.[26] This does not mean that no political considerations at all enter into the ICJ appointment process, but only that such influences will reflect the generalised desire of certain States to influence the direction of public international law, rather than their desire to win a particular case.

By contrast, investment arbitrators are appointed to tribunals for a single case, are almost always appointed on the nomination of a single party to the dispute, and are selected after the nominating party is aware of the relevant facts of the case and the likely legal issues that the tribunal must decide.[27] Unsurprisingly, the investment arbitration appointment process is a highly contentious one, with parties often approaching it as a means of gaining advantage in the upcoming proceedings, rather than as a means of ensuring the best understanding of the applicable law.[28]

This fundamental difference between the means of appointment of ICJ judges and investment arbitrators further undermines any claim investment arbitration tribunals might otherwise have to being able to serve as authoritative norm-adopting interpreters of international investment law. Investment arbitration tribunals unquestionably have the authority to decide the dispute before them, and in doing so they must interpret and apply the applicable law.[29] However, an investment arbitration tribunal's decision on the content of this law ultimately just represents the opinion of individuals appointed to resolve a specific dispute. It does not create a norm to be followed by subsequent tribunals.

It should be emphasised, though, that the inability of investment arbitration awards to create binding norms is not necessarily a weakness of international investment arbitration. Not every situation, after all, is ideally addressed through an objective and universally binding interpretation of the law. The structural differences between the roles of investment arbitrators and ICJ judges, then, merely indicate that a difference exists, not that one is an unsuccessful version of the other.

Indeed, any portrayal of investment arbitrators as unsuccessful judges would make incomprehensible the continuing endorsement of international investment arbitration by States. States agreeing to international investment arbitration, that is, simply do not do so with the expectation that arbitrators will reach their decisions in the same way as would ICJ judges. This is just not the way that States have structured the international investment law dispute resolution system.

Recognition of the differences in structure between the roles of ICJ judges and investment arbitrators, then, should not lead to discussions of how the role of the investment arbitrator can be reformed to make it resemble more closely that of the ICJ judge. It should, instead, lead to an analysis of what is distinctive about the structure of the role of the investment arbitrator, and what that distinctiveness indicates about how the role of the investment arbitrator should be performed.

With respect to the use of non-binding instruments, the most important aspect of the structure of the role of the investment arbitrator concerns the appointment process already described. While ICJ judges are appointed to long-term positions in which they address disputes between many parties, investment arbitrators are appointed to address a single dispute, at a time that the parties are already aware of the legal and factual issues that the tribunal will likely have to address. Because of this structure, parties selecting an investment arbitrator pay significant attention to the substantive legal views of any potential appointee. Doing so allows each party to ensure that substantive views of particular importance to it are represented in the tribunal's deliberations.

Appointing arbitrators in this way, however, would make no sense if an investment arbitrator's role was to arrive at a detached and generalisable understanding of the content of the applicable law. It is a structure that strongly emphasises the arbitrator's substantive views on the law, and it provides no protection against a tribunal composed of individuals who all share a minority understanding of that law.

The structure of the appointment process of investment arbitrators, then, is best understood as allocating to them a responsibility to engage in what can be called the 'substantive interpretation' of the applicable law. They must certainly decide in accordance with the law, as anything else would be inconsistent with the status of arbitration as a legal dispute resolution mechanism.[30] However, in arriving at their determination of what the content of that law is, they have no obligation to conform to any view they do not share, no matter how broadly accepted that view might be.[31]

It is this important difference between the roles of ICJ judges and investment arbitrators that justifies the conclusion that investment arbitrators are not bound by the constraints of Article 38 of the ICJ Statute. The Statute identifies rules designed for a judge, and as a representative of a broader legal community a judge is obligated to conform his or her opinions to developing trends within past case law and within the reasoning of his or her fellow judges.[32] An investment arbitrator, however, is not a judge, but is instead an individual appointed to reach his or her own conclusions on points of fact and law. The roles are different, and hence the rules in accordance with which roles must be performed are different as well.

The remainder of this chapter will look more closely at the manner in which investment arbitrators can legitimately rely upon non-binding instruments in reaching their interpretations of the content of international investment law. Two types of instruments will be addressed, identified in accordance with the manner in which they can legitimately be relied upon by an arbitrator. The term 'authoritative instruments' will be used to refer to those non-binding instruments that serve as authoritative guides to the normative principles that underlie international investment law. The term 'persuasive instruments' will be used to refer to those non-binding instruments that have their impact through the strength of the arguments they contain.

3 The use of authoritative instruments in investment arbitration

3.1 The legitimacy of the use of authoritative instruments by investment arbitration tribunals

Although it has been argued above that investment arbitration tribunals are not bound by the constraints of Article 38 of the ICJ Statute, it does not follow that Article 38 is therefore irrelevant to a discussion of the use of non-binding instruments by investment arbitration tribunals. Article 38, after all, is the outcome of an extended deliberation by prominent experts as to the instruments that should be used by an international tribunal when determining the content of international law.[33] Consequently, even though it is not binding on investment arbitration tribunals, it may reflect an approach to the topic that is compelling in its own right.[34] The following discussion will, therefore, begin with Article 38's approach to the use by tribunals of authoritative instruments, and will explain why Article 38's approach is not one that IIA tribunals should adopt.

The most notable aspect of the approach of Article 38 of the ICJ Statute to authoritative instruments is the starkly different treatment that is given to two different types of instrument: (a) authoritative commentaries; and (b) State-generated 'soft law' instruments. Under Article 38(1)(d), 'the teachings of the most highly qualified publicists' can legitimately be used as a guide to the content of international law. No mention at all is made, however, of a similar use of non-binding State-generated soft law instruments.

It is not difficult to see why tribunals should be allowed to consult authoritative commentaries (i.e. 'teachings'), as doing so allows the tribunal to draw from expertise it might not itself possess. More questionable, though, is allowing tribunals to use commentaries written by individuals with no role in the creation of international law, while simultaneously precluding the use of non-binding instruments generated by the very entities that create international law in the first place. Intuitively, if either of these two groups is likely to possess reliable insights into the current content of international law, it will be States.

One simple rationale for this exclusion of soft law instruments derives from the practicalities of State control over the content of international law. That is, allowing tribunals to rely on non-binding instruments generated by States would potentially undermine the ability of States to control their international obligations. After all, the potential range of State-generated instruments that could be taken to constitute soft law is enormous.[35] Consequently, if tribunals could rely on soft law instruments, almost any instrument generated by a State could be used by a tribunal to influence its determination of the content of international law. This would significantly undermine the distinction States have attempted to maintain between those instruments by which they are legally bound, and those by which they are not.

On the other hand, however, denying the relevance of soft law instruments to the content of international law leaves a great deal of State action difficult to understand. That is, many non-binding instruments generated by States are clearly meant to be norm-creating, and are taken seriously by States to an extent that would be difficult to understand if those instruments were meant to have no impact on States' international legal obligations.[36] Even more significantly, States are known to use soft law instruments both to supplement hard law instruments and to undermine them, actions that would be pointless if it was possible to determine the content of international law without consulting soft law instruments.[37] In order to determine the true content of international law, then, so this argument concludes, it is essential to consider soft law instruments, which play a different role in the formation of international law than hard law instruments, but nonetheless play a role.

In the context of the ICJ Statute, it is clear why concerns about the need to respect State control over international law would be given priority, as the ICJ is a norm-adopting body capable of determining the content of international law. It is less clear, however, that this same concern is equally powerful with respect to investment arbitration tribunals. Investment arbitration tribunals, after all, are not norm-adopting, but instead merely deliver awards that express the views of the tribunal's members regarding the content of international law. These views are not only not binding on other tribunals, but will simply be rejected by any subsequent tribunal with a different intellectual composition.[38]

Nonetheless, this does not mean that an investment arbitration award is merely a forum in which a tribunal announces its decision, as an award must also present the reasoning behind the decision.[39] This requirement gets little attention, but it adds an important element to the role of the investment arbitrator. Given that an investment arbitration tribunal is not norm-adopting, its decision has no direct relevance for future tribunals. Consequently, the existence of this requirement can only be understood as reflecting an obligation on the part of investment arbitration tribunals to attempt to ensure that the parties to the dispute can both understand and accept the decision they have received. Achieving this goal is clearly more likely if a tribunal appeals to a broad range of conduct by States as a means of supporting its decision than if it merely invokes the reasoning of its constituent members, all of whom were appointed in a highly adversarial context.[40]

There is, then, clear justification for the use of both authoritative commentaries and authoritative soft law instruments by investment arbitration tribunals. A tribunal's use of authoritative commentaries can both increase the likelihood that its understanding of international law is correct, and increase the persuasiveness of its award for the parties, while the tribunal's invocation of soft law instruments in its award can increase the persuasiveness of the award for the parties, whether or not those instruments constitute sources of international law.

Nonetheless, even if the use of authoritative instruments by investment arbitration tribunals is accepted, this does not clarify precisely how they should be used. The following three sections of this chapter will, therefore, address this question, first by establishing the current use of authoritative instruments by investment arbitration tribunals, and then by examining whether that current use is appropriate.

3.2 The current use of authoritative instruments in investment arbitration

A study of citations in published investment arbitration awards was undertaken for this chapter, with cited writings being sorted into 'academic' and 'institutional' categories.[41] 'Academic' writings were those that expressed the views of one or a small number of authors, and were relied upon because of the individual reputations of the authors. 'Institutional' writings were those developed through an organised process involving groups of individuals, entities or States, that had collaborated to produce a single writing. That writing might not fully reflect the views of any single participant, but was intended to contribute to the codification and/or development of the law. Such writings were relied upon because of the institutional context in which they were developed, rather than because of the expertise of the participants.

Two notable results emerge from the study. First, awards on the whole adopt an approach to citation that is more appropriate to norm-adopting judicial decisions than to investment arbitration awards intended to be persuasive to the parties to the dispute. That is, rates of citation in general are low, with tribunals usually content merely to express an opinion, without then supporting that opinion through citation to authoritative instruments.

Second, when authoritative instruments are cited by tribunals, the instruments in question are rarely State-generated soft law instruments. Such writings constituted only 18 per cent of all citations to institutional writings,[42] with only two soft law instruments being cited in more than one investment arbitration award: the UNIDROIT Principles of International Commercial Contracts,[43] cited four times, and National Treatment for Foreign-Controlled Enterprises,[44] cited twice.[45]

By contrast, 12 non-State-generated institutional writings were cited in more than one investment arbitration award, with one publication alone, the International Law Commission's Articles on Responsibility of States for Internationally Wrongful Acts, being cited in 36 awards. Indeed, the dominance of the International Law Commission in the category of institutional writings is itself notable, with the Commission generating three of the four most cited writings, and 67 per cent of citations of all institutional writings. Citation of the International Law Commission, that is, was three times more common than citation of instruments produced by States themselves, and 13 times more common than citation of the next most highly cited institution, the International Law Association.

Academic writings were also cited significantly more often than State-generated soft law instruments, and indeed were also cited more often than non-State-generated institutional writings.[46] The category of 'academic writings', of course, includes both writings cited by tribunals as authoritative instruments and writings cited as persuasive instruments. As a result, it is not possible to draw strong conclusions on the use of academic writings as authoritative instruments based purely on rates of citation. A single writing may, after all, be relied upon by one tribunal as an authoritative instrument, but by another as a persuasive instrument. Nonetheless, the following general observations can be made.

Within the specialist topic of international investment law, a unique position has been achieved by Christoph Schreuer's *The ICSID Convention: A Commentary*, which was cited in 60 separate awards. Three other specialist international investment law writings also repeatedly invoked by tribunals were Rudolf Dolzer and Christoph Schreuer's *Principles of International Investment Law*, cited eight times, Rudolf Dolzer and Margrete Stevens' *Bilateral*

Investment Treaties, cited eight times, and Campbell McLachlan, Laurence Shore and Matthew Weiniger's *International Investment Arbitration: Substantive Principles*, cited seven times. In addition, two general commentaries on public international law were repeatedly cited by tribunals: Ian Brownlie's *Principles of Public International Law*, cited 16 times, and Lassa Oppenheim's *International Law*, cited nine times.

Overall, then, investment arbitration tribunals have been unwilling to invoke State-generated soft law instruments in support of their conclusions, even though they have not hesitated to invoke the support of non-State-generated institutional writings where available. In addition, despite the relative youth of international investment arbitration, certain texts have already begun to emerge as authoritative instruments, with Christoph Schreuer's *The ICSID Convention: A Commentary* and the International Law Commission's Articles on Responsibility of States for Internationally Wrongful Acts rapidly becoming the most authoritative writings within the field.

The following two sections of the chapter will examine more closely what the structure of the role of the investment arbitrator indicates should be the approach adopted by investment arbitration tribunals to the citation of authoritative sources, and whether the citation practices just identified are indeed appropriate for international investment arbitration.

3.3 Citation of soft law instruments in investment arbitration awards

As mentioned in the previous section, investment arbitration tribunals have rarely cited authoritative soft law instruments, preferring instead either to cite non-State-generated institutional writings, or to just blankly state their own conclusions on the content of the applicable law, without citation of any authoritative support.[47] This section of the chapter will argue that proper attention to the structure of an investment arbitrator's role indicates clearly that this practice is misguided, and that soft law can play an important part in fulfilling a tribunal's obligations to the parties. As a result, tribunals should be citing soft law at a much higher rate than they currently do.

The central consideration in this respect relates to the nature of substantive interpretation, which up to this point has been described as allowing each arbitrator to determine for him- or herself what he or she believes to be the content of the applicable law. This description has been based primarily on the role of the parties in the appointment process of arbitrators, and the ability this role gives parties to appoint arbitrators who hold particular legal views.

Focus solely on the control of the parties over the appointment process, however, results in an incomplete understanding of the investment arbitrator's role, which is not simply to be an agent of the party that appointed him or her. Instead, while a single party may be responsible for the appointment of an investment arbitrator, it is nonetheless clear that after appointment investment arbitrators owe equal obligations to both parties.[48] This is reflected in the fact that the parties do not have unconstrained freedom in their selection of an arbitrator, and a lack of impartiality between the parties is a valid ground on which an appointment can be challenged.[49]

A minimal interpretation of this requirement of impartiality would not support a finding of impartiality based solely on an arbitrator's substantive views of law, but such an interpretation would be inconsistent with the importance of those views in the arbitrator selection process. An investment arbitrator, that is, is to a significant extent selected by his or her appointing party as a means of getting certain views represented on the tribunal, not merely because of any expertise he or she may possess. Because of this, a dogmatic insistence by an investment arbitrator on his or her own views constitutes privileging the views of that abritrator's appointing party over those of the other party to the dispute. Such a privileging is inconsistent with the arbitrator's obligation of impartiality between the parties.

Recognition of this fact, however, does not entail that an arbitrator should simply abandon substantive interpretation, and attempt to deliver an 'objective' and generally acceptable decision on the content of the applicable law. Doing so would, after all, be inconsistent with the centrality of the parties to the investment arbitrator appointment process.

Instead, the obligation of an investment arbitrator to be impartial between the parties indicates a limitation within which substantive interpretation must be implemented. That is, while an investment arbitrator is empowered to reach his or her own conclusions on the content of the applicable law, this must be done within the boundaries of any consensus of the parties. Only in this way can an arbitrator exhibit proper consideration to the views of the party that had no role in his or her appointment, while still fulfilling an arbitrator's responsibility to reflect the views for which he or she was appointed.

Soft law instruments, however, play an important role in identifying the views of States, beyond those limited occasions on which they are willing to be legally bound. States, after all, must be presumed to have entered into soft law instruments in good faith. Consequently, where a soft law instrument either acknowledges an obligation on the part of signatory States to pursue a certain goal, or recognises the legitimacy of State action to achieve such a goal, this indicates a normative consensus reached by all States party to the instrument.

In the context of a treaty-based arbitration, then, in which an investor has been given the power to institute and control its own claim, but must do so within the legal regime established between the Home and Host States, soft law instruments can play an important role in establishing the content of the applicable law. Such instruments cannot themselves create binding legal obligations, but this does not make them irrelevant for the purposes of substantive interpretation, where they can establish the existence of a normative consensus between the Home and Host States, that must be respected by arbitrators acting impartially between the parties.[50]

3.4 Citation of other authoritative instruments in investment arbitration awards

Although investment arbitration tribunals rarely invoke authoritative soft law instruments in support of their reasoning, the same reticence has not extended to authoritative instruments not generated by States. Instead, citation to such instruments, whether 'institutional' or 'academic', is a routine feature of investment arbitration awards. This practice might seem unproblematic, given that citation to 'teachings' is a standard practice in public international law adjudication and is expressly sanctioned by Article 38 of the ICJ Statute. However, it will be argued here that the specific context of contemporary international investment law means that such writings simply cannot be relied upon as authoritative instruments, and can instead only be invoked for their persuasive value.

Authoritative writings have an obvious appeal for investment arbitration tribunals, as they eliminate the need for the tribunal to determine for itself the content of the applicable law. While ordinarily the tribunal would be obligated to undertake an extended analysis of any potentially significant legal issue, the existence of a clear statement from an authoritative writing allows the tribunal simply to invoke the authoritative writing and proceed without further analysis or argument. This not only makes the tribunal's job easier, but also reduces the likelihood that the tribunal's award will be controversial, as it can be seen to be based upon a trustworthy source.

The legitimacy of a tribunal's reliance on authoritative writings, however, is inextricably tied to the role these writings play in the tribunal's reasoning. Authoritative writings are not, that is, mere sources of persuasive arguments, but are instead invoked by tribunals as guides to the content of the applicable law. Any writing can provide an argument that a tribunal decides to use, but only an authoritative writing can provide a conclusion that a tribunal can legitimately adopt. Mere invocation of the authoritative writing justifies the tribunal's conclusion. No further argument is necessary.

It is, however, important to emphasise that authoritative writings do not themselves create law, but only serve as guides to its content. The consequence of this is that no writing can be authoritative where the content of the law is highly contested. A *reliable* guide in such a situation is simply impossible, as it is inherently unclear which view on the content of the law will prevail. A writing may still be highly persuasive to a particular tribunal, and it may be persuasive on a contested issue because it is authoritative on other issues. Nonetheless, it cannot legitimately be invoked as authoritative on the contested issue, because to attribute to a writing the ability to resolve conflicts on the content of law is to grant it the power to create law, rather than merely to serve as a guide to it.

'Contested', however, is the most apt description of the state of contemporary international investment law. Investment arbitration tribunals contradict one another on issues of law, commentators criticise the holdings of tribunals, and those same commentators routinely disagree with one another.[51] Moreover, this disagreement exists not just with respect to certain new and unresolved issues within the field, but on even the most central topics.[52] In such a situation of ongoing and wide-ranging dispute, it is simply impossible for any writing to serve as a *reliable* guide to the content of the law.[53]

The problem this creates is that investment arbitration tribunals nonetheless demonstrably do cite to certain writings as though they were authoritative. That is, they rely upon the conclusions of writings that they present as authoritative, and do not themselves present and evaluate the arguments that underlie those conclusions. In doing so, these tribunals treat as authoritative writings those that are in reality only capable of providing persuasive arguments, and as a result inadvertently transform those writings into sources of international investment law, a role they cannot legitimately perform.

The practice adopted by investment arbitration tribunals of invoking writings as authoritative guides to the content of international investment law, then, simply cannot be justified. Only once the field of international investment law has matured and settled to a significant degree will it be possible for any writing to serve as authoritative. Until that time, writings, whether 'institutional' or 'academic', can only legitimately serve as persuasive sources of arguments to be considered by investment arbitration tribunals.

4 The use of persuasive instruments in investment arbitration

4.1 The legitimacy of the use of persuasive instruments by investment arbitration tribunals

Scholarship has traditionally had a privileged place within international law, with tribunals in all jurisdictions regularly relying on leading commentaries as means of establishing the content of the law.[54] To a large degree this practice was a response to the lack of an international judiciary, as tribunals addressing questions of international law were unable to invoke decisions by authoritative international tribunals.[55] Instead, they were required either to rely upon the views of prominent commentators or be seen as merely expressing a personal opinion on what international law should be. Since these tribunals were either domestic courts with no particular expertise in international law, or arbitral tribunals with no recognised legitimacy beyond the dispute they were addressing, the ability to invoke highly regarded scholarship was widely embraced.[56]

The creation of a broad range of international tribunals in the twentieth century changed this situation significantly, of course, as it became increasingly possible to resolve questions of international law through direct reliance on decisions of international tribunals.[57] As a result, the direct impact of scholarship on the jurisprudence of international law has unquestionably declined.[58]

What is important for present purposes, however, is not the degree to which scholarship remains influential in international law, but the manner in which its ongoing influence is exerted. That is, as discussed above, non-State-generated writings can legitimately be relied upon by tribunals either as authoritative guides to the content of the law, or as persuasive sources of arguments about the law. Article 38 of the ICJ Statute, however, only mentions one of these two uses, sanctioning the use of scholarship in so far as it is authoritative, but impliedly excluding its use as merely persuasive.

This distinction might seem surprising, as a tribunal that considers only authoritative guides to the content of the law will be unlikely to deliver as sound and well-reasoned a decision as one that also considers arguments advanced by specialists as to how the law should be understood or developed. The inclusion of this distinction within Article 38 of the ICJ Statute can be readily understood, however, if the Article is considered in the context in which it was originally advanced.

Article 38 of the ICJ Statute, that is, was developed to direct the interpretative practices of the ICJ, a norm-adopting judicial tribunal with a central role in establishing and developing the content of international law.[59] However, the existence of such a tribunal unavoidably entails a risk that its decisions will develop in a direction that is at odds with the wishes of States, the traditional forces behind the creation of international law. Article 38, then, by allowing the ICJ to rely only on those non-State-generated instruments that serve as reliable indicators of the content of State-generated law, reflects a desire to minimise the risk that States will lose control over the development of that law. It is, in short, a rule expressly designed for a norm-adopting tribunal, rather than one designed to ensure that the best ruling is reached on the content of international law.

This understanding of Article 38, however, makes clear that the distinction it adopts between authoritative and persuasive instruments is not easily extended to investment arbitration tribunals. After all, investment arbitration tribunals are, as argued above, not norm-adopting. Consequently, the existence of the system of international investment arbitration does not entail the same risk that States will lose control over the development of the law as is created by the existence of the ICJ. This is not to say that no risk exists at all, but the non-normative nature of investment arbitration awards, combined with the ability of States to select arbitrators for each investment arbitration tribunal, means that the risk is significantly lower.

The primary concern that motivated the exclusion of persuasive instruments from Article 38 of the ICJ Statute, then, simply does not apply in the international investment arbitration context. Nonetheless, it does not follow from this that investment arbitration tribunals should rely upon persuasive instruments, as there may be reasons unique to investment arbitration tribunals that make a parallel exclusion appropriate. Before this question is examined, however, the next section of this chapter will examine the current practice of investment arbitration tribunals with respect to citation of non-State-generated writings.

4.2 The current use of persuasive instruments in investment arbitration

It is often argued that investment arbitration tribunals cite non-State-generated writings at a far higher rate than is typical of international legal tribunals, and this observation is supported by the study undertaken for this chapter.[60] Indeed, while the ICJ has adopted an informal policy of never citing academic writings in majority decisions, such citations are a standard feature of the drafting of investment arbitration awards.[61]

Of course, the mere existence of a difference in citation rates between investment arbitration and other international tribunals is not necessarily meaningful, as it may simply reflect different attitudes to citations in the public international law and international investment law communities. However, the considerable overlap between these two communities makes this explanation unlikely, as public international law specialists, including former ICJ judges, are regular members of investment arbitration tribunals.[62] Moreover, investment arbitration tribunals composed partly of public international law specialists display no particular unwillingness to cite academic writings.[63]

The most likely explanation for this observable difference in citation rates, then, is that the individuals serving on investment arbitration tribunals perceive the role of such tribunals as in some way significantly different to the role of other international legal tribunals. No other explanation would appear able to explain the different attitude to citations displayed by the same individuals when serving on investment arbitration and on other international legal tribunals. However, closer examination of the citation practices of investment arbitration tribunals is necessary if the nature of this perceived difference is to be properly clarified.

For example, while investment arbitration awards regularly cite non-State-generated writings, this fact in itself says nothing about the way the cited writings are actually being used by tribunals. After all, as argued above, tribunals can rely upon such writings either as authoritative guides to the content of the applicable law, or as sources of persuasive arguments relating to the applicable law.

In this respect the great diversity of writings cited by investment arbitration tribunals appears significant. Of the approximately 300 distinct writings cited by investment arbitration tribunals as of mid-2011, only 69 were cited in more than one award. This great diversity of writings supports a conclusion, then, that investment arbitration tribunals are primarily invoking non-State-generated writings for their persuasive value. It is clearly implausible, after all, that such a large number of authoritative writings exists within such a relatively youthful field.

Such an interpretation of investment arbitration tribunal citation practices becomes less plausible, however, once the manner in which tribunals cite non-State-generated writings is examined. That is, if non-State-generated writings were being cited by investment arbitration tribunals for their persuasive value, such citations would be expected to appear as part of analytic discussions in which tribunals examined the primary arguments available on particular points of law, and cited writings they found insightful and useful on the topic. That is, after all, the only context in which persuasive writings are relevant to a tribunal's award.

However, this is simply not the manner in which investment arbitration tribunals cite non-State-generated writings. Investment arbitration awards certainly include extended passages of analytic discussion, but this discussion is rarely supported by more than an occasional citation of a non-State-generated writing. Indeed, it is standard for multiple pages of discussion to be offered with the tribunal never expressly considering even a single argument advanced in an academic or institutional writing. Moreover, when non-State-generated writings are cited, it is rarely as part of the tribunal's analysis, but is instead a means of validating the tribunal's conclusion, by indicating clearly that this conclusion is one that has also been reached by a specialist commentator.

That is, the standard approach by investment arbitration tribunals to the citation of persuasive instruments is defensive. The citation is not added to the award because the writing cited is believed by the tribunal to be authoritative, but neither is it included because the tribunal is analysing an argument originally advanced in the cited writing. Instead, the citation serves merely to defend against potential criticism of the award. It adds nothing to the quality of the award itself, but is offered to reassure readers of the award who are not persuaded by the tribunal's own reasoning that its conclusion is nonetheless defensible.

Such reassurance, however, is not necessary for those international legal tribunals with which investment arbitration tribunals have attempted to align themselves. Those tribunals, after all, are norm-adopting. Consequently, they do not need to defend their conclusions against criticism.[64] The problem that exists for investment arbitration tribunals is that they are attempting to replicate the low-citation drafting style of norm-adopting tribunals, but are unable to avoid the reality that they are not themselves norm-adopting. As a result, they are forced to defend their reasoning to a degree not necessary for norm-adopting tribunals, and use citation of non-authoritative writings as a means of doing so.

The citation practices of investment arbitration tribunals, then, can be explained by the fact that investment arbitration tribunals have attempted to locate themselves in a middle-ground between norm-adopting tribunals capable of relying only on citation of authoritative writings, and non-norm-adopting tribunals required to rely heavily on persuasive writings. Unfortunately, no such tenable middle-ground exists, and as a result investment arbitration awards have generally suffered from having both too little authority and too little persuasiveness.

Because this weakness derives from the standard citation practices used in investment arbitration awards, it can only be resolved through a significant change in those practices. The concluding section of this chapter will, therefore, examine what the structure of international investment arbitration indicates should be the citation practices adopted by investment arbitration tribunals.

4.3 Citation of persuasive instruments in investment arbitration awards

This chapter has argued that the structural differences between investment arbitration tribunals and norm-adopting bodies such as the ICJ have important consequences for the appropriate use in investment arbitration awards of non-binding documents and literature. Investment arbitration awards cannot establish new law, as they lack the institutional context necessary to have this effect. However, they are also not fora in which arbitrators are invited to express their personal views on the proper understanding and content of international investment law. Instead, investment arbitration awards have the important role of explaining to the parties the tribunal's decisions on any relevant points of law, in order that the parties can both understand and accept the tribunal's conclusions.

It has already been argued that this obligation of investment arbitration tribunals to draft persuasive awards underlies the legitimacy of the use by investment arbitration tribunals of soft law instruments. This same obligation, however, also entails that investment arbitration tribunals have a responsibility to use persuasive writings to a far greater degree than is the case in current arbitral practice. An award cannot be persuasive, after all, if it does not clearly and compellingly express the reasoning on which its conclusions are based. The obligation to draft a persuasive award, then, gives rise to two responsibilities for investment arbitrators with respect to persuasive writings.

First, an investment arbitrator must be sufficiently aware of the available persuasive literature on each legal issue to be decided that he or she can justifiably be content both that the most important applicable arguments have been considered and that his or her conclusions are correct. As a result, an arbitrator cannot just rely upon his or her pre-appointment views, but must instead reconsider those views during the appointment through a re-examination of the relevant persuasive literature. In addition, however, an arbitrator also cannot restrict his or her examination of the persuasive literature to only those writings relied upon by the parties in their submissions. The parties, after all, have cited persuasive writings as a means of winning a dispute, not in order to provide the tribunal with the literature necessary for an informed decision on the law. Each tribunal member, then, must undertake an independent examination of the relevant persuasive literature if he or she is to fulfil an arbitrator's responsibility to deliver an informed and considered decision on the law.

Second, an investment arbitration award must be drafted in a form that explains clearly and compellingly why the tribunal reached the conclusions that it did. As a result, it must convey both that the tribunal undertook the research necessary to reach an informed decision on the law, and that the authors of the award have defensible reasons for adopting the understandings of the law upon which they have relied. It must, therefore, include both thorough citation of the variety of persuasive writings that the tribunal have considered, and explicit analytical discussions of the most important arguments those writings presented. Only an award of this form has any probability of convincing an unsuccessful party that its loss resulted from anything other than poor litigation strategy.

5 Conclusion

The manner in which investment arbitration tribunals should and should not use non-binding documents and literature in their awards has as yet received little attention in investment arbitration scholarship. At most, commentators have combined a simple observation of the fact that tribunals do indeed cite literature with a discussion of soft law instruments that is indistinguishable from discussions that occur in the public international law context. The goal of this chapter is to demonstrate that this is a mistake. International investment arbitration has its own distinctive structure, and consequences flow from that structure for the manner in which non-binding documents and literature can and should be used. International investment law has developed significantly since its genesis as a department of public international law, and it is only by considering it in its new context, and in particular the central role in its contemporary development of international investment arbitration, that it can really be understood.

4 The minimum standard of treatment and the protection of foreign investors during an armed conflict

1 Introduction

While arguments have often been made that the interconnections between States that develop as a result of global capitalism will increasingly undermine the willingness of States to enter into armed conflict, war has steadfastly remained a prominent feature of the international landscape.[1] It is, then, initially surprising that despite the remarkable growth that has occurred in the law of international investment over the past two decades, little certainty yet exists as to the legal rules that govern State treatment of foreign investors during an armed conflict. International investment arbitration case law involving damage arising from an armed conflict is almost non-existent,[2] and few commentators have seen this issue as one worth addressing.[3]

The practical irrelevance of this issue, however, has primarily been caused by the economic structure that has dominated international investment until recent years. With foreign investors overwhelmingly coming from developed States and investing in developing States, the military inequalities and geographic distance between Home and Host States made it highly unlikely that any armed conflict would arise between them.[4]

The economic structure of international investment, though, is changing. Significant foreign investment outflows can now be seen from many developing States that traditionally only received foreign investment, and few States anywhere in the world have been unwilling to alter their laws and economies in order to attract foreign investment.[5] The combination, that is, of the continual spread of foreign investment into newer and less politically stable markets, and the increased participation of all States in the sending of foreign investment abroad, is significantly increasing the likelihood that future disputes will arise in which an investor alleges that it was mistreated by a Host State during an armed conflict with its Home State.[6]

The goal of this chapter, however, is not to deliver an encyclopaedic survey of all the laws that are potentially relevant to international investment during an armed conflict.[7] It is instead to use a discussion of the obligations of a Host State to investors from a State with which it is engaged in an armed conflict as a means of analysing the relationship between the minimum standard of treatment (MST) of aliens under international law and the protection of foreign investors.

The discussion will be divided into two sections. Section 2 will focus on the protection available to international investments through public international law. After discussing the right of States to sequestrate enemy-owned private investments during an armed conflict, it will offer an analysis of the MST as found in customary international law. It will argue that although the MST remains unchanged from the formulation it was famously given in the 1926 decision in *Neer v Mexico*,[8] the increased recognition given to non-State entities by public international law means that many actions that States could formerly legally take towards enemy-owned private investments would now violate the MST. Section 2 will then conclude by arguing that the MST remains applicable to enemy-owned private investments even during sequestration.

Section 3 will then address the protections potentially available to enemy-owned private investments from international investment treaties. However, rather than surveying every common investment treaty clause that might have an application during an armed conflict, it will instead concentrate on two fundamental issues. First, it will argue that investment treaties presumptively remain applicable after the outbreak of hostilities between Contracting States. Second, it will argue that the prohibition on indirect expropriation commonly found in investment treaties may, in some situations, require Host States to compensate foreign investors whose investments were sequestrated, even when compensation is not required by the standards of public international law applicable in an armed conflict.

2 Public international law

Contemporary international investment law is dominated by treaties.[9] Nonetheless, while this means that many claims by investors that they were mistreated by Host State governments will be resolved through the interpretation of specifically negotiated treaty language, the non-treaty rules of public international law are not thereby made irrelevant. The coverage of investment treaties, after all, is not universal, and the rules of public international law remain applicable whenever a dispute arises in which the Home and Host States have not concluded an applicable treaty.[10] Moreover, even though conclusion of a treaty gives States the opportunity to determine for themselves what standards should be applied in the treatment of their investors, many investment treaties simply incorporate the standards of public international law, rather than replacing them.[11] As a result, it is impossible to understand the legal rules applicable to international investment during an armed conflict solely by considering the operation of standards commonly found in investment treaties, and an understanding of the protections available to international investments through public international law is essential.

While public international law contains few rules specifically addressing the treatment of foreign investments by a Host State, the treatment of foreign investors is uniformly accepted to be governed by the customary international laws applicable to the treatment of all aliens abroad.[12] As a result, whenever the standards of non-treaty public international law are applicable to the treatment of a foreign investor by a Host State, the Host State will be constrained in its actions by the MST. Elucidation of this standard and its operation in the context of an armed conflict will be the focus of this section of the chapter.

Subsection 2.1 of this chapter will discuss the permission given to a Host State under the rules of armed conflict to 'sequester' any enemy-owned private investments within its territory upon occurrence of an armed conflict. It will subsequently be argued that although the rule permitting sequestration is an exception to the treatment normally permissible under the MST, the MST remains otherwise applicable to the Host State's treatment of the investment during the course of the armed conflict. Subsection 2.2 will, therefore, offer an analysis of the MST, and will argue that the MST is best understood as reflecting the requirements of 'social' obligations between States, dictating the actions that it is 'appropriate' for States to take to one another, rather than those that are 'right' or 'wrong' in any more fundamental sense.

Subsection 2.3 will then elucidate the traditional understanding of the content of the MST, as most famously captured in the 1926 decision of the US-Mexico General Claims Commission in *Neer v Mexico*, while subsection 2.4 will use the social understanding of the MST developed in subsection 2.2 to clarify the impact on this traditional standard of the increased recognition given to non-State entities in contemporary public international law. Lastly, subsection 2.5 will discuss the impact on the MST of the contemporary prevalence of international investment treaties, and subsection 2.6 will examine the applicability of the contemporary MST to Host State treatment of enemy-owned investments during an armed conflict.

2.1 Treatment of enemy-owned private investments under the law of armed conflict

It is perhaps unsurprising that although there have long existed 'laws of war', regulating the actions States can and cannot legitimately take during an armed conflict, the rules constraining a Host State's treatment of enemy-owned private investments during an armed conflict are significantly less restrictive than the MST applicable in peacetime. Armed conflict is, after all, a quintessentially State-focused activity, creating a period in which the interests of individuals are often called to be made subject to the needs of the State. Nonetheless, while pre-modern rules of armed conflict left enemy-owned private investments entirely unprotected from Host State action, treating them in effect as investments owned by the government of the enemy State, as early as the time of Vattel recognition was given to the idea that enemy-owned private property and enemy-owned public property were entitled to significantly different treatment.[13]

This distinction between property owned by an enemy government and that owned by its citizens is now solidly recognised in international law.[14]

Nonetheless, enemy-owned private property is still treated differently under the laws of armed conflict than is both property owned by investors from the Host State itself and property owned by investors from non-enemy States.[15] Consequently, even if neither the foreign investor nor the investment itself is directly involved in assisting the Home State in the conflict, the investor cannot be assured of being allowed to operate its investment in the same manner as was possible before the armed conflict occurred.

The primary legal obstacle in this respect is the acceptability under the laws of armed conflict of the 'sequestration' by the Host State of any enemy-owned private property contained within its territory.[16] That is, while the Host State may not simply expropriate all enemy-owned private investments operating within its territory, the outbreak of an armed conflict gives it the right to take control of such investments for the duration of the conflict, with the subsequent operation of the investment being managed by a 'sequestrator' appointed by the Host State.[17] In addition, even upon conclusion of the conflict, the investment need not be returned directly to the investor, but is instead subject to any arrangements agreed between the States involved in the conflict.[18]

During the course of an armed conflict, that is, enemy-State investors lose at least some of the protections granted by public international law to all other foreign investors in the Host State, and are instead under a special legal regime that gives them significantly less protection than is available during peacetime.

This does not mean, however, that enemy-State investors are entirely unprotected, as the investment has merely been sequestrated, not expropriated, and so remains owned by the foreign investor.[19] The Host State, as a result, has an obligation to preserve the investment while it is under sequestration, and will ultimately be liable to the investor where damage has occurred to the investment as a result of conduct by the sequestrator that was either negligent or wilful.[20]

Importantly, however, it is the Host State, and not the sequestrator, that is the primary bearer of the obligation to preserve the investment.[21] Appointment of a sequestrator, therefore, does not absolve the Host State of responsibility for any damage that it may itself cause to the investment, independently of any actions by the sequestrator. Instead, damage caused to the investment directly by the Host State may be compensable even if the sequestrator was neither negligent nor wilful in failing to prevent that damage.

Nonetheless, while the Host State is obligated to preserve the sequestrated investment, this cannot be understood to mean that every action taken by the Host State during sequestration that damages the investment gives rise to a right of compensation on the part of the investor. Such a rule is clearly too broad. A State can damage an investment, after all, merely by passing perfectly legitimate laws that impede the investment's ability to compete in its relevant market. In such a case, the investment as tangible property remains unaffected, but the investment *as an investment* has unquestionably lost value.

Requiring compensation for any and all damage that the Host State causes to a sequestrated investment, that is, would actually privilege the investment over its domestic competitors. The Host State could, after all, do nothing that would impede the competitive position of the sequestrated investment, without incurring an obligation to pay the enemy-State investor compensation upon termination of the armed conflict. A sequestrating State, then, despite its obligation to preserve the sequestrated investment, can clearly take some actions that will damage, or even destroy, the investment.

The resolution to this apparent conflict is to note that the Host State plays two separate roles during a sequestration. As a sequestrating power it has an obligation to preserve the investment, which is executed through the acts and decisions of the sequestrator that it appoints. As a Host State, however, it has no particular responsibilities towards the sequestrated investment, and must merely act in accordance with whatever its other legal obligations may be.

These split responsibilities explain the conflicting liability rules that apply to a State's actions during a sequestration. Where damage is alleged to have resulted from the management decisions of the sequestrator, compensation will be available to the foreign investor if the decisions in question were either negligent or wilful. By contrast, where the damage caused to the investment resulted from actions of the State *as a State*, traditional public international law standards will be applicable, and the competence and good faith of the sequestrator will be irrelevant.

However, while this conclusion identifies public international law as the source of the standards controlling Host-State treatment of enemy-owned private investments during an armed conflict, it does not follow from this that it is the MST, rather than some other rule, that applies. Subsection 2.2, therefore, will examine more closely the nature of the MST, as a means of clarifying why the MST should be held to be applicable even during an armed conflict.

2.2 The social structure of the minimum standard of treatment

One of the standard distinctions drawn in legal theory, and one that is often referenced in discussions of public international law, is the difference that exists between the structures that underlie the creation and enforcement of domestic legal obligations and those that underlie the creation and enforcement of purely social obligations.[22] Domestic laws, for example, are developed by bodies formally separate from the larger community over which the laws will be applied, while social rules evolve informally through recognition by the individuals in the social group as to what does and does not constitute appropriate behaviour. Similarly, the enforcement of domestic laws involves a body separate from the community against which the rules are to be enforced applying generally applicable sanctions decided in advance of any specific case, while social rules are enforced directly by members of the social group, with sanctions decided by each individual member based on what he or she believes to be appropriate.

As has often been noted, the structures underlying public international law more closely resemble those underlying social obligations than they do those underlying domestic legal obligations.[23] International laws, that is, are developed through a consensus-based recognition of the practice of States, rather than by any form of independent deliberative body.[24] Similarly, international legal obligations are enforced by sanctions individually developed and individually applied by States, and not by any form of pre-established independent body applying clearly mandated and pre-decided sanctions.[25]

While this observation is most commonly made during discussions of whether public international law is 'really law', that is an issue that does not need to be resolved for present purposes.[26] Instead, far more important is that the close resemblance between the structures underlying the creation and enforcement of social rules and those underlying the creation and enforcement of public international law justifies drawing a close parallel between the content of public international law and the content of social rules within a social group. That is, public international law is best understood as reflecting what States regard as acceptable behaviour by a member of the international community of States, rather than as a set of formally constructed rules of the type familiar from domestic legal systems. In turn, the functioning of public international law rules will be better understood through a model of social rules governing relations within a social group, than it will be through a model based on the independently derived and independently enforced obligations familiar from domestic law.[27]

Importantly, the claim being made here is *not* that the rules of public international law are in reality 'social' rules, rather than 'legal' rules. That distinction is simply irrelevant to the argument being advanced. Rather, the argument is that because domestic law, public international law and the rules governing a social group are all normative systems, it may be possible to illuminate the functioning of one of those normative systems, namely public international law, by drawing an analogy with the functioning of another of those systems. Therefore, because the structures underlying public international legal obligations more closely resemble those underlying social obligations than they do those underlying domestic legal obligations, any such analogy is more appropriately drawn with the normative operation of social groups than it is with the operation of domestic legal systems. However, it does not follow from the existence of a structural difference between domestic law and public international law that they cannot both constitute forms of 'law'. This conclusion could only be reached if it had also been demonstrated that only normative systems structurally similar to domestic law can constitute 'legal systems', and that question is simply beyond the scope of the current discussion.

Accepting this analysis of the structure of public international law, however, has important consequences for a proper understanding of the MST. That is, the MST should not be understood as a traditional legal rule, modelled along the lines of domestic law, imposing invariant standards of conduct on those subject to it. Rather, the MST is best understood as though it were a type of social rule, reflecting the minimum 'socially acceptable' behaviour between States. As the remainder of this subsection will demonstrate, this understanding of the MST has significant consequences for its functioning.

First, while the very notion of a 'minimum standard' of the treatment of aliens might seem to entail a connection with the fundamental notions regarding the treatment of individuals contained in human rights, acknowledging the social basis of the MST makes clear that no such connection exists.[28] Human rights, even when formulated in treaties between States, are ultimately obligations to the individuals holding those rights, and are not obligations to the States of which those individuals happen to be citizens.[29] The MST, by contrast, is an obligation owed by each State to the international community of States as a whole.[30] It concerns the treatment to be given by each State to the citizens of other States, but it is nonetheless not an obligation owed to those citizens themselves.[31] Consequently, while human rights may in some cases require precisely the same actions from States as are required by the MST, the two obligations will be parallel, and not identical.

Second, the social basis of the MST also clarifies that the MST is not an inherently uniform standard, equally applicable to all citizens abroad. A standard of 'social acceptability' inherently varies to reflect the interests of the individuals composing the social group. Consequently, if the community of States regards the mistreatment of one group of citizens as more harmful to State interests than the mistreatment of some other group, then conduct that might violate the MST with respect to the former group might not violate it with respect to the latter. By way of example, the MST may allow Host States to take certain actions with respect to foreign tourists in their territory when an armed conflict begins that they are not allowed to take with respect to foreign investors in the same situation.

Third, just as the MST will vary depending on the specific citizens affected by the conduct of the Host State, so it will vary depending on the specific context in which the conduct occurs. The social acceptability of any action depends not only on the inherent acceptability of the action itself, but also on whether the action was acceptable in the circumstances in which it was taken. Consequently, as is clear from the acceptability of sequestration during an armed conflict, it may be that some actions that constitute a violation of the MST when taken during peacetime, do not violate the MST when taken during an armed conflict.

Fourth, once it is accepted that considering the context of a State's conduct is essential in determining that conduct's acceptability under the MST, it must also be acknowledged that an essential part of that context is the availability to the State in question of any more acceptable action. That is, whether or not conduct represents a good faith effort to meet the rules of a social group will significantly affect whether that conduct will be found by other members of the group to be socially acceptable. Some conduct, of course, may be so unacceptable that even good faith cannot redeem it. However, above this absolute minimum, good faith plays an important role in determining the social acceptability of any action taken. In terms of public international law, for example, it may be that actions taken by a wealthy State capable of doing better would violate the MST while precisely the same action taken in parallel circumstances by a State lacking the capacity to do otherwise would not.[32]

Lastly, and importantly for the analysis provided in the remainder of this section, the social basis of the MST also entails that the proper method for determining the content of the MST will vary if membership of the international community expands beyond that of States. Traditionally, it was beyond question that only States played any role in generating the rules reflected in public international law.[33] As a result, the MST was determined solely by the views of States themselves as to the treatment they should and should not give to aliens within their territory. Since the beginning of the twentieth century, however, public international law has increasingly recognised the separateness of non-State entities from their State of origin, and the resulting independent existence of non-State entities as subjects of international law.[34] This means, however, that if this recognition has now reached the point at which either some or all non-State entities can legitimately be regarded as members of the rule-generating community at the heart of public international law, then the MST can no longer be determined solely by the views of States. It must instead also consider the views of non-State entities on what States may and may not legitimately do to aliens within their territory.

Recognition of the social basis of the MST, however, provides only broad guidance as to the essential structural features of the MST, rather than details as to its application. As a result, any such recognition can only be an initial step in analysing the applicability of the MST to enemy-owned private investments during an armed conflict. Subsection 2.3, therefore, will examine more closely the practical application of the MST, through a discussion of the most prominent formulation of the MST given in case law, namely that contained in *Neer v Mexico*. Subsection 2.4 will then continue this analysis by addressing the degree to which the *Neer* formulation, initially announced in 1926, remains an accurate account of the MST as it exists today.

2.3 The traditional formulation of the minimum standard of treatment

Despite the centrality of the MST to international political relations, no specific formulation of it has ever been expressly agreed by the international community.[35] As a result, tribunals and commentators remain free to this day to determine for themselves both what the MST means as a general rule of public international law and precisely which actions by States will and will not violate it.

However, while this lack of clarity has resulted in significant ongoing disagreement about both the meaning and the practical application of the MST, one early formulation has become central to all subsequent analyses.[36] Consequently, while an extensive survey of the available case law on the MST is beyond the scope of this chapter, an analysis of the 1926 decision of the US-Mexico General Claims Commission in *Neer v Mexico* will provide a useful guide to the understanding of the MST that has dominated public international case law and commentary for almost a century.

It should initially be acknowledged that the Commission in *Neer* was considering neither mistreatment of a foreign investor nor mistreatment of an alien during an armed conflict. Rather, the Commission was addressing a case in which the Mexican authorities were alleged to have failed to investigate properly the murder of a US citizen who at the time of his death had been working in Mexico.[37] Nonetheless, since the *Neer* formulation of the MST has subsequently been accepted as applicable to a highly factually diverse range of disputes, it can appropriately be treated as a generally applicable account of the MST, rather than one restricted to the specific factual context in which it was announced.

According to the Commission's formulation of the MST, then,

> the treatment of an alien, in order to constitute an international delinquency, should amount to an outrage, to bad faith, to wilful neglect of duty, or to an insufficiency of governmental action so far short of international standards that every reasonable and impartial man would readily recognize its insufficiency.[38]

It is important to emphasise at the outset that the precise words in which the Commission formulated its account of the MST should not be analysed too closely. The Commission itself, that is, was clear that it was not attempting to 'announce a precise formula' for the MST.[39] Moreover, the *Neer* standard is only important because of the influence it has had on subsequent jurisprudence and commentary, and that subsequent jurisprudence and commentary has steadfastly refused to treat the four categories listed by the Commission as in any way exhaustive. The proper approach to analysing the *Neer* standard, then, is not to attempt to clarify the meanings of the specific words in which it was formulated, but rather to identify the large-scale features that made this description of the MST seem such a plausible one to the Commission, and that have in turn made it so appealing to so many tribunals and commentators.

With that qualification in mind, two primary points must be emphasised about the content of the *Neer* formulation of the MST. First, consistent with the social basis of the MST emphasised in this chapter, the *Neer* standard gives no recognition to any sort of absolute value, whether in the form of human rights or even just moral wrongs. Instead, the entire focus of the *Neer* standard is on actions that are in some way socially inappropriate, whether because they involve 'bad faith', a 'wilful neglect of duty',[40] or merely fall substantially short of the 'standards' the relevant social group believes to be applicable. Even the initial reference to 'an outrage', a term that could potentially be used to refer to an action that violates an absolute norm, is nonetheless also a term commonly used to refer to actions that seriously violate standards of social acceptability.[41] Under the *Neer* standard, that is, the substance of the MST is not determined by any absolute standards of appropriate treatment of non-State entities, but instead will vary with changes in contemporary beliefs regarding what a State can and cannot legitimately do to citizens of another State.[42]

The second important point to acknowledge about the *Neer* standard is that it is not aspirational. That is, although the MST under *Neer* is substantively linked to currently prevailing beliefs about how a State can treat citizens of other States, it does not require that States actually act appropriately towards those citizens. Rather, States possess a considerable freedom to act inconsistently with 'international standards' without incurring any liability under the MST. Only if a State's actions are either wilfully bad, constitute an 'outrage', or are so far below the applicable standards that 'every reasonable and impartial man would readily recognize [their] insufficiency' is any liability imposed. The MST under *Neer*, that is, does not impose an obligation of 'good governance' on States, but is literally a 'minimum' standard: it forbids behaviour that is so far below expected standards that it cannot be tolerated, but mandates tolerance of everything else.

As traditionally formulated, then, the MST imposed very few restrictions on the actions that States could take towards aliens. 'International standards' could be violated with impunity, so long as the violation was not too extreme, and the limited category of actions that States could not take with respect to aliens was determined exclusively by the changing political interests of States. Considerations of human rights or even morality were only relevant if States chose to make them so.[43] The *Neer* formulation of the MST, that is, reflects an understanding of public international law as determined exclusively by the international community of States, and reflects solely the views of those States as to what is and is not acceptable behaviour.

Since the time of the *Neer* decision, however, NSEs have received increasing recognition under public international law, independent of their ability to serve as representatives of their Home States.[44] Subsection 2.4 will, therefore, examine the impact of this change on the MST, and whether it entails that the views of NSEs on the treatment of enemy-owned private investments during an armed conflict must now be considered alongside those of States when determining what the MST does and does not allow.

2.4 The impact on the minimum standard of treatment of the increased recognition given to non-State entities in contemporary public international law

Arguably, the defining feature of the development of public international law in the twentieth century was the growing recognition of the need to treat non-State entities as something more than mere representatives of States.[45] While public international law, that is, began the twentieth century considering non-State entities exclusively through the lens of the States of which they were citizens, it ended with a proliferation of documents recognising the existence of inherent human rights,[46] State officials being criminally tried for State-sanctioned actions taken during armed conflicts,[47] and both individuals and corporations possessing the power to bring claims directly against States at international tribunals.[48]

These changes in the status of non-State entities under public international law might initially appear to justify a conclusion that public international law is no longer purely a concern of States, and that as a result non-State entities now have a legitimate role to play in determining the content of the MST. Such a conclusion would, however, seriously misrepresent the nature of the change that has occurred. Non-State entities still do not possess an international legal personality equivalent to that of States, and so simply are not yet full members of the international community.[49] Indeed, even in the context of international human rights, the area of public international law in which the independence of non-State entities from their Home States is most clear, non-State entities only possess those legal rights that have been formally recognised by States, and can only enforce those rights against States if States have given them permission to do so.[50] On a purely formal level, that is, public international law remains focused exclusively on States, and non-State entities only exist as citizens of State members of the international community.

Nonetheless, while the structure of public international law may not have changed, the substance has changed fundamentally. Many documents granting rights or other recognition to non-State entities are clearly just reflections of the policy choices of States, and so fit easily into the traditional State-centred model of public international law.[51] The language of many contemporary human rights documents, however, is importantly different. These documents increasingly state that the rights to which they are giving legal recognition are not merely desirable features of the international legal landscape, but are instead inherent rights of individuals that pre-exist their formal legal recognition by States.[52] Recognition by States, that is, remains essential for those rights to have international legal effect, but not only does that recognition not create the rights in question, it is not given by States as a matter of choice, but of obligation.

The impact on the MST of this obligatory nature of the recognition of inherent human rights is fundamental. States retain their role as the sole formal sources of public international law, and so the focus of the MST remains on the prevention of actions that seriously violate the standards of behaviour applicable within the international community of States. However, the acknowledgement by States that the recognition of inherent human rights is an obligation and not a choice entails that inherent human rights are a primary concern of the international community. Consequently, the serious violation of such a right will constitute a violation of the MST even if no international legal document yet makes States directly liable for failing to secure that right.[53]

In terms of the *Neer* standard, then, nothing in the increased recognition given to non-State entities in contemporary public international law justifies a conclusion that the *Neer* standard no longer accurately represents the MST.[54] The *Neer* standard, after all, is merely a description of the *form* of the MST, reflecting the exclusive focus of public international law on the interests and actions of States. That focus, however, has not changed. What has changed is the *substance* of the MST, or, in other words, those actions that will constitute an 'outrage', or that will fall far enough below 'international standards' that they will give rise to a violation of the MST. These actions now include not only conduct expressly recognised as unacceptable by the international community of States, but also those actions that constitute a serious violation of inherent human rights.

Nonetheless, while many human rights documents now recognise the rights they address as inherently possessed by individuals, the same is not true of international investment treaties. The language of investment treaties, that is, usually expressly acknowledges that the purpose of the treaty is to secure an economic benefit, and not to give obligatory recognition to pre-existing rights held by investors.[55] While the above analysis, then, clarifies that the *Neer* standard remains the applicable measure for determining violations of the MST from Host State treatment of enemy-owned private investments, it does not address the substance of that standard when no human rights violations have occurred. Subsection 2.5, therefore, will analyse the substance of the MST as it applies to international investment, in the light of the large number of investment treaties that have come into effect since the time of the *Neer* decision.

2.5 The application of the minimum standard of treatment in the context of international investment

Subsection 2.4 argued that despite the increased recognition given to non-State entities in contemporary public international law, the degree of international legal personality that non-State entities currently possess is insufficient to justify any claim that non-State entities are now members of the international legal community, whose views and interests must be taken into account in determining the content of the MST. For this reason, it was concluded, the *Neer* standard continues to be an accurate account of the MST.

Similarly, however, the current existence of a large number of international investment treaties expressly giving investors both substantive protections and procedural rights does not justify concluding that the *Neer* standard has been replaced in the context of international investment law. The *Neer* standard, after all, reflects the State-centred *structure* of public international law, not its substantive content, and international investment treaties remain agreements between States, reflecting State views and interests, and benefiting investors only to the extent that States wish to benefit them. The *Neer* standard, therefore, remains an accurate account of the MST in the State-centric context of international investment.

Nonetheless, just as it was argued in subsection 2.4 that the continuing applicability of the *Neer* standard as a description of the MST has not prevented human rights treaties changing the MST's substantive content, so it follows that although the *Neer* standard remains applicable in the international investment context, the substantive content of the MST may have been changed by the standards incorporated into international investment treaties. Any such change would only be applicable to foreign investors, and would not change the substantive content of the MST more broadly, but as was noted in subsection 2.2, the social underpinnings of the MST entail that the substantive content of the MST may vary from one context to another, even if the same formal standard remains applicable.[56]

The relevant consideration in this respect is the *Neer* standard's recognition that the MST will be violated by State conduct that is 'so far short of international standards that every reasonable and impartial man would readily recognize its insufficiency'.[57] The *Neer* decision itself never clarifies precisely what is meant by the term 'international standards', and one reading of this term is as a reference to any binding international legal obligation. However, this interpretation cannot be correct, as even a minor violation of binding legal obligations gives rise to legal liability, while liability for violation of 'international standards' under the MST only occurs when the violation is extreme. The best interpretation of 'international standards', then, is that it is a reference to the level of conduct that the community of States has recognised as *appropriate*, even though not legally required, in any given context.

Given this understanding, the role of international investment treaties in determining the content of the MST becomes clear. The contemporary prevalence of such treaties does not change the *form* of the MST, and the *Neer* standard remains applicable in the international investment context. However, persistent inclusion of a particular standard in an adequately wide range of investment treaties will indicate that the standard in question has been recognised by the international community of States as reflecting *appropriate* treatment of foreign investors.[58] As a result, while treatment of investors inconsistent with that standard would not *necessarily* violate the MST, treatment far below it would.

In the context of international investment, then, the conduct of a Host State can violate the MST in three ways. First, conduct that would violate the MST with respect to any alien will violate the MST with respect to a foreign investor. Second, conduct that seriously violates the inherent human rights of a foreign investor violates the MST. Lastly, conduct that is significantly below any standard adopted in an adequately broad range of international investment treaties will also violate the MST.

With this clarification of the functioning of the MST in the international investment context in mind, subsection 2.6 will address directly the application of the MST to enemy-owned private investments during a time of armed conflict.

2.6 Conclusion: the application of the minimum standard of treatment to enemy-owned investments in times of armed conflict

Section 2 commenced by noting that during an armed conflict, public international law permits Host States to take certain actions against enemy-owned investments that would unquestionably violate the MST if taken during peacetime. Most notably, Host States may sequestrate enemy-owned investments for the duration of the conflict.

One conclusion that might be drawn from this fact is that the MST no longer applies to the relations between belligerent States during an armed conflict. Instead, a special legal regime unconnected to the MST becomes operative, and the MST only returns to relevance once the armed conflict concludes and the special legal regime terminates. Indeed, some support for such a view might be argued to be given by one of the public international law documents most directly concerned with the protection of aliens during an armed conflict, the Fourth Geneva Convention,[59] which not only places few express restrictions on the treatment of enemy-owned private property during an armed conflict, but explicitly allows States to take 'measures of control and security' with respect to such property.[60]

The social basis of the MST developed above, however, makes clear that such a view is mistaken, as the obligation reflected in the MST is not an obligation owed solely to the Home State of the investor, and thus subject to extinction when relations between the Home and Host States break down. It is, rather, one owed to every member of the international community of States, as reflecting the standards of conduct expected from all members of that community. Since, then, States involved in an armed conflict remain members of the international community, they also remain bound by the obligations entailed by membership of that community. This includes treating aliens within their territory in accordance with the MST.

Of course, as argued above, the conduct required by the MST varies depending on the context in which the conduct is to occur.[61] Consequently, even though the MST remains applicable during an armed conflict, it does not follow that the obligations imposed by the MST in such a period are identical to those imposed by it during peacetime. Indeed, the acceptability under the MST of sequestration during an armed conflict is a perfect example of this.

Importantly, however, what makes sequestration acceptable under the MST is not anything about sequestration itself, but only that it is regarded by the international community of States as acceptable behaviour during an armed conflict. The MST, after all, reflects only the social acceptability of actions to the international community of States. For this reason, any determination of the requirements of the MST during an armed conflict is only possible through an examination of contemporary State practice regarding the treatment of enemy-owned private investments during an armed conflict. Information on how investments are treated in any other context, or arguments based on deduction from fundamental principles, cannot suffice.

This point being made, an empirical study of this nature is beyond the scope of the present chapter, which is focused solely on clarifying the fundamental rules on the treatment by Host States of enemy-owned private investments during an armed conflict. The remainder of the chapter, therefore, will focus instead on the impact of an armed conflict on international investment treaties. Contemporary international investment law, after all, is dominated by treaties, and where an investment treaty is operative between a Home and a Host State, the rules it contains will take priority over any derived from the MST.

3 International investment treaties

While the rules contained in any investment treaty between a Home and a Host State will take precedence over the rules of public international law discussed in section 2, the existence of an armed conflict has substantial effects on both the bindingness and the content of treaty obligations.[62] As a result, even though an investment treaty exists between a Home and a Host State, the manner of operation during an armed conflict of any obligations contained in that treaty cannot be taken for granted.

This section of the chapter will, therefore, address the operation of investment treaties during an armed conflict. Subsection 3.1 will argue that although it has long been accepted that commercial treaties terminate if armed conflict commences between the States party to the treaty, this rule should not be applied to a contemporary international investment treaty unless the treaty itself indicates that it was intended to terminate. Subsection 3.2 will then examine whether sequestration of enemy-owned investments would violate treaty provisions regarding indirect expropriation, even when it is conducted in accordance with the law of armed conflict.

3.1 The impact of armed conflict on investment treaties

The role that treaties play in moderating aspects of the relationship between States might initially suggest that when that relationship breaks down, and an armed conflict arises, treaty obligations between all States opposed in the conflict cease to be binding upon them. The relationships reflected in such treaties, after all, have ceased to exist, and the States concerned cannot now be presumed to be willing to take actions that will benefit their enemies. Indeed, prior to the twentieth century the accepted rule under public international law was precisely that treaties terminated upon commencement of hostilities.[63]

As the twentieth century progressed, however, it became increasingly clear that this traditional rule was ill-designed for the globalised world in which States were now operating. Not only were more and more issues being addressed by both bilateral and multilateral treaties, thereby increasing significantly the potential impact of a rule terminating treaties upon commencement of an armed conflict, but non-State entities now played a central role in the treaty-making process, both as beneficiaries of treaties and as motivators for them being signed.[64] The political reasons that justified the termination of treaties upon commencement of an armed conflict, however, did not as clearly apply to treaties addressing the interests of non-State entities as it did to those that focused solely upon the concerns of States.

By mid-twentieth century, then, a new approach developed, most famously articulated by Arnold McNair in his *Law of Treaties*, which rejected the traditional presumption that all treaties terminated upon commencement of an armed conflict.[65] In its place, the new approach emphasised instead the need to attend to the specific language and nature of each treaty, as a means of identifying what the States party to the treaty intended to happen if an armed conflict arose between them.[66] Only if the evidence indicated that the treaty was intended to terminate, would it terminate.[67]

Thus, for example, treaties directly addressing the conduct of States during an armed conflict, such as the Geneva Conventions, would be presumed not to terminate, absent very clear textual or other evidence they were intended to do so.[68] Similarly, treaties designed to have a permanent effect, such as by transferring territory from one State to another, would again be presumed not to terminate.[69] On the other hand, treaties relying upon the existence of goodwill between the Contracting States, such as those providing economic benefits or privileged immigration access, would be presumed to terminate if hostilities between the States in question commenced.[70] Lastly, no matter what the subject matter of the treaty, if the language of the treaty clearly stated the intent of the Contracting States, or the *travaux préparatoires* otherwise made it clear, then that intent would determine the impact of any armed conflict on the treaty's operation.[71]

Nonetheless, while McNair's analysis certainly constituted an important advance over the traditional rule, the exclusive focus it retains on the intentions of the Contracting States is problematic in the context of contemporary public international law. As argued above, that is, while the form of public international law remains concerned exclusively with the actions and intentions of States, its substance now recognises the relevance of non-State entities to a degree that was not yet true in McNair's time.[72] Consequently, any rule that focuses solely on ascertaining the intentions of the States party to a treaty ignores the relevance of the interests of non-State entities to how many contemporary treaties operate.

Indeed, this new relevance of non-State entities to the operation of treaties has been at least implicitly acknowledged by the International Law Commission in its 2011 Articles on the Effects of Armed Conflicts on Treaties.[73] The Articles reiterate McNair's view that an individual analysis must be undertaken for each treaty to determine if it terminates upon the outbreak of hostilities, but expressly reject McNair's focus on the intentions of the Contracting States.[74] Instead, while primary importance is still given to the language of the treaty, the Commentaries to the Articles qualify this importance by requiring that where no 'conclusive' answer is provided by that language, a final answer should be reached by considering, among other things, the treaty's subject matter.[75] The subject matter, however, is relevant not because of what it reveals about the intentions of the Contracting States, but because of what it reveals about the rights and obligations the treaty involves. That is, treaties 'concerning private rights', for example, are presumed to remain in effect during an armed conflict not because this is what the Contracting States would have intended, but because they are treaties *concerning private rights*.[76]

For this reason, then, it is clear that contemporary investment treaties also remain in effect during an armed conflict.[77] As a formal matter, of course, contemporary investment treaties are the product of a relationship between States, and include promises between those States rather than promises directly to non-State entities. On a substantive level, however, contemporary investment treaties are more accurately understood as involving the relationship between States and non-State entities than they are the relationship between Contracting States. The ultimate goal of an investment treaty, after all, is to motivate private action, not to secure particular treatment from one State to another, and they are entered into with the explicit goal of inducing non-State entities to rely upon the promises they contain. As a result, contemporary investment treaties simply do not implicate the relationship between States in the way that justified the traditional rule that treaties terminated when that relationship broke down and an armed conflict commenced. Contemporary investment treaties, therefore, must be presumed to remain in force even when an armed conflict commences between the Home and Host States.

Because of limitations of space, this chapter will not address the range of investment treaty provisions that may impact on a Host State's treatment of enemy-owned private investments in an armed conflict.[78] Instead, it will conclude with a discussion of the common investment treaty provision that relates most directly to the preceding discussion of the MST and the sequestration of enemy-owned private investments. The sequestration of investments, after all, arguably constitutes an indirect expropriation, an act for which most contemporary investment treaties require compensation be paid to the investor.[79] Indeed, under the jurisprudence developed by investment arbitration tribunals, compensation would be owed for indirect expropriation even in some situations in which the sequestration was performed unproblematically, and compensation was not required by the standards of public international law applicable in an armed conflict. Subsection 3.2 will, therefore, address when sequestration of an enemy-owned private investment constitutes indirect expropriation, and thus when a Host State may be obligated to pay compensation for a sequestration, even though its actions were in full conformity with the public international law rules regulating the treatment of enemy-owned private investment during an armed conflict.

3.2 Sequestration as indirect expropriation

An indirect expropriation occurs when a Host State interferes with an investment owned by a foreign investor in such a way that the investor is effectively deprived of the benefits of owning the investment.[80] While a 'direct' expropriation requires that the investor lose title to the investment, an 'indirect' expropriation can be found to have occurred even though ownership of the investment always formally remains with the investor.[81] Protection against indirect expropriation is not only an aspect of customary public international law, but is also a standard feature of contemporary investment treaties, which usually require that compensation be paid to the investor whenever an indirect expropriation occurs.[82]

The complication this creates is that the legality under public international law of a properly conducted sequestration of an enemy-owned private investment does not mandate the legality of precisely the same action under an investment treaty containing a prohibition on indirect expropriation. That is, the reason sequestration of enemy-owned investments during an armed conflict does not constitute indirect expropriation under public international law is that special rules apply under public international law during an armed conflict. However, unlike the public international law rules relating to indirect expropriation, investment treaties will usually remain fully applicable even when an armed conflict arises between the Contracting States. Consequently, if a properly conducted act of sequestration constitutes an act of indirect expropriation under an applicable investment treaty, the sequestrating State will be obligated by that treaty to compensate the investor for the indirect expropriation, even though it is not required to do so by the standards of customary public international law.

Considerable disagreement still exists within international investment law as to the requirements for a finding of indirect expropriation, but two elements are now uniformly accepted.[83] First, tribunals have repeatedly emphasised that an indirect expropriation does not occur every time a Host State interferes with the ownership rights of an investor. Instead, 'the test is whether that interference is sufficiently restrictive to support a conclusion that the property has been "taken" from the owner'.[84] Second, the State's interference with the ownership rights of the investor cannot merely be 'ephemeral', but must instead amount to 'a lasting removal of the ability of an owner to make use of its economic rights'.[85]

Both these standards, however, are problematic from the perspective of the sequestration of an enemy-owned private investment during an armed conflict. Every sequestration, after all, will unavoidably involve serious interference with the ownership rights of the investor, who is forced to cede all control over the investment to a government-appointed sequestrator. Similarly, while an armed conflict may certainly be quick, protracted armed conflicts are hardly unknown, and one tribunal has held that temporary State interference with an investment for a mere 4 months can justify a finding of indirect expropriation.[86] Consequently, while the facts of each case would determine whether a particular sequestration constituted a compensable act of indirect expropriation, it is nonetheless clear that some sequestrations will meet the standards currently accepted in international investment law.[87]

By entering into investment treaties, then, States significantly limit the generous freedoms that public international law allows them during an armed conflict. The existence of these constraints, however, is fully consistent with both the increasing recognition in public international law of the independence of non-State entities from their State of origin, and the ultimate purpose of investment treaties, which is to offer selected investors security and compensation beyond the minimal levels provided by public international law.

4 Conclusion

Despite occasional optimistic comments to the contrary, there is little indication that armed conflict will soon disappear from the world stage. This reality creates significant problems for an increasingly globalised world economy, in which international investment constantly searches for new opportunities, and States worldwide court investors with promises of the beneficial treatment their governments will provide. When an armed conflict occurs, investors who entered a State with no consideration of their origin beyond the tax or treaty benefits it might provide, can suddenly find themselves labelled an 'enemy', and subjected to restrictive measures that would not be legally permissible in peacetime.

This chapter has not attempted to address every aspect of the legal rules governing the treatment of enemy-owned private investments during an armed conflict, but has instead concentrated on the impact on this area of public international law of the increasing recognition that is being given to the independence of non-State entities from their States of origin. Public international law remains, of course, a State-focused enterprise, and non-State entities lack the formal ability to influence directly the legal rules that govern how they are treated by States. Nonetheless, the days in which public international law allowed States to treat non-State entities as nothing but representatives of the States from which they came are long gone, and even in the State-centric field of the law of armed conflict States now bear significant obligations to treat non-State entities as independent entities, entitled to be treated fairly no matter their origin.

5 The history and development of the most-favoured nation clause

1 Introduction

Contemporary international investment law is characterised by fragmentation.[1] Disputes are heard by a variety of tribunals,[2] which often are constituted solely for the purpose of hearing a single claim.[3] The law applicable in a dispute is usually found in a bilateral agreement, applicable only between the two States connected to the dispute, rather than in a multilateral treaty or customary international law.[4] Moreover, the international investment community itself is profoundly divided on many issues of substantive law, meaning both that the interpretation given to international investment law by a tribunal will be determined largely by those who sit on it, and that even the most authoritative texts are recognised as representing only their authors' own views, rather than constituting a clarifying statement of the law as it actually stands.[5]

Given this context of fragmentation, it is perhaps unsurprising that States negotiating investment treaties have consistently incorporated one of the traditional means of bringing uniformity to international obligations, the Most-Favoured Nation (MFN) clause.[6] An MFN clause in an investment treaty is fundamentally a promise between the two States party to the treaty that neither State will give to investors[7] from any third-State more favourable treatment than that given to investors from the other State party to the treaty.[8] If more favourable treatment is provided to investors from a third-State, an obligation arises to provide equivalent treatment to those investors benefiting from the MFN clause.[9]

While MFN clauses in investment treaties do not directly limit the fragmentation of international investment law, they can serve to harmonise the law under which foreign investors from different States operate.[10] Absent MFN clauses, States will compete with one another to ensure that their investors receive the most favourable treatment given by a particular State, thereby generating a diversity of legal regimes. MFN clauses, by contrast, ensure that whenever benefits are given to investors from one State, they must also be provided to investors from any other State with an applicable MFN clause, thereby ensuring equality of treatment.[11]

But, while MFN clauses are potentially a means of reducing the level of fragmentation in international investment law, they carry a significant risk of over-interpretation.[12] MFN clauses are often described as being primarily a means of eliminating discrimination within a given market.[13] However defensible such a description is in general terms, a teleological interpretation[14] of this type risks allowing the goal of market equalisation to override the operation of the MFN clause itself.[15] That is, it encourages tribunals to lay aside technical arguments as to the operation of the clause and simply interpret it in the way that will most effectively eliminate market discrimination. Indeed, this effect can already be seen in the discussions of MFN clauses given by some investment arbitration tribunals and commentators.[16]

The goal of the next three chapters is to reduce the dangers inherent in such teleological interpretations by clarifying certain boundaries to the operation of MFN clauses in international investment law.[17] Of course, although MFN clauses are a common feature of international investment agreements,[18] the language in which they are expressed can differ significantly, and such differences will affect their operation.[19] Nonetheless, while attention must ultimately be paid to the specific language adopted in each clause, this does not mean that nothing can be said regarding the operation of such clauses generally.[20] Rather, it simply means that any limitations described in these chapters can be eliminated or varied by States through the language they choose for their specific MFN clause.

Section 2 of this chapter will discuss the historical development of MFN clauses in international agreements in order to provide the background against which the current use of MFN clauses in international investment agreements should be understood. Section 3 then concludes the historical discussion by examining the place that MFN clauses have achieved in contemporary international investment law. Section 4 will then turn to the analysis of MFN clauses themselves by discussing the limits to the operation of MFN clauses that have already been recognised by non-investment international tribunals. The limitations discussed in this section are important to investment law not only because they have been expressly adopted by a series of investment arbitration tribunals, but because the operation of MFN clauses in international investment law is ultimately a specialised development of the operation of such clauses in international law more generally.[21] Consequently, although these limits were not originally recognised in the international investment law context, they are nonetheless applicable to MFN clauses in international investment agreements.

Chapter 6 will then present an original analysis of MFN clauses, explaining certain limitations that must be recognised in the operation of MFN clauses in international investment law. These boundaries are identified as: (a) the general inapplicability of such clauses to treaty provisions already in place when the MFN clause was adopted; (b) the need to evaluate the alleged 'favourability' of treatment by referring to the broad class of investors from the Home State,[22] rather than the particular investor invoking the MFN clause; and (c) the ability of an MFN clause to deprive an investor of access to the terms of the Basic Treaty.[23]

Finally, Chapter 7 will then examine in more depth the meaning of 'favourability' in the MFN context, and the consequences that can be drawn for the functioning of MFN clauses from a proper understanding of what truly constitutes 'more favourable treatment' of foreign investors.

2 The historical development of most-favoured nation treatment

Study of the historical development of MFN clauses in international agreements is of more than academic interest for any attempt to clarify the boundaries within which such clauses must operate. Proponents of the non-discrimination interpretation of MFN clauses, after all, routinely cite to this history as evidence of the overriding anti-discrimination purpose of MFN clauses.[24] As shown in this section, however, a close examination of this history reveals a very different use of MFN clauses by States in which MFN clauses are used tactically as a means of gaining advantage over competitors, rather than due to any idealistic commitment to non-discrimination. Consequently, while a correct understanding of the historical development of MFN clauses cannot by itself demonstrate that the non-discrimination interpretation of contemporary MFN clauses is incorrect, it does serve to remove a convenient justification for adoption of this approach. Moreover, an awareness of the varied purposes a State can have in adopting an MFN clause underlines clearly the need to attend to the specific details regarding each MFN clause, rather than relying for interpretative purposes on some pre-decided teleological conclusion.

Although MFN clauses have come to particular prominence in the economic sphere, nothing about their operation restricts them to economic matters, and indeed their original genesis appears to have been in a far broader socio-political context. While the precise origin of the MFN clause is still contested, one commentator has traced its use back as far as the early Holy Roman Empire,[25] while others cite its development as occurring sometime in the medieval period.[26] Realistically, however, as an MFN clause fundamentally constitutes just a promise from one State to another that no third-State will receive better treatment in some specific substantive field, no conclusive 'birth-date' is likely to be ascertainable. Such promises have, after all, likely been made for as long as States have entered into agreements with one another.

Nonetheless, whatever the origins of the MFN clause, it was unquestionably with the rise of international commerce that they gained their importance in international law.[27] While the expression 'most-favoured nation' only became common in the seventeenth century,[28] the rise of international commerce in the late medieval period saw States adopting MFN clauses as a means of ensuring that their traders would compete in foreign markets on at least equal terms with traders from third-States.

What is important for present purposes, however, is not the long history of the MFN clause, but the limited form taken by early instances of the clause. While contemporary MFN clauses are generally recognised as being applicable to any benefit granted within a specified substantive area,[29] including those benefits granted after the MFN clause comes into effect,[30] early MFN clauses referenced specific benefits already being received by specific third parties and constituted solely an agreement to extend those specific privileges to the beneficiary of the MFN clause.[31] That is, MFN clauses were initially not generalised promises that no third-State would at any time be treated more favourably than the beneficiary of the MFN clause. They were, rather, grants to the beneficiary of the MFN clause of specific benefits already received by specific third-States.

Early MFN clauses, thus, were unilateral, specific and retrospective. Rather than constituting an agreement by both States that each would provide MFN treatment to the other, they were instead an agreement by one State alone to extend MFN treatment to the other (i.e. they were unilateral). Moreover, they were not a generalised promise that no third-State would receive better treatment than that given to the State benefiting from the MFN clause. Rather, they identified specific benefits that were already being provided to a third-State, and constituted an undertaking that these same benefits would also be provided to the State benefiting from the MFN clause (i.e. they were specific). Lastly, because they applied only to the specific benefits identified in the clause, they applied solely to treatment already being given to one or more third-States. They did not, that is, require the State offering MFN treatment to maintain the equality of the State benefiting from the MFN clause by also extending to it any benefits granted to third-States in the future (i.e. they were retrospective).

Early MFN clauses, then, did not reflect any form of principled commitment to equality of treatment or impose serious constraints upon the freedom of a State to control its economic policies. Instead, they served solely as a mechanism for a sufficiently important trading partner to secure from a State benefits that were currently being received by major competitors. The State granting MFN treatment, however, remained completely free to provide more favourable treatment to States not mentioned in the clause, and also to provide additional benefits to the named third-States in the future. MFN clauses at this time, then, were used only as a means of expansive drafting in a context of limited information, ensuring that the beneficiary State received all benefits currently received by its major competitors, rather than only those of which it was at that time aware.

However, a significant change occurred to the structure of MFN clauses in the seventeenth and eighteenth centuries, by which time the growth in global trade and commerce had resulted in these clauses becoming a standard feature of international economic agreements.[32] While earlier MFN clauses had been unilateral, creating benefits for only one of the parties to the agreement, in this later era they began to be predominantly bilateral in operation, creating benefits for both States concerned.[33] In addition, they were now also usually both general and prospective, applying to any benefit given to any third-State within a particular substantive field,[34] usually tariffs, and to both already-existing benefits and those given in the future.[35]

Nonetheless, while States were at this point using MFN clauses as a generalised means of ensuring that their traders were not discriminated against in particular markets, it remains inaccurate to describe MFN clauses of this time as reflecting an attempt by States to eliminate market discrimination.

MFN clauses were, after all, even at the height of 'free trade fervor' in the mid-nineteenth century, used tactically by States. They were incorporated into agreements when doing so would provide political benefits, and excluded when it would not.[36]

This tactical use of MFN clauses became most explicit in the treaty-making activities of the United States in the nineteenth century.[37] On its emergence into international commerce in the late eighteenth century, the United States had found itself in an international market heavily geared against it.[38] As a producer of primarily agricultural products, the United States relied on exportation of such products to generate the income necessary to pay for the importation of manufactured products from Europe.[39] However, European nations had erected large tariff barriers against the importation of agricultural products, and unless the United States could negotiate lower tariffs, its products could not compete in European markets.[40] Negotiating lower tariffs was certainly possible, but if the United States agreed to include MFN clauses in its treaties, as had become standard by that time, each negotiated reduction would automatically be transferred to every other State with which the United States had an MFN clause.[41] In effect, the United States would gain tariff reductions from just one State, but in exchange would give them to every State in Europe.

The solution adopted by the United States was what came to be known as the conditional MFN clause.[42] Prior practice regarding MFN clauses had established that as soon as more favourable treatment was provided to any third-State, the State benefiting from the MFN clause immediately gained the right to the same treatment, without having to offer anything in return.[43] That is, MFN clauses were unconditional in their operation. The conditional MFN clauses included within US treaties, however, required that in order for the State benefiting from the MFN clause to gain access to any more favourable treatment granted to a third-State, it had to offer the United States a concession equivalent to that given by the third-State.[44] If no equivalent compensation was offered, no obligation to extend the more favourable treatment to the beneficiary arose.[45] Since the United States was the ultimate judge of what constituted equivalent value, the conditional MFN clause was effectively just an invitation to renegotiate the terms of the original treaty.[46]

The justification publicly offered by the United States for its insistence on the use of conditional MFN clauses was that providing a benefit to a State via an MFN clause without securing equivalent compensation to that given by the original recipient of the benefit actually privileged the beneficiary of the MFN clause.[47] It therefore created precisely the inequality of treatment that MFN clauses were intended to eliminate.[48] More realistically, of course, the true explanation for the United States' adoption of this policy is likely found in the power the policy gave it to decide for itself when it would and would not give MFN treatment.[49]

Contrary to any understanding of MFN clauses of this period as reflecting a commitment to non-discrimination, European States had no objection in principle to conditional MFN clauses.[50] Indeed, although it was the United States that came to be identified with the use of the conditional MFN clause,[51] it was in fact France that had initially proposed to the United States that a conditional MFN clause be adopted for their 1778 treaty.[52] Consequently, it is unsurprising that for a short period the conditional clause became the norm even within Europe.[53]

Nonetheless, in reality, the United States was the only State that truly benefited from conditional MFN treatment, with the conditional MFN clauses adopted by European States ultimately having the same substantive effect as unconditional clauses.[54] While the inability of European States to benefit from conditional MFN clauses is partly explained by the relatively few instances of more favourable treatment being given within Europe at that time, a more fundamental obstacle arose from the fact that all the major trading States other than the United States were already enmeshed in an extensive network of unconditional MFN clauses when they began adopting conditional clauses. The problem this created is that a single unconditional MFN clause will completely undermine the operation of a conditional MFN clause.[55]

By way of example, presume that Germany signs a series of treaties incorporating conditional MFN clauses. As a result of these clauses, if Germany provides a benefit to, for example, Italy, then that same benefit must also be provided to those States benefiting from applicable MFN clauses, upon payment of the same compensation originally paid by Italy. As a result, Germany gains benefits that it would not have gained had its MFN clauses been unconditional.

However, if Germany also has in place a treaty with Finland that includes an unconditional MFN clause, then Finland has the right to receive the benefit in question without paying any compensation. The difficulty this creates for Germany is that while it initially provided the benefit to Italy for a cost, it has now provided the same benefit to Finland free of charge. Consequently, all the States with which Germany has applicable conditional MFN clauses can also claim the benefit free of charge, this being the compensation paid by Finland.

Because of the effect unconditional MFN clauses have on conditional clauses, a State that has signed even a single unconditional MFN clause will gain no benefit from negotiating conditional MFN clauses. Only the fact that the United States was a new State entering into its first round of treaties allowed it successfully to adopt conditional MFN clauses, and only a continued insistence on this policy allowed them to remain effective.[56] Indeed, the one time that the United States was forced to admit that an MFN clause to which it had agreed was unconditional, it terminated the treaty as soon as the first claim was made under it.[57]

While European States were ultimately prevented from following the American policy of conditional MFN clauses, however, they were still able to approach unconditional MFN clauses tactically.[58] For example, although unable to insist on compensation for the provision of benefits through an

MFN clause, European States would at times grant tariff reductions crafted to apply to a very specific type of product.[59] They would then argue that the reduction in question was not given in violation of any applicable MFN clause, as any State could meet the criteria in question, even though only one happened to do it currently.[60] Similarly, in 1891 Austria and Germany kept tariff reductions they had negotiated with one another secret until further treaties had been concluded with third-party States. This secrecy allowed them to negotiate compensation via treaty for reducing tariffs to these third-party States, even though the States in question would have been entitled to receive the same reductions without compensation through applicable MFN clauses.[61] More generally, European States would attend closely to the order in which they negotiated treaties as a means of controlling the benefits that they would gain or give through any applicable MFN clauses.[62]

As a result of such practices, by the end of the nineteenth century the MFN clause had largely fallen out of favour with States.[63] Indeed, hostility to the MFN clause was so strong in France that all its treaties containing MFN clauses were denounced, and a law was passed forbidding the French government from entering into any future treaties containing MFN clauses.[64]

But this hostility to the MFN clause was relatively short lived, and MFN clauses regained their popularity in the period between the two World Wars.[65] Indeed, in 1923 even the United States came to endorse the unconditional form of the MFN clause.[66] Notably, though, this was not because of a newfound appreciation of the benefits of multilateral non-discrimination, but because the United States' continued use of conditional MFN clauses had become counterproductive in the face of the hostility of its trading partners.[67] As a result, a practice of bilateral, prospective, general and unconditional MFN clauses began and has remained the dominant approach to the present day.[68]

As the above discussion shows, MFN clauses have simply never been the generalised non-discrimination provisions that some contemporary commentators have portrayed them as being. They were originally developed as a means of gaining specific advantages already offered to specific third-States, and, even when the generalised form of MFN treatment became dominant, the clause was used tactically as a means of ensuring market benefits rather than as a principled means of promoting multilateral non-discrimination.

The above discussion, however, has almost exclusively focused on the application of MFN clauses to tariff barriers, as until very recently this was almost their exclusive role.[69] With the rise to importance of international investment law, however, MFN clauses have moved into a very different context: one that is particularly problematic for the teleological non-discrimination interpretation of their operation. As section 3 will emphasise, international investment law by its nature has far greater effects upon State action than does the mere setting of tariff levels for imported products. Consequently, failing to recognise the appropriate limits on the operation of MFN clauses within international investment law, and interpreting them solely in accordance with predetermined teleological goals, risks seriously impacting the appropriate regulatory activities of States.

3 Most-favoured nation clauses and bilateral investment treaties

While section 2 addressed the development of MFN clauses in international agreements, no attention has yet been given to their specific role within international investment law. Indeed, the exclusive focus on the use of MFN clauses in international trade characterises most commentary on the topic, for the simple reason that tariff reduction was traditionally the almost-exclusive context in which such clauses were used.[70]

The growth of international investment law in the second half of the twentieth century, however, has created a new field in which MFN clauses have just as central a role as in the regulation of tariffs.[71] Since a treaty will usually take years to renegotiate, a State with an investment treaty that does not include an MFN clause risks shackling its investors to an agreement that has since been superseded by more favourable agreements negotiated with other States.[72]

Of course, as the obligation to provide MFN treatment only arises from treaties, it was not until international investment law came to be dominated by treaties that MFN clauses achieved their current importance within the field. Traditionally, international investors had been protected through the operation of customary international law, which contained restrictions limiting the freedom of Host States[73] in their treatment of foreign investors.[74] The effectiveness of this law, however, depended to a significant degree upon the identity that initially existed between those States serving as the sources of foreign investment and those serving as the recipients. That is, because States receiving foreign investments also had citizens and corporations of their own investing in other countries, each State actively participating in international investment had an interest in agreeing to at least minimal protections of foreign investors.

Moreover, even where a developing State was the recipient of foreign investment, the activities of the investors in question were often governed by the developed State from which the investors came, rather than the developing State in which they were investing. This was because the vastly superior bargaining power of capital-exporting States allowed them to insist upon consular jurisdiction treaties, in accordance with which nationals of a developed State would remain under its sole jurisdiction even when operating in a developing State.[75] Consequently, the investor-friendly policies of developed States would apply even where the Host State in question applied fundamentally different rules to its own investors.

However, the growth of genuinely global business in the twentieth century, the rise to influence of socialist thought, and the wave of decolonisation that occurred immediately after the Second World War combined to produce the collapse of the largely pro-investor consensus that had long underwritten the customary law on the protection of international investments.[76] The decades immediately after the Second World War, therefore, saw a series of actions taken by a variety of States, particularly those newly independent from colonial powers, that would previously have been regarded as inconsistent with international law.[77]

It was against this background that, from the late 1950s, States wishing to ensure protection for their citizens investing abroad ceased relying primarily upon customary international law and turned instead to the signing of BITs.[78] While BITs generally act as a supplement to customary international law, rather than as a replacement for it, investors operating under the protection of a BIT need not rely on the vague and elementary protections offered by customary international law and can instead point to specific promises made by the Host State regarding the treatment they will receive.[79] In addition, if the BIT includes consent to direct investor-State arbitration for any alleged violation of its terms (as is now standard), investors have the additional certainty that the rights granted in the BIT can indeed be enforced, even against an unwilling State.[80] This system of BITs has proven so effective that there are now over 2000 BITs in force, enshrining individualised agreements regarding investor protection between countries from all corners of the world, representing all levels of economic development.[81]

Nonetheless, while the innovation of BITs gave any two States the ability to tailor promised investment protections to the specific relationship existing between them, it also created yet another forum in which States could compete for advantage. After all, as the goal of a BIT is to encourage foreign private investment, it cannot achieve its purpose unless foreign investors know of both its existence and its contents.[82] Consequently, BITs are routinely widely publicised and publicly available.[83] The consequence of this publicity is that each BIT negotiation is conducted with both States fully aware of the terms of the other BITs that its potential treaty partner has already signed.[84] Any State negotiating a BIT will, therefore, do so with full knowledge of what it must do in order to ensure that its investors are treated at least as well as, and ideally better than, those of any third-State.

The high level of publicity attached to BITs, therefore, largely eliminates their usefulness as a means of securing already-existing treatment, as such treatment can easily be identified and specifically requested. However, it makes their role as protector against more favourable future agreements even more important, as the public availability of the contents of a BIT will ensure that States negotiating future agreements with either State party to the original BIT will attempt to achieve more favourable terms than the original BIT included.[85] Consequently, it is unsurprising that BITs characteristically include MFN clauses.[86]

MFN clauses in BITs, however, are of a particularly voracious variety. Although in some treaties they will be restricted in their operation to a particular article, overwhelmingly MFN clauses in BITs are generalised promises of MFN treatment with respect to all areas addressed by the BIT, modified sometimes by certain limited carve-outs.[87]

The difficulty caused by this generality of MFN clauses in BITs is that contemporary international investment agreements address an enormously wide variety of potential government actions and are framed in very broad and vague language.[88] Consequently, there are few, if any, areas of governmental regulation that can be said to be beyond the reach of a contemporary BIT.[89] As a result, while the traditional promise of MFN treatment with respect to tariffs only constrained governmental action in a very narrow field, a generalised MFN clause in a BIT can potentially be applicable to any action taken by a government that affects a foreign investor.[90] In their move from the world of trade and tariffs to the protection of international investments, MFN clauses have gained the power to impact significantly upon the broad policy-making freedom of States.[91]

The importance of MFN clauses has, of course, long been clear, and attempts to standardise the interpretation of MFN clauses by means of international agreements have already twice been undertaken. In the 1920s, the forerunner of the International Law Commission, the Committee of Experts for the Progressive Codification of International Law, undertook the first examination of the possibility of a multilateral convention on the operation of MFN clauses.[92] Ultimately, however, the Committee concluded that 'international regulation of these questions by way of a general convention, even if desirable, would encounter serious obstacles' and, consequently, decided not to proceed.[93] Similarly, the International Law Commission itself addressed the operation of MFN clauses in a project commenced in 1967,[94] resulting in the 1978 Draft Articles on Most-Favoured-Nation Clauses.[95] However, despite several attempts to develop these draft articles into a multilateral treaty, no formal action was taken, and again the idea of a treaty on the operation of MFN clauses was ultimately abandoned.[96]

While the work of both these committees is certainly important, in neither case did the work explicitly discuss the role of MFN clauses in international investment agreements, instead focusing primarily on their role in international trade.[97] This was an understandable emphasis, as international investment law did not attain its current position of importance until after the International Law Commission had concluded its work.[98] Nonetheless, the significantly different context provided by international investment law limits the usefulness of the work produced by these two committees for the interpretation of MFN clauses in BITs. Indeed, it was in recognition of the new importance of international investment law, and the importantly different context it provides for MFN clauses, that the International Law Commission decided in 2008 to resume its work on MFN clauses, with particular consideration given to their operation in international investment agreements.[99]

Up to this point, this chapter has argued that the teleological non-discrimination interpretation of MFN clauses is both inconsistent with the reality of the MFN clause's history, and potentially enormously problematic when imported into international investment law. Nothing has yet been said, however, regarding the boundaries within which MFN clauses should be understood to operate. Section 4 will, therefore, focus upon the limitations on the functioning of MFN clauses that have already been recognised by tribunals applying public international law. The decisions of these tribunals have been recognised as also applicable within international investment law, and thus provide the already-existing limitations on the teleological interpretation of MFN clauses that currently dominates the field.

4 The boundaries of most-favoured nation clauses as recognised by international tribunals

Although there were relatively few decisions by international tribunals regarding the operation of MFN clauses prior to the investment arbitration decisions of the late twentieth century, three decisions from this earlier period are foundational for any understanding of the boundaries of MFN clauses. The importance of these decisions lies not just in the temporal priority they have over all later decisions, but in the approach they took to resolving the MFN-based questions they faced. In each decision, the tribunal in question rejected a broad teleological approach to the interpretation of MFN clauses and instead recognised a specific limitation within which MFN clauses must be seen as operating in international law. As a result, the decisions of these tribunals provide three essential elements for any subsequent discussion of the boundaries of MFN clauses in international investment law.

4.1 Anglo-Iranian Oil*: the treaty-boundedness of most-favoured nation clauses*

One of the great risks of an MFN clause, the precise purpose of which is to allow a party to an agreement to receive treatment not actually promised in that agreement, is that it will be read as operating in an almost unconstrained fashion. Since an MFN clause constitutes a promise not to treat any third party more favourably, an unrestricted MFN clause might be taken to apply to any more favourable treatment given to a third party, with few limitations deriving from the context in which that treatment occurs. As a result, an already enormously powerful clause would potentially be transformed into a replacement for the treaty itself, gathering any more favourable treatment offered to any third party while avoiding any restrictions.

One element of this problem was addressed by the ICJ in its decision in the *Anglo-Iranian Oil Company* case of 1952.[100] The dispute arose out of the nationalisation of the Iranian oil industry, and the consequent losses suffered by the UK-based Anglo-Iranian Oil Company.[101] For the losses suffered by the company during the nationalisation, the United Kingdom was seeking compensation from Iran under treaties concluded between the United Kingdom and Iran in 1857 and 1903.[102]

The question faced by the ICJ, however, was not the substantive question regarding the obligation of Iran to pay compensation, but rather whether it had jurisdiction even to hear the United Kingdom's claim.[103] Under Article 36 of the ICJ Statute, the Court's jurisdiction can be established in two ways.[104] First, both parties to the dispute can consent to the case being heard at the ICJ.[105] Iran had refused its consent, and so the United Kingdom did not rely upon this basis for jurisdiction.[106]

Instead, the United Kingdom was attempting to rely upon the second basis for ICJ jurisdiction, known as its 'compulsory jurisdiction'.[107] Under this approach, States are permitted to lodge a declaration with the Secretary-General of the United Nations regarding the types of disputes they are willing to have brought before the ICJ.[108] Once this consent is lodged, no further consent need be given for the ICJ to have jurisdiction in any specific case. As Iran had indeed given its consent to the ICJ's compulsory jurisdiction, if the United Kingdom could establish that its claim fell under this consent, the ICJ would have jurisdiction despite Iran's unwillingness to agree to have the Anglo-Iranian dispute itself heard at the ICJ.[109]

The complication that arose for the United Kingdom was that Iran's consent to the compulsory jurisdiction of the ICJ, which it had lodged in 1930, had been specifically restricted to disputes arising out of treaties concluded subsequent to that date.[110] Therefore, as the United Kingdom based its claim on treaties concluded in 1857 and 1903, the ICJ prima facie did not have compulsory jurisdiction over the case.[111]

One of the arguments offered by the United Kingdom in its attempt to avoid this obstacle involved the invocation of MFN clauses included in both the 1857 and 1903 treaties.[112] According to the United Kingdom, access to the ICJ constituted more favourable treatment than the dispute resolution mechanisms available under the Basic Treaties themselves.[113] Therefore, since Iran had consented to allow some third-States to bring claims against it at the ICJ, these States were receiving more favourable treatment than was being given to the United Kingdom, and hence the MFN clauses in the Basic Treaties required that the United Kingdom be allowed to bring its case at the ICJ.

If one accepts the United Kingdom's substantive contention that access to the ICJ constitutes more favourable treatment than the dispute resolution procedures offered under the Basic Treaties, then this argument certainly has facial plausibility. Nonetheless, it was rejected by the ICJ. Importantly, however, this was not based on the ground that ICJ jurisdiction was not more favourable than the dispute resolution provisions in the Basic Treaties.[114] Instead, the Court emphasised that whatever impact an MFN clause might have on the provisions of the treaty within which it is contained, it simply cannot alter the terms of any other document.[115] That is, the operation of an MFN clause is restricted to the treaty in which it is contained. On one level this is an obvious conclusion, fully in line with the traditional doctrine of *res inter alios acta*.[116] However, its importance for the purposes of interpreting MFN clauses is clarified by the fact that this rule can, as it arguably did in this case, result in the beneficiary of an MFN clause not actually receiving more favourable treatment to which it is unquestionably entitled through the MFN clause.

As emphasised by the ICJ, the restriction on Iran's consent to the ICJ's compulsory jurisdiction that the United Kingdom was attempting to remove was not included within either of the Basic Treaties. Instead, it was included in a completely separate document.[117] Consequently, since the operation of the MFN clauses in the Basic Treaties was restricted to the Basic Treaties themselves, they could not remove the restriction on Iran's consent to the ICJ's compulsory jurisdiction.[118]

It simply did not matter, therefore, for the purposes of the ICJ's jurisdiction, whether access to the ICJ constituted more favourable treatment than Iran was providing to any third-State, and hence whether the United Kingdom had a treaty-based right to bring its claim before the ICJ. The United Kingdom may indeed have possessed this right, but it simply was not a right that the ICJ had the jurisdiction to vindicate.

It is thus simply inaccurate to categorise the *Anglo-Iranian Oil Company* decision as constituting a rejection of the view that MFN clauses can apply to dispute resolution procedures, as some commentators have done.[119] The ICJ simply never addressed this point.

By drawing this distinction between the existence of a right to more favourable treatment and the jurisdiction of a tribunal to determine whether that right exists, the ICJ thus recognised an important constraint on the operation of MFN clauses. Mere invocation of an MFN clause does not gain the beneficiary all more favourable treatment currently being provided to third-States, as would a general non-discrimination clause. Unless that treatment can in some way be incorporated into the treaty in which the MFN clause is contained, it is simply unavailable to the beneficiary of the MFN clause, whether it is indeed more favourable or not.[120]

4.2 Rights of Nationals of the United States of America in Morocco: *the temporality of most-favoured nation clauses*

Only 1 month later, in *Rights of Nationals of the United States of America in Morocco*,[121] the ICJ recognised a further important limitation on the operation of MFN clauses with respect to their essential temporality. The case concerned a disagreement between the United States and France regarding the extent of US consular jurisdiction in Morocco,[122] at that time under the control of France.[123] While France contended that US consular jurisdiction only extended to civil disputes, the United States argued that it also extended to criminal disputes.[124] As one of its arguments, the United States attempted to invoke an MFN clause included in an agreement between itself and Morocco in an attempt to gain access to broad grants of consular jurisdiction included in treaties concluded by Morocco with Spain and with the United Kingdom.[125]

The difficulty for the United States was that even if it was accepted that the grants of broader consular jurisdiction to Spain and the United Kingdom did indeed constitute more favourable treatment than that given to the United States, the treaties delivering that treatment were no longer in effect.[126] The United States, therefore, was not attempting to argue merely that an MFN clause gains the beneficiary State any more favourable treatment given to third-States, but that once a State gains a certain form of treatment via an MFN clause, it retains that treatment even if the third-State in question ceases to receive it. As viewed by the United States, MFN provisions should be understood as a means of drafting by reference, with incorporated treatment retained as though there were explicit language in the treaty requiring that it be given.[127]

While such an argument might have had some strength at a time when MFN clauses were understood to operate purely retrospectively, incorporating only treatment already given to third-States when the MFN clause came into effect, the ICJ appropriately rejected it in the contemporary context of prospective MFN clauses.[128] Instead, the Court emphasised in its decision that rather than being a form of incorporation by reference, contemporary MFN clauses are properly understood as a means of ensuring equality between the State beneficiary of the MFN clause and the third-State receiving the more favourable treatment in question.[129] However, to allow the United States to retain the arguably more favourable treatment even after it was withdrawn from Spain and the United Kingdom would actually privilege the United States over its competitors, a goal inconsistent with the purpose of a contemporary MFN clause.

In this ruling, then, the ICJ further reiterated that MFN clauses are not an unrestricted means of States gaining the best form of treatment possible. Rather, they operate not only within the limits of the treaty in which they are contained, but also within the temporal limitations of the treatment being sought. MFN clauses, that is, have their effect on an ongoing basis. Treatment is not incorporated once and then forever maintained. It is instead incorporated anew at each moment the more favourable treatment is available to the third-State. Consequently, once the more favourable treatment is withdrawn from the third-State, it is no longer available to be incorporated via the MFN clause and is therefore lost to the beneficiary of the clause as well.

4.3 The Ambatielos *arbitration:* ejusdem generis

One final limitation that has been recognised by international tribunals addresses the risk created by the impact on the operation of MFN clauses of the broad range of issues about which States enter into international agreements. A State may, for example, be willing to subject itself to binding dispute resolution in the field of human rights, while remaining completely unwilling to do so where purely economic claims are brought. However, if the State has included an MFN clause within an economic treaty it has signed, the beneficiary of that clause may argue that States signatory to the human rights treaty are receiving more favourable treatment due to the availability of binding dispute resolution. Unrestricted interpretations of general MFN clauses, then, create the risk that States will find themselves obligated to extend benefits willingly granted in one area of law into a completely different area of law from which they may have been expressly excluded.

While the situation as just described was not itself faced by the tribunal in the *Ambatielos* arbitration,[130] the *ejusdem generis* principle that the tribunal enunciated has served to resolve this risk.[131] By virtue of this principle, an MFN clause 'can only attract matters belonging to the same category of subject as that to which the clause itself relates'.[132] The *Ambatielos* arbitration concerned a claim brought by Greece against the United Kingdom on behalf of a Greek shipowner, Nicolas Eustache Ambatielos.[133] Ambatielos had purchased nine ships from the British government, but after a delay in delivery of the ships Ambatielos had experienced difficulties in making the agreed payments.[134] When sued by the British government in English courts for the monies owed, Ambatielos brought a counterclaim arguing that there had been a verbal agreement regarding the dates of delivery of the ships, and that he was therefore owed compensation for losses suffered as a result of their late delivery.[135]

After losing at the level of the trial court, Ambatielos appealed to the Court of Appeals, seeking to introduce new testimony from a British government official regarding the existence of the alleged verbal agreement.[136] In accordance with British procedural rules, the Court of Appeals excluded this testimony, as it had not been presented at the original trial.[137] The Court subsequently held against Ambatielos.[138]

Ambatielos turned to the Greek government for assistance, and, after decades of failed negotiations,[139] Greece attempted to bring the dispute before the ICJ.[140] The ICJ, however, held that it did not have jurisdiction over the substance of the claim due to a pre-existing arbitration clause, and that Greece and the United Kingdom were obligated to proceed to arbitration.[141]

The existence of an MFN clause in a treaty between Greece and the United Kingdom became a central issue in the arbitration when Greece attempted to invoke that clause in order to incorporate a promise made by the United Kingdom in treaties with third-States to treat nationals 'in accordance with "justice," "right," "equity" and the "principles of international law"'.[142] According to Greece, the refusal by the Court of Appeals to admit the testimony of the British government official regarding the agreed dates of delivery constituted a violation of this standard.[143]

The United Kingdom's defence included the argument that an MFN clause 'can only attract matters belonging to the same category of subject as the clause itself relates to', and that as the clause invoked by Greece applied only to 'matters relating to commerce and navigation', it could not be applied to issues regarding what the United Kingdom termed 'the administration of justice'.[144]

Adopting the *ejusdem generis* principle, the tribunal accepted the United Kingdom's argument that an MFN clause only gives a right to more favourable treatment that is given in those fields to which the MFN clause itself relates.[145] Consequently, in order for Greece to use the MFN clause to incorporate the standard to which it had appealed, it was necessary that 'the administration of justice' be one of the 'matters relating to commerce and navigation'.[146] The tribunal held that it was indeed such a matter, but ultimately also held that the United Kingdom's actions nonetheless did not constitute a violation of the principle in question.[147]

The importance of the *Ambatielos* decision for the present discussion does not, however, relate to the final holding of the tribunal, but rather to its endorsement of the *ejusdem generis* principle. By recognising the role of this principle as an essential element of the interpretation of MFN clauses, the tribunal placed a further important constraint on the operation of such clauses.[148] That is, just as MFN clauses are only able to affect the terms of the treaty in which they are contained, so they are substantively circumscribed by the nature of that treaty. The mere ability of the beneficiary of an MFN clause to identify treatment received by a third-State that would also benefit its activities, in so far as they are covered by the MFN clause, does not entail that it has a right to such treatment. MFN clauses are not a generalised means of ensuring market equality.[149] So long as the market inequality arises as an incidental consequence of treatment delivered in an area of law other than the one covered by the MFN clause, the MFN clause has no effect.[150]

5 Conclusion

Through these three cases, the ICJ and the *Ambatielos* tribunal went a significant way towards delineating the boundaries of the functioning of MFN clauses in public international law. However, while these boundaries are also applicable to MFN clauses in international investment law, the decisions in which they were recognised do not themselves address that field. As Chapter 6 will argue, however, the structure of international investment law itself imposes significant additional boundaries on the operation of MFN clauses.[151] Consequently, any understanding of the operation of MFN clauses in international investment agreements must attend to the specific structure of international investment law and cannot rely solely upon discussions of the functioning of MFN clauses in public international law generally.

6 The operation of the most-favoured nation clause in international investment law

1 Introduction

Chapter 5, having introduced the public international law background of MFN clauses, Chapter 6 will now address the manner in which MFN clauses should be understood to operate in the specific context of international investment law. It will argue that the structure of contemporary international investment law, including particularly the adoption of investment arbitration as the primary dispute resolution mechanism within the field, results in three important characteristics of the operation of MFN clauses in the international investment law context. First, it will argue that MFN clauses in international investment agreements should generally be understood as granting access solely to more favourable treatment provided after the agreement is negotiated, and not to any pre-existing more favourable treatment.[1] Second, it will argue that the 'favourability' of a particular type of treatment should be evaluated not with respect to the specific investor invoking an MFN clause, but with respect to the entire class of investors covered by the clause. Lastly, it will argue that MFN clauses do not merely provide to the beneficiary any more favourable treatment provided to a third party, but also simultaneously exclude the beneficiary's access to the treatment originally promised. Moreover, these three characteristics can sometimes combine in a way that results in an investor actually being harmed by an MFN clause rather than being benefited by it.

2 The instantaneous effect of a most-favoured nation clause

While no one would question that an MFN clause can have an impact on the rights and obligations included within a BIT, MFN clauses in international investment agreements must be understood as having an instantaneous effect, independent of any need for the beneficiary of the clause to invoke the clause's existence. That is, where State A and State B have signed a BIT containing an MFN clause, the instant State B gives more favourable treatment to State C than to State A, State A instantly becomes entitled to the higher level of treatment given to State C.[2]

That MFN clauses operate instantaneously is not in itself a controversial claim, as it is fully consistent both with the accepted approach adopted in public international law and in decisions by investment arbitration tribunals.[3] Simply because an MFN clause entails an obligation not to provide more favourable treatment to a third party than is provided to the beneficiary of the MFN clause, the moment more favourable treatment is provided, the State providing the more favourable treatment is in breach of its treaty obligations.

There are, however, two ways in which an MFN clause could be understood as having an immediate effect, which are referred to here as the 'right to claim' understanding and the 'instantaneous obligation' understanding. Subsections 2.1 and 2.2 will detail these two approaches and subsection 2.3 will then argue that only the 'instantaneous obligation' approach to MFN clauses is consistent with the nature of contemporary international investment law.

2.1 The 'right to claim' understanding of most-favoured nation obligations

The first potential way of understanding the immediate effect of an MFN clause is that as soon as more favourable treatment is provided to a third party, the beneficiary of the MFN clause gains the 'right to claim' equivalent treatment for itself. That is, no immediate obligation arises for the State providing the treatment to the third-State to also provide it to the beneficiary of the MFN clause, but once the beneficiary requests equivalent treatment, it must be provided.[4]

The 'right to claim' understanding makes a significant degree of sense in the context of international agreements, as it maximises the predictability and transparency of MFN obligations,[5] thereby minimising the impact of such clauses on the policy-making freedom of States. After all, while there will be cases in which it is clear that treatment given to a third-State is more favourable than that given to the beneficiary of the MFN clause, in many cases it will be disputable.[6] States attempting to act in such a situation will face pressure to be conservative in the obligations they undertake with third parties, out of concern that they may unwittingly also obligate themselves to provide the same treatment to any States with which they have an applicable MFN clause. By contrast, if the beneficiary is required to make a claim for the more favourable treatment before it is owed, the granting State is assured of knowing at all times precisely what its obligations are.

In addition, because no obligation to provide the more favourable treatment existed until the claim was made, there is no risk of large backdated damages claims, extending through years in which the State in good faith did not believe any obligation to provide the treatment in question existed.

However, the 'right to claim' understanding is significantly less desirable for the beneficiary of the MFN clause than it is for the State providing the more favourable treatment. After all, since the beneficiary is required to claim any treatment before it has a right to receive it, the beneficiary will need constantly to monitor the treatment provided by the granting State to third-States in order to ensure that it is not missing any benefit it should be receiving under the MFN clause.[7]

The 'right to claim' understanding of MFN obligations, then, ultimately maximises State policy-making freedom, but does so by minimising the benefits MFN clauses provide, as it creates a significant risk that the beneficiary of an MFN clause will often not in fact be receiving the most favourable treatment given by the State with which it has an MFN agreement.

2.2 The 'instantaneous obligation' understanding of most-favoured nation obligations

By contrast, the 'instantaneous obligation' understanding of MFN clauses eliminates any necessity for the beneficiary of the MFN clause to monitor the actions of the State with which it has an MFN agreement. However, it also significantly increases the impact of an MFN clause on State policy-making freedom.

Under this approach, if State A and State B have entered into an MFN agreement, as soon as State B provides more favourable treatment to State C, it is obligated also to provide it to State A. State A need do nothing to gain this more favourable treatment, and in turn any claim it makes against State B for benefits it should have received under the MFN clause will be backdated to the moment the more favourable treatment was given to State C.

The 'instantaneous obligation' understanding, then, emphasises that States entering into an MFN agreement have done so voluntarily, and that the existence of such an agreement is simply inconsistent with allowing one party to the agreement to violate it, so long as its counterparty remains unaware.[8]

2.3 The justification for the 'instantaneous obligation' understanding in investment arbitration

Within the context of investment arbitration there are clear justifications for adopting the 'instantaneous obligation' understanding rather than the 'right to claim' understanding. There is, for example, unambiguous investment arbitration case law on this issue, and each tribunal that has addressed the question has adopted the 'instantaneous obligation' understanding.[9]

In addition to mere adherence to prior case law, however, additional substantive reasons exist to support the adoption of the 'instantaneous obligation' understanding within investment arbitration, arising specifically from the incorporation of investors into the investment arbitration process.

By incorporating direct investor-State dispute resolution into a BIT, the parties to the BIT have thereby created a separation between the parties to the BIT and the parties to any dispute resolution procedure that may result from a violation of the BIT. Indeed, the existence of this distinction has traditionally served as a primary rationale for the adoption of investor-State arbitration, as it is argued that allowing an investor to bring its claim directly against the Host State serves to depoliticise the dispute by removing the Home State from the proceedings.[10]

However, if the 'right to claim' understanding were to be adopted in investment arbitration, the Home State would be required to claim MFN treatment in order for its investors to receive it. The Home State would, therefore, be reintegrated back into the dispute resolution process in a way that would raise precisely the politicisation concerns that initially served to motivate the adoption of investor-State arbitration. The 'right to claim' understanding, then, is simply inconsistent with one of the primary rationales underlying the adoption of investment arbitration.

It might be argued that due to the delegation of dispute resolution authority to investors, commencement of arbitral proceedings by an investor should be treated as a 'claim' by the investor's Home State to any more favourable treatment. However, there may clearly be situations in which a Home State does not wish allegedly more favourable treatment to be claimed. Of most immediate relevance, the Home State may not wish the MFN clause in a BIT to be applied to dispute resolution clauses, as it has itself agreed to more favourable dispute resolution procedures with third-States than exist under the BIT, including the MFN clause. It does not, therefore, want investors from the State counterparty to the MFN agreement to be able to access those procedures.

It is, to be blunt, simply implausible to think that merely through the incorporation of direct investor-State arbitration into a BIT, the States party to that BIT intended to give investors the power effectively to rewrite the terms of a carefully negotiated treaty. The commencement of an arbitration by an investor, then, simply cannot be regarded as a 'claim' by its Home State of any more favourable treatment currently offered by the Host State to third-States.

Under the 'right to claim' approach, then, no tribunal could decide in favour of an investor with respect to an MFN clause unless the Home State had explicitly supported the investor's MFN argument. Yet such a requirement is not only clearly inconsistent with the desire to depoliticise investment disputes, it is also inconsistent with the delegation of dispute resolution to the investor, as it subjects a significant portion of the investor's argument to an effective veto by the Home State.

The very structure of investment arbitration, then, with its incorporation of direct investor-State arbitration, requires that MFN clauses in international investment agreements be interpreted in accordance with the 'instantaneous obligation' understanding, as a result of which any more favourable treatment delivered by State B to State C is instantly owed to State A, without requiring any form of claim to the treatment to be made by State A. Section 3 will demonstrate how this aspect of MFN clauses in international investment law creates an important boundary for their functioning in this field that does not apply to MFN clauses in public international law generally.

3 The predominantly forward-looking nature of most-favoured nation clauses in investment arbitration

Section 2 addressed one element of what can be called the 'temporality' of MFN clauses, or the way in which they are fundamentally enmeshed in considerations regarding time. As seen in that discussion, MFN clauses in investment arbitration must be understood as having their effect the instant more favourable treatment is provided to a third-State. This section will demonstrate the impact of this instantaneous effect on the applicability of MFN clauses to more favourable treatment already existing when the MFN clause came into effect. Specifically, it will be argued that an MFN clause in an investment treaty should not usually be understood as giving the beneficiary of the clause access to more favourable treatment in a pre-existing third-State treaty, although it can give access to pre-existing non-treaty treatment. This is a particularly important limitation on the operation of MFN clauses in international investment law, as there has traditionally been no controversy regarding the applicability of MFN clauses to pre-existing treatment.[11]

3.1 The role of intent in interpreting most-favoured nation clauses in investment treaties

The approach to MFN clauses advanced in this chapter relies heavily upon arguments regarding what can plausibly be said to have been intended by the States party to a BIT when they decided to incorporate an MFN clause into their treaty. There is, however, a significant difference of opinion among legal commentators regarding the relevance to treaty interpretation of the subjective intentions of the Contracting States. This subsection, therefore, lays out the justification for appealing to party intent in interpreting MFN clauses.

Although it is uncontested that Articles 31 and 32 of the VCLT[12] are the touchstone for interpretation of any BIT,[13] there is still significant disagreement among commentators regarding their precise meaning. While few, if any, commentators would deny that the VCLT gives primacy to the text of a treaty over any textually unexpressed intentions of the Contracting States, disagreement exists regarding how strong this preference for 'text' over 'intention' actually is. Most controversially, commentators are split regarding whether clear evidence that the text as adopted does not accurately reflect the intentions of the Contracting States should suffice to overrule otherwise clear treaty language, or if States must instead simply live with the agreements they sign.[14]

The source of this disagreement lies in the language adopted in Articles 31 and 32 of the VCLT. It is unquestionably true that Article 31 gives primacy to the text of the treaty, rather than to the subjective intentions of the parties, adopting as its fundamental rule that treaties be interpreted 'in accordance to the terms of the treaty in their context and in light of its object and purpose'.[15] While this rule is admittedly framed in a way that gives recognition to the intentions of the parties, requiring interpretation in accordance with the 'object and purpose' of the treaty, this recognition applies solely with respect to interpretation of the written language. Consequently, it cannot justify giving any reading to a clause not directly based upon the actual language of the treaty.

The complication arises, however, when proper consideration is given to Article 32 of the VCLT, regarding the use of 'supplementary means of interpretation', such as 'the preparatory work of the treaty'.[16] Article 32 lays out a two-step process in which an interpretation is initially developed under Article 31, but is then tested against supplementary means of interpretation to either 'confirm' the interpretation arrived at under Article 31 or to derive a different interpretation where the interpretation arrived at under Article 31 left the treaty language either 'ambiguous or obscure' or 'manifestly absurd or unreasonable'.[17]

It is the recognition in Article 32 of the VCLT that supplementary means of interpretation can be used to 'confirm' an interpretation reached under Article 31 that creates the difficulty for a purely textualist interpretation of the VCLT, as this option is listed separately to situations in which the treaty language remains 'ambiguous' or 'absurd'.[18] That is, it is not first necessary for the interpretation reached via Article 31 to be clearly flawed in some way for supplementary means of interpretation to be used to 'confirm' its correctness.

There is, however, little point in confirming the correctness of an interpretation if that interpretation cannot be rejected when shown to be wrong. It must, therefore, be the case, as recognised by commentators such as Stephen Schwebel, former President of the ICJ, that clear evidence of the intentions of Contracting States can override even apparently clear treaty language.[19]

Even on this understanding of the VCLT, of course, the text retains its centrality in interpretation. Otherwise Article 31's emphasis on the text would be nonsensical. However, this emphasis on the text can be understood as simply requiring a high level of certainty regarding the subjective intentions of the parties to the treaty if apparently clear language is to be overridden. That is, clear treaty language overrides vague indications of contrary party intent, but where party intent is sufficiently clear, even apparently clear treaty language must give way to it.

The subjective intentions of the States party to a BIT are, therefore, always important in the interpretation of the provisions of the BIT, including an MFN clause, even though they remain subsidiary to the language of the BIT itself.

3.2 Party intent as to the extension of most-favoured nation clauses to already-existing more favourable treatment

Once it has been accepted, however, that party intent can correct even otherwise clear treaty language, an important conclusion can be drawn regarding the operation of MFN clauses. Specifically, it will be argued in this subsection that parties usually cannot plausibly be understood to have intended an MFN clause in an investment treaty to grant the beneficiary of the clause access to more favourable provisions present in other investment treaties already in effect when the Basic Treaty came into force.[20] Consequently, even where the text of the MFN clause would itself seem to allow such an application, the clear intent of the parties should be taken to override the language of the clause.

The justification for this preclusion of already-existing treaty provisions from coverage by an MFN clause in a BIT derives directly from the instantaneous obligations that arise as a result of such clauses, as discussed above. To illustrate with an example, presume that in 1995 States A and B sign an investment treaty including an MFN clause, as well as including a fair and equitable treatment clause[21] restricted in certain ways. However, States B and C had already signed, in 1992, an investment treaty containing an unrestricted fair and equitable treatment clause. If the MFN clause in the A-B treaty is understood as applying to treaty provisions already in existence when the A-B treaty comes into force, then investors from State A are actually covered by an unrestricted fair and equitable treatment clause, despite the restrictions explicitly incorporated into the A-B treaty.

The implausibility that parties to the treaty intended this situation derives not from the fact that the parties to the A-B BIT are receiving treatment other than that promised them in the BIT, as that is an inherent consequence of the operation of an MFN clause. Rather, the implausibility results because, due to the instantaneous effect of MFN clauses, the removal of the restrictions on the fair and equitable treatment obligation included in the A-B treaty occurred the instant the A-B treaty came into force. That is, there was no point at which the fair and equitable treatment clause expressly negotiated between States A and B was actually in effect between them. Such a situation, however, simply makes incomprehensible the inclusion of the restrictions in question within the treaty.[22]

Nevertheless, as established above, sufficiently strong evidence of party intent can suffice to override otherwise clear treaty language.[23] Consequently, the sheer implausibility that States A and B negotiated treaty language that would have absolutely no effect might justify precluding the application of the MFN clause in the A-B treaty to the fair and equitable treatment clause in the B-C treaty. That is, although the language of the MFN clause itself is unrestricted, an exception is read into the clause that prevents it being applied to any more favourable treaty provisions already in effect at the time the A-B treaty came into force.

The difficulty with such an argument is that, as noted in the historical survey in Chapter 5, MFN clauses have traditionally been recognised as applying to already-existing treatment.[24] Indeed, it has been argued that one of the primary purposes of an MFN clause is to reassure treaty negotiators that they have secured the best available treatment for their State, rather than leaving them with the burden of discovering every form of treatment the counterparty to the treaty is providing to third-States.[25]

It is at this point that the distinctively public nature of investment treaties becomes important. Unlike most treaties, investment treaties are expressly designed to be broadly publicised. After all, States enter into investment treaties as a means of attracting private investment from abroad.[26] The entire purpose of such a treaty, then, would be undermined were it to be kept secret, or even just not made broadly available. As a result, information on the investment treaties signed by States is easily available, even to the extent of the full text of treaties being available on publicly accessible websites.[27]

The consequence of this public nature of investment treaties for the interpretation of MFN clauses is that it is simply implausible that States incorporated an MFN clause into their treaty as a protection against unknown already-existing BIT-based treatment. The information on such treatment is simply too easily accessible.[28] To return to the example above, if unrestricted fair and equitable treatment had been discussed in the negotiations between States A and B, State B could have insisted that State A grant some countervailing benefit. However, if it is subsequently incorporated via an MFN clause, no compensation is given, and State B has effectively granted unrestricted fair and equitable treatment free of charge. Absent evidence to the contrary, then, it is simply implausible to read an MFN clause in a BIT as referring to already-existing provisions in a third-State BIT.

The precise nature of the position being maintained here should be emphasised. It is not being argued that the MFN clause in the A-B BIT should be understood as including an exception specifically precluding its applicability to the already-existing B-C BIT. Rather, the exception in question is a generalised one, referring to any pre-existing BIT-based treatment. It does not require that the parties have identified the BITs in question in any way.

It is important to note, however, that since this argument is premised upon the publicity attached to BITs, it will be far less applicable to non-treaty-based treatment or to treaties that have not received significant publicity. Where the treatment granted to a third-State constitutes, for example, an administrative practice, any tribunal addressing the applicability of an MFN clause must undertake an analysis of the accessibility to the Contracting States of information on the practice. Only if the availability of information on the practice reaches a level corresponding to the publicity attached to BITs will the current argument be applicable.[29]

Nonetheless, as argued above, using the intentions of the parties to override otherwise clear treaty language is only appropriate when those intentions can be clearly ascertained, and it might be argued that the mere implausibility that States would knowingly agree to an MFN clause that automatically deleted negotiated treaty language does not rise to the level of certainty required by the VCLT. After all, it is certainly possible that the individuals negotiating the treaty simply adopted the general MFN clause without a full awareness of its effects. In such a situation, however, there would be no intent to exclude pre-existing BIT provisions.

Subsection 3.3 will, therefore, offer an alternative argument that requires consideration of available evidence, rather than merely invoking a presumption. These two arguments have different impacts on the interpretation of MFN clauses, but both would suffice to preclude the application of MFN clauses to already-existing more favourable BIT provisions in at least some situations.

3.3 Interpretation of most-favoured nation clauses and the interconnectedness of treaty rights

While the argument advanced in subsection 3.2 would justify a blanket exclusion of pre-existing BIT provisions from the application of MFN clauses, it is also possible to make an argument for a more limited exclusion, but one that is based on a stronger evidential foundation. As a result, even if the blanket exclusion argued for above is rejected, a more limited exclusion might still be applicable.

The argument for this more limited exclusion centres on interpretation of the term 'treatment' as used in an MFN clause. MFN clauses, after all, are a promise that no more favourable 'treatment' will be given to investors from any third-State than is given to investors from the beneficiary State. What constitutes 'treatment' under an MFN clause, however, is never specified, and hence must be determined by each tribunal that is faced with an MFN-based argument.

The standard approach to evaluating an MFN-based argument involves comparing the specific treaty provisions invoked by the investor.[30] That is, if the investor is attempting to use the MFN clause in the Basic Treaty to alter that treaty's dispute resolution provisions, a conventional analysis would involve comparing those provisions with the dispute resolution provisions in the third-State treaty. If the latter are judged to be more favourable, then the MFN clause is held to be applicable.

Such an approach relies upon a contention that each treaty provision in a treaty constitutes an identifiable form of treatment, independent of the other clauses in the treaty. Without such a premise, a one-to-one comparison of treaty provisions could not suffice to show that investors under the third-State treaty are receiving more favourable 'treatment' than investors under the Basic Treaty. Of course, the alternative of viewing the 'treatment' received by an investor as constituting every provision of the applicable treaty, acting together, is itself unworkable, as it would make any meaningful comparison impossible. Consequently, inclusion of an MFN clause would be nonsensical, as it could never be successfully invoked.

A third approach serves as the foundation for the argument to be presented in this subsection. This approach emphasises that treaty negotiation is not a clause-by-clause matter, with each provision being agreed before another is addressed. Rather, treaty negotiation is fundamentally a more interrelated enterprise, with substantively unconnected elements of the treaty often being used as trade-offs: one party getting its preferred language in the first clause in exchange for the other party getting its preferred language in the second clause.[31]

Because of this interconnectedness of treaty negotiation, an agreement between State A and State B to include, for example, restrictions on access to investor-State arbitration in the A-B BIT, need not reflect an unwillingness of one of the States to grant unrestricted access to investor-State arbitration. For example, it may simply be that what State B requested from State A in exchange for unrestricted access to investor-State arbitration was something State A was unwilling to give. That is, the existence of the restriction might represent a failure of negotiation rather than an agreed level of treatment.

This does not mean that there is no identifiable 'treatment' of investors that was agreed between A and B. Rather, it means that the 'treatment' consists of a combination of the restricted dispute resolution procedure included in the treaty, and the provision(s) with which it was connected during negotiations. The dispute resolution procedure, that is, was agreed as part of a broader package, and it is this broader package that constitutes the 'treatment' of the investor from the perspective of an MFN clause.[32]

Of course there will rarely be information available to a tribunal as to which aspects of the treaty were connected in this way during negotiations. Consequently, it might seem that this broader conception of 'treatment' is of no use to a tribunal faced with an MFN-based argument. However, it is unnecessary for a tribunal actually to identify which treaty provisions were used as trade-offs against one another. Rather, all the tribunal must do is find adequate evidence that such a trade-off took place.

For example, the tribunal may note that in the B-C BIT, entered into prior to the A-B BIT, State B was willing to agree to unrestricted investor-State dispute resolution. Absent evidence of a change in policy by State B between negotiation of the two BITs, it is then reasonable to conclude that State B was willing to agree to unrestricted investor-State arbitration in the A-B BIT. Similarly, the tribunal may find that there is no evidence that State A was unwilling to agree to unrestricted investor-State arbitration. As a result, a rebuttable presumption must arise that unrestricted investor-State arbitration was an option during negotiations for the A-B BIT, but that restrictions were imposed anyway.

The tribunal need simply conclude that since both parties were willing to agree to unrestricted investor-State arbitration, but nonetheless ultimately imposed restrictions, the most plausible explanation is that the dispute resolution provisions were not negotiated independently, but were instead linked to another provision or provisions during negotiations. The limitations on dispute resolution were part of a broader package of treatment, in which those limitations were imposed as a result of a failure to agree to alternative terms on one or more other provisions.

Nonetheless, whatever other provisions were included in this broader 'treatment', the available evidence indicates that unrestricted dispute resolution was expressly rejected by the parties. As argued in subsection 3.2, though, if the MFN clause in the A-B BIT is interpreted as applying to provisions in the pre-existing B-C BIT, the restrictions on dispute resolution in the A-B BIT will never come into force. Consequently, given that information on the B-C BIT was easily accessible to both States, it would have made no sense for States A and B to agree on limited investor-State arbitration as part of a broader package of 'treatment', only to have those limitations removed as soon as the A-B BIT came into effect. This would involve giving away for free something for which a price was clearly being asked during negotiations.

This second argument, therefore, also justifies interpreting the MFN clause in the A-B BIT as not applying to the dispute resolution provisions of the B-C BIT. However, it does so in a more limited fashion than the first argument.

That is, while a conclusion derived from this second argument has the benefit of being based on evidence, rather than on a mere presumption, it is also thereby limited in that if the evidence is not sufficient, the argument fails. There might be, for example, evidence that at the time the A-B BIT was negotiated, State A had a policy opposing unrestricted investor-State arbitration. In such a situation, an alternative explanation for the incorporation of restricted investor-State arbitration into the BIT exists, and it is unnecessary to appeal to negotiation trade-offs. As a result, there would be inadequate justification for interpreting the MFN clause in the A-B BIT as not applying to the dispute resolution provisions of the B-C BIT.

It is also important, however, to emphasise precisely what is precluded by this argument, as it differs from what is precluded by the first argument. The first argument resulted in a blanket exception of the application of the MFN clause to all pre-existing BIT provisions. The exception created by this second argument, on the other hand, relates not to pre-existing BIT provisions, but to a particular type of provision. That is, it is based on a conclusion by the tribunal that the parties most probably considered and rejected unrestricted investor-State arbitration. As a result, it is the substantive agreement to unrestricted investor-State arbitration that is excluded from the application of the MFN clause, not mere appeal to the B-C BIT. Subsection 3.4 will address the importance of this distinction between the two arguments.

3.4 Most-favoured nation clauses and subsequent adoptions of already-existing more favourable treatment

Subsections 3.2 and 3.3 have offered two approaches to the issue of the application of MFN clauses to treatment of a third-State already in existence at the time the treaty containing the MFN clause comes into effect. As will be demonstrated below, however, these two arguments have significantly different effects on the impact of the subsequent adoption by a State of already-existing more favourable treatment.

Even if it is determined, for example, that investors from State A should not receive the unrestricted access to investor-State arbitration already available to investors from State C when the A-B BIT came into effect, State B may nonetheless subsequently negotiate a further BIT with State D that also includes unrestricted access to investor-State arbitration. The question this raises is whether investors from State A could then gain unrestricted access to investor-State arbitration through the B-D treaty, even though they were precluded from doing so through the B-C treaty.

The difference in this context between the two arguments offered above arises from the rationales on which each argument is based. The first argument is based upon a determination that the MFN clause in the A-B BIT must be understood not to refer to already-existing third-State BIT provisions, due to the implausibility that the parties would have adopted a treaty provision with the knowledge that it would have absolutely no effect.

Yet a subsequent adoption by State B of precisely the same treatment with respect to State D would not have the effect of making the original negotiation of the language in the A-B BIT pointless. After all, had the B-C treaty never existed, there would be no question that the MFN clause in the A-B BIT would be applicable to the terms of the B-D BIT. A tribunal that adopted the first argument in refusing to apply the MFN clause in the A-B BIT to give investors from State A the unrestricted access to investor-State arbitration included in the B-C treaty would nonetheless remain perfectly free to grant that access via the B-D treaty.

By contrast, the second argument, focusing upon the interconnectedness of treaty negotiation, ultimately relies upon a conclusion that the States party to the BIT containing the MFN clause had considered and rejected a particular type of provision. As a result, a tribunal adopting this second argument as a ground for rejecting the applicability of the MFN clause in the A-B BIT to the dispute resolution procedures in the B-C BIT does so on the ground that the MFN clause in the A-B BIT simply cannot be a means of incorporating unrestricted investor-State arbitration into the A-B BIT. The subsequent adoption of precisely the same substantive treatment in the B-D treaty, therefore, would fail by precisely the same argument.[33]

Ultimately, then, while both of the arguments advanced here provide a justification for holding MFN clauses to be inapplicable to at least some types of pre-existing treatment, they are nonetheless importantly different, and significantly different impacts will result from a tribunal's adoption of one of the arguments rather than the other.

4 Non-State beneficiaries of most-favoured nation clauses in investment treaties as classes, not individual claimants

So far, this chapter has addressed potential exclusions of the applicability of MFN clauses to substantive treaty promises, but no analysis has as yet been made regarding the nature of the beneficiaries of an MFN clause. While for most non-investment treaties this question may have an obvious answer, it is a more complex issue in the international investment law context, as MFN clauses in BITs do not generally refer to the Contracting States but to their 'investors'.[34]

In response to this situation, it might be argued that MFN-based claims should be approached as though they require that any evaluation of the 'favourability' of treatment be done with reference to the particular individual bringing the claim. The claimant, after all, is the 'investor', and hence presumably the subject of the reference in the MFN clause. The goal of this section is to demonstrate that this approach is mistaken, and that evaluations of the favourability of treatment must be made with respect to the class of investors from which the claimant in an arbitration has come, rather than with respect to the claimant itself.

The initial indication that it is the class of investors from which the claimant in an arbitration comes that is the beneficiary of an MFN clause in a

BIT comes simply from the language adopted in such a clause. The claimant, after all, is not only not a signatory to the BIT, but is also nowhere referenced in it. That is, rather than including a promise that MFN treatment will be provided to this specific investor, the BIT will include merely a generalised reference to 'investors', a class to which this particular investor belongs. It might nonetheless be argued that although the collective term 'investors' is used, it is used as a means of referring individually to each member of the class, rather than referring collectively to the class as a whole. In the same manner, someone who says 'I fed my children dinner' is not saying that they somehow gave food to an abstract class of children, of which their individual children happen to be members. Rather, the clear meaning is that they provided food individually to each of their children. If the collective reference to 'investors' in a BIT is understood as also operating in this individualised manner, then the relevant reference for the evaluation of favourability would remain the claimant investor, rather than the broader class from which it came.

However, the 'instantaneous obligation' understanding of MFN clauses in investment treaties simply makes such an individualised interpretation of the term 'investor' unworkable.[35] Presume, for example, that in 1990 State A and State B entered into a BIT that includes an MFN clause. Then, in 1995, State B entered into a BIT with State C that includes a more favourable fair and equitable treatment provision than the one included in the A-B BIT. As a result of the instantaneous effect of MFN clauses, that more favourable fair and equitable treatment provision is incorporated into the A-B BIT in 1995, as soon as the B-C BIT comes into force.

Importantly, however, some investors from State A will not even have invested in State B as of 1995. In addition, few of those who have invested prior to 1995 will have a claim against State B as of that date. As a result, no facts about investors from State A, their investments, or the bases of their claims can be relevant to determining whether the treatment provided to investors from State C is indeed more favourable than that provided to investors from State A. The information is simply not there to be considered.

Only an evaluation of favourability with respect to investors from State A as a class can possibly support a conclusion that the broader fair and equitable treatment provision included in the B-C BIT was also applicable to investors from State A as of 1995. This is precisely the conclusion mandated by the instantaneous effect of MFN clauses.

The consequence of this is that the proper evaluation to be undertaken by a tribunal addressing an MFN-based claim is not whether the treatment claimed by the investor would be more favourable to the specific investor bringing the claim. It must, rather, be whether the treatment in question would be more favourable to investors from the claimant's Home State as a class.

As section 5 argues, however, moving the focus of a favourability evaluation from the claimant to the class of investors from which the claimant comes can cause an enormous change in the impact an MFN clause has on an investor. Indeed, it can have the consequence that an MFN clause will actually harm a claimant, rather than benefit it.[36]

5 The 'exclusionary effect' of a most-favoured nation clause

That MFN clauses only serve to provide 'more favourable' treatment to investors might be taken to imply that there is no circumstance in which a respondent State in an arbitration would be able to invoke an MFN clause as a defence against an investor's claims. After all, if the application of an MFN clause to a particular type of third-State treatment would harm an investor, that treatment would hardly be 'more favourable' for it. However, as section 4 argued, this view is fundamentally flawed, as it bases the evaluation of the favourability of third-State treatment on the individual claimant in an arbitration, rather than on the class from which the claimant comes. Section 5 will demonstrate that MFN clauses can in fact harm an investor and hence can indeed be used by respondent States as a defence against an investor's claims.

Presume that in 1990 State A and State B signed a BIT that includes an MFN clause, as well as a consent to investor-State arbitration restricted to claims for expropriation. Subsequently, in 1995, State B signed a BIT with State C that includes a consent to investor-State arbitration for a wide variety of claims, but not including expropriation. Presuming that this latter consent is indeed more favourable than the narrower consent in the A-B BIT, the instantaneous effect of MFN clauses means that as of 1995 State B is obligated to consent to arbitration with investors from State A in accordance with the terms of the consent to arbitration included in the B-C BIT.

It is important to note that the MFN clause in the A-B BIT only constitutes a promise that investors from third-States will not be treated better than investors from State A. As discussed in the historical survey in Chapter 5, MFN clauses are a means of providing equality with competitors, not superiority.[37] The MFN clause in the A-B BIT only obligates State B to provide investors from State A with treatment equal to that received by investors from State C. It does not obligate State B to provide them with better treatment.

Investors from State C, however, cannot bring expropriation claims to investor-State arbitration, as such claims are not covered by the consent to arbitration in the B-C BIT. Consequently, were investors from State A able to retain their right to bring expropriation claims, while also gaining the right to bring claims under the terms of the B-C BIT, they would actually be receiving better treatment than investors from State C.

It must be, therefore, that as soon as State B is obligated to consent to arbitration with investors from State A in accordance with the consent to arbitration in the B-C treaty, those investors simultaneously lose the right to bring claims under the consent to arbitration in the A-B treaty. That is, MFN clauses obligate a State to provide any more favourable treatment given to third parties, but in so doing exclude the treatment originally promised in the treaty in which they are contained. This element of the operation of MFN clauses is what is here called the exclusionary effect of an MFN clause.

This may initially appear to be a minor point, given that the MFN clause will only incorporate treatment given to third parties where that treatment is more favourable to the beneficiary of the clause. However, as made clear in section 4, the proper standard for determining whether an MFN clause incorporates treatment into the BIT in which it is contained is not whether the treatment in question would be more favourable to the investor bringing the arbitration, but whether it would be more favourable to the class referred to in the MFN clause, such as investors from State A.

To return to the example, it would presumably be more favourable to investors from State A as a class to have access to a broad dispute resolution provision, even one that does not include expropriation. There is, after all, no way of knowing in advance the specific grounds on which investors may need to bring a claim. Consequently, the broader consent to investor-State arbitration in the B-C BIT now represents State B's obligation to arbitrate with investors from State A, replacing the narrower consent originally included in the A-B BIT.

This will have the effect, however, of preventing any investor from State A from bringing to arbitration a claim of expropriation. The effect of the MFN clause in the A-B BIT will, therefore, by no means be 'more favourable' to investors whose only claim is one of expropriation, as they will lose their ability to bring any claim at all.

The exclusionary effect of an MFN clause, then, once understood in the context of the class-based nature of MFN beneficiaries under BITs, can actually serve to make MFN clauses harmful to specific investors. In turn, it can give respondent States a reason to invoke MFN clauses as a defence to an investor's claim, in opposition to the traditional view that they are merely a mechanism to be used by investors.

6 Conclusion

MFN clauses have gained their current importance in international investment law primarily because of the interaction between such clauses and investor-State arbitration. Nonetheless, investment arbitration tribunals have done little to explicate the operation of MFN clauses in the international investment context, focusing instead on the perceived teleological nature of such clauses. However, this teleological non-discrimination approach to the interpretation of MFN clauses is both inconsistent with the historical development of MFN clauses and fails to recognise certain limitations on MFN clauses that follow necessarily from their incorporation into international investment agreements.

A full understanding of MFN clauses makes clear that they are enormously powerful instruments that can impede significantly a State's otherwise legitimate regulatory activities. Nonetheless, despite the power of MFN clauses, they are almost routinely incorporated into contemporary BITs, as though they constitute little more than a political statement of friendship with no legal consequences. It is, however, to be hoped that once the operation of MFN clauses in international investment agreements is more clearly understood, they will be used more circumspectly.

7 Dispute resolution procedures and the favourability of treatment under a most-favoured nation clause[1]

1 Introduction

The preceding two chapters have attempted to develop an understanding of the operation of MFN clauses that takes proper account of the distinctive features of contemporary international investment law. They did not, however, address two of the most important issues in the interpretation of MFN clauses in that context, namely what does and does not constitute 'treatment' of an investor, and what makes one form of such treatment 'more favourable' than another. Yet MFN clauses are fundamentally comparative, and as a result it is impossible for them to be interpreted and applied correctly without a clear understanding of what must be compared and the basis on which that comparison must be made. The goal of this chapter is to demonstrate that a proper understanding of both of these issues can be gained through a re-examination of the jurisdictional decision in the most famous case on the operation of MFN clauses in international investment law, *Maffezini v Spain*.[2]

The 2000 jurisdictional decision in *Maffezini v Spain*, in which an arbitral tribunal held that an MFN clause in a BIT could allow an investor to access dispute resolution procedures different than those in the BIT under which it was bringing its claim, has long been recognised as a foundational decision in the interpretation of MFN clauses. Prior to *Maffezini*, MFN clauses had been a largely uncontroversial importation into international investment law from the world of trade law, where they had long been used as a means of equalising tariffs charged to imported goods.[3]

After *Maffezini*, however, MFN clauses also became useful for eliminating one of the major obstacles faced by an investor attempting to bring a claim against a Host State government, namely that often the investor does not choose the forum in which it must pursue its claim, or the conditions placed on its access to that forum. Instead, the consent of the Host State to arbitrate directly with an investor is often included in a BIT, which the investor had no role in negotiating. The investor must, therefore, simply accept or reject the form of arbitration it is being offered. By holding that an MFN clause can be applied to dispute resolution procedures, rather than just to the substantive promises in a BIT, however, the *Maffezini* tribunal gave to investors a limited power to change the terms of the arbitration they were being offered, at least to the extent that 'more favourable' terms were being offered by the Host State to investors from any third-State.

Unsurprisingly, since the decision in *Maffezini*, a series of investors has attempted to take advantage of this newfound power, although with mixed results. Some tribunals have mirrored the *Maffezini* decision and allowed investors to avoid procedural obstacles that had been placed in the way of an investor's access to arbitration,[4] while others have refused to follow *Maffezini*, mapping out instead an alternative approach to the issue.[5]

Problematically, however, rather than attempting to examine and explain the proper application of MFN clauses to dispute resolution procedures, tribunals have instead repeatedly relied on broader claims regarding treaty interpretation. As a result, that is, although tribunals have regularly alluded to questions such as whether dispute resolution procedures constitute 'treatment' under an MFN clause and what makes one dispute resolution procedure more favourable than another, no tribunal has yet seriously examined them. Instead, decisions can ultimately be divided into two very broad streams. Stream One, consisting of those decisions that have adhered to the *Maffezini* line of reasoning, reflects a strongly textualist approach to treaty interpretation, backed up by a presumption that international arbitration is inherently 'more favourable' than domestic courts for the resolution of international investment disputes. By contrast, Stream Two emphasises the importance of understanding the intentions of the Contracting States when interpreting treaty language, backed up by an assertion that an intent-focused approach to interpretation is particularly important where what is being interpreted is the limits of a State's consent to arbitration.

This chapter will not focus, however, on an analysis of the caselaw on the application of MFN clauses to dispute resolution procedures, as a means of establishing that one or the other of these streams is correct. Instead it will attempt to demonstrate that a close analysis of the functioning of MFN clauses in the dispute resolution context can provide insights that are acceptable to both streams, but that have nonetheless thus far been ignored. Specifically, it will argue that important insights into the applicability of MFN clauses to dispute resolution procedures can be gained through an analysis of the nature of 'treatment' under an MFN clause, and of what makes one dispute resolution procedure more favourable.

Althouth this chapter is intended to offer an original analysis of the application of MFN clauses to dispute resolution procedures, Section Two will attempt to establish the consistency of this analysis with existing arbitral caselaw by demonstrating that the foundations of the analysis offered here can also be discerned in the jurisdictional decision in *Maffezini*.

Importantly, however, it will not be argued that the jurisdictional decision in *Maffezini* was itself correct, but rather that one important element of that decision reflects an important insight into the functioning of MFN clauses in the dispute resolution context. Unfortunately this insight has largely been overlooked by tribunals since *Maffezini*, and indeed was insufficiently analysed by the *Maffezini* tribunal itself. Nonetheless, it is through the incorporation of this insight into the *Maffezini* decision that the original analysis offered in this chapter can be solidly connected to the ongoing debate between tribunals on the proper application of MFN clauses to dispute resolution procedures.

Section 3 will then present the original argument that is the centre of this chapter, focusing on the question of the relationship of dispute resolution procedures to the 'treatment' being received by an investor, as that term has meaning in the MFN context. It will be argued that tribunals have mistakenly focused on whether dispute resolution procedures should themselves be classified as 'treatment' under an MFN clause, when the preferable approach is to examine the manner in which dispute resolution procedures affect the substantive 'treatment' received by investors. That is, neither the tribunals in Stream One nor those in Stream Two dispute that the substantive promises in a treaty constitute 'treatment' of investors under an MFN clause. Consequently, if the 'favourability' of a substantive treaty promise is affected by the dispute resolution procedure adopted to enforce it, then the impact of an MFN clause on dispute resolution procedures can be evaluated without even addressing the contentious question of the application of MFN clauses to dispute resolution procedures themselves.

Specifically, it will be argued in Section 3 that MFN clauses in BITs must be understood as a means of ensuring that investors from third-States are not placed in a superior competitive position in the market of the Host State through actions taken by the Host State. Consequently, evaluations of the 'favourability' of substantive promises in a treaty must focus on how the existence of those promises affects the competitive position of investors from the Home State in the market of the Host State. It will then be argued, however, that this means that the 'favourability' of any 'treatment' by the Host State delivered to investors cannot be evaluated by consideration of the nature of the substantive treatment alone, but must instead also consider the reasonable subjective perceptions of the affected investors of the likely efficacy of the dispute resolution procedures through which that substantive treatment is to be enforced.

This argument having been made, Section 4 will then analyse the practical impact of this understanding of MFN clauses on two issues of contemporary controversy. First it will be argued that this understanding of MFN clauses clarifies that a State need never have agreed to use a certain dispute resolution procedure in order for that procedure to be made available to an investor through the operation of an MFN clause. Rather, all that is required is that access to this procedure be an appropriate means of equalising the 'treatment' received by investors in the market of the Host State. Second it will be argued that the interpretation of MFN clauses offered in this chapter has the consequence that an MFN clause can expand the definition of 'investor' or 'investment' included in a BIT, and thereby grant access to the dispute resolution procedures included in that BIT to individuals not covered by the original terms of the BIT itself.

Finally, Section 5 will offer a short critique of the consent-based approach to the application of MFN clauses to dispute resolution procedures, the primary alternative to the approach pioneered by the *Maffezini* tribunal. In addition, it will offer an important qualification to the ability of investors to use an MFN clause to access dispute resolution procedures other than those included in the Basic Treaty.

2 *Maffezini v Spain*: the ability of dispute resolution procedures to affect the 'treatment' received by investors

While the applicability of MFN clauses to dispute resolution procedures only came to real prominence with the 2000 jurisdictional decision in *Maffezini*, it was not the first time that the issue had been faced by an international tribunal. Indeed, as discussed in Chapter 5, it had already been raised three times in prominent twentieth century State-State disputes, before both the ICJ and an independent arbitral body.[6] In each case, however, the tribunal ultimately decided the dispute on other grounds, thereby leaving the question unresolved.[7] It was in this situation of uncertainty that in 1997 a case was filed at ICSID by an Argentine citizen who had invested in Spain.

Emilio Maffezini, an Argentine national, had been the holder of a 70 per cent share in a Spanish company, Emilio A Maffezini SA ('EAMSA'), that had been founded to produce and distribute chemicals within Spain. The remaining 30 per cent of the shares had been held by a Spanish government-controlled company, Sociedad para el Desarrollo Industrial de Galicia Sociedad Anónima SA ('SODIGA').[8] EAMSA ultimately failed before commencing production and, after unsuccessful negotiations, Maffezini initiated arbitration at ICSID, arguing that alleged mistreatment he had suffered at the hands of SODIGA could be legally attributed to the Spanish government.[9]

The primary obstacle faced by Maffezini was that under the terms of the Argentina-Spain BIT, upon which he was relying for Spain's consent to ICSID arbitration, investors could only commence ICSID arbitration in two situations: (a) where the Host State directly consented to the proceedings; or (b) where the investor had initially filed suit in the domestic courts of the Host State, and a period of 18 months had passed with no order being issued on the merits.[10] However, Spain had not consented to arbitrate at ICSID with Maffezini, and Maffezini had not spent 18 months pursuing his claim in local courts.[11] Consequently, under the jurisdictional provisions of the Argentina-Spain BIT, an ICSID tribunal could not hear Maffezini's claim.

Maffezini, however, cited the inclusion within the Argentina-Spain BIT of an MFN clause, as well as the existence of a BIT between Chile and Spain that granted investors immediate access to ICSID arbitration, without any requirement first to spend time in the domestic courts of the Host State.[12] According to Maffezini, the ability of Chilean investors to access ICSID arbitration immediately constituted more favourable treatment than that available under the Argentina-Spain BIT. Consequently, he argued, the MFN clause in the Argentina-Spain BIT entitled him to avoid the requirement first to spend time in Spanish courts.[13]

The tribunal accepted Maffezini's argument and allowed his claim to proceed. For the purposes of this chapter, however, the most notable aspect of this decision is not that the tribunal accepted that MFN clauses can apply to dispute resolution procedures, even though this was the first time any international tribunal had reached this conclusion.[14] More important is the rationale the tribunal advanced to explain its decision.

The MFN clause in the Argentina-Spain BIT made no explicit reference to dispute resolution procedures, merely providing a generalised promise that no more favourable treatment would be provided to investors from any third-State '[i]n all matters subject to this Agreement'.[15] While on its face this clause might seem to cover dispute resolution procedures, as one of the 'matters subject to this Agreement', Spain had argued 'since it is the purpose of the most favoured nation clause to avoid discrimination, such discrimination can only take place in connection with material economic treatment and not with regard to procedural matters'.[16] This interpretation was, however, rejected by the tribunal, which emphasised that the dispute resolution procedures in a treaty are 'essential ... to the protection of the rights envisaged under the pertinent treaties; they are also closely linked to the material aspects of the treatment accorded'.[17]

While much commentary has been made on the *Maffezini* decision, little attention has been given to the fact that despite holding that the MFN clause in the Spain-Argentina BIT altered the dispute resolution procedures available to Maffezini, the *Maffezini* tribunal does not directly dispute Spain's claim that an MFN clause is only applicable to the substantive promises in the BIT. Rather, the tribunal holds that the dispute resolution procedures are so intimately tied to the substantive promises included in the treaty that those procedures can be altered by the MFN clause even if they are not substantive themselves.[18]

Unfortunately, the *Maffezini* tribunal does not expand on this reasoning, and so does not explain why it should follow from the simple fact that dispute resolution procedures are 'essential' to the protection of the substantive rights included in a treaty, that they are therefore also covered by an MFN clause that arguably only covers substantive treaty promises. Instead, the tribunal simply invokes what it argues to be the inherent 'favourability' of investment arbitration to foreign investors, and holds that because of this inherent favourability the MFN clause in the BIT gives Maffezini the right to avoid the requirement to spend 18 months in Spanish courts.[19] Nonetheless, by invoking the distinction between the status of dispute resolution procedures as 'treatment' of investors, and the 'essential' role of those procedures in delivering the 'treatment' received by investors, the *Maffezini* tribunal implicitly recognises that dispute resolution procedures can affect the 'treatment' received by investors even if they do not constitute a form of 'treatment' themselves.

Subsequent decisions by other tribunals that have found MFN clauses to apply to dispute resolution procedures have gone no further in providing the missing reasoning in the *Maffezini* decision, routinely invoking precisely the same emphasis on the centrality of dispute resolution procedures to the protection of substantive rights.[20] Moreover, almost all such tribunals have failed to reiterate *Maffezini*'s important distinction between whether dispute resolution procedures constitute part of the 'treatment' of investors by the Host State, or merely affect that treatment.[21]

Section 3, however, will examine closely this argument made by the *Maffezini* tribunal, and will offer an interpretation of the ability of generalised MFN clauses to alter dispute resolution procedures that does not require a conclusion that such procedures constitute a separable form of 'treatment' of investors. Instead, it will argue that the issue is best analysed by concentrating on the impact of dispute resolution procedures on the 'favourability' of substantive treaty promises, the latter being something that no one disputes constitute a form of 'treatment' under an MFN clause.

3 Dispute resolution procedures and the 'favourability' of 'treatment' under a most-favoured nation clause

The *Maffezini* decision has been subjected to a great deal of criticism, addressing both its unsupported presumption that international arbitration is somehow inherently more favourable to investors than domestic litigation, and its attempt to limit its own effects by manufacturing out of whole cloth a series of 'policy'-based exceptions to the application of MFN clauses to dispute resolution procedures.[22] It will be argued here, however, that whatever other faults the *Maffezini* decision might have, it correctly focuses on an important issue for the application of MFN clauses to dispute resolution procedures, namely the intimate connection between the substantive promises in a treaty and the dispute resolution procedures through which those promises can be enforced.

Unfortunately, the *Maffezini* decision itself provided no serious examination of why this connection should be seen to result in a conclusion that a generalised MFN clause is applicable to dispute resolution procedures. As already noted, some tribunals subsequent to *Maffezini* have attempted to rationalise this holding by arguing that dispute resolution procedures therefore constitute an element of the 'treatment' to which investors are subject. Whether dispute resolution procedures constitute 'treatment' under an MFN clause is, however, a view that has been seriously challenged.

While this section does not include an argument supporting the conclusion that dispute resolution procedures constitute an element of the 'treatment' to which investors are subject, its central purpose is instead to advance a different argument that nonetheless builds upon the position of the *Maffezini* tribunal. That is, it will argue that a close examination of the meaning of 'treatment' in the context of MFN clauses supports a conclusion that generalised MFN clauses do indeed alter the dispute resolution procedures available to foreign investors. However, this is not because such procedures constitute an element of the 'treatment' to which investors are subject, which might or might not be true. Rather, it is because such procedures alter the 'favourability' of substantive treaty promises, which no one disputes constitute 'treatment' of investors.

3.1 Dispute resolution procedures as 'treatment' of investors

Perhaps the most consistent feature of the ongoing discussion of the applicability of MFN clauses to dispute resolution procedures is the uniform presumption, by both tribunals and commentators, that the substantive promises in a treaty constitute a form of 'treatment' of investors. That is, both commentators and tribunals appear to work from a presumption that an MFN clause must apply to something, and its position in a treaty indicates that the main things to which it must apply are the promises that a treaty contains.

It is important to note, however, that there is no necessary reason why this presumption should be correct. While it is certainly implausible that an MFN clause in a treaty has no relationship to the substantive promises the treaty contains, a conclusion means that the MFN clause is directly applicable to substantive treaty promises elides the important distinction between the promises contained in a treaty, and any actions taken by a State to fulfil those promises. That is, it is by no means implausible that the 'treatment' to which MFN clauses apply includes not the substantive promises in a treaty themselves, but only those actions the State takes to fulfil those promises.

On this understanding of MFN clauses, the mere existence of an allegedly 'more favourable' promise in a third-State treaty would give investors from the Home State no right to claim such a promise for themselves. Instead, only when the Host State took action to fulfil that promise could more favourable treatment be found. Moreover, even then only the specific actions taken by the Host State could be claimed, even if the State thereby only partially fulfilled its treaty promise to the third-State investors.

Such an understanding of the operation of MFN clauses would be incorrect, but no attempt has thus far been made in case law or commentary to explain why this is so. An analysis of why treaty promises should be found to constitute 'treatment' under an MFN clause, however, rather than only subsequent fulfilment actions by the Host State, provides important insights into the operation of MFN clauses and helps explain why generalised MFN clauses should be understood as altering the dispute resolution procedures available to foreign investors.

As is standard in interpreting treaty language, the first step in ascertaining the meaning of 'treatment' in the MFN context is to consider the 'ordinary meaning' of the term.[23] Such an examination of the meaning of 'treatment', however, reveals the important fact that 'treatment' of an individual is not merely behaviour that affects the individual, but rather is behaviour 'towards' that individual.[24]

There is little question that the actions taken by a State to fulfil its investment treaty obligations will meet this requirement. After all, the obligations in question are for the State to act in certain ways towards investors, so the fulfilment of these obligations cannot but involve the State taking actions specifically directed at investors.

The situation is less clear, however, with respect to treaty promises themselves. It will not, after all, suffice to demonstrate that treaty promises have an impact upon investors for them to constitute 'treatment' of investors, as any action can have an impact upon entities other than those at which it is directed. It must, rather, be demonstrated that even though the promises included in a BITs are formally made only to the investors' Home State, they nonetheless are in some significant manner directed at the Home State's investors themselves.[25]

This requirement is clearly met, however, as the fundamental purpose of an investment treaty is to motivate private entities to undertake investments. They take the form of a traditional agreement between States, but unlike most treaties their primary focus is on motivating private behaviour through promising State action, rather than on a mutual exchange of promises to benefit each State. Consequently, although a promise in a BIT is formally made to the investors' Home State, and hence is directed at the Home State, it is nonetheless also clearly directed at investors themselves, as it is their actions that the Host State wishes to influence.

The manner in which promises in investment treaties constitute 'treatment' of investors is, however, important to note. Such promises constitute 'treatment' of the Home State of the investor simply because they are a promise made to the Home State, and hence clearly an action taken 'towards' it. The same argument cannot, however, be made with respect to investors themselves, as in entering into the treaty the Host State makes no promises at all directly to the investors. Rather, promises in an investment treaty are only directed at investors, and hence only constitute 'treatment' of investors, because they constitute an attempt on the part of the Host State to induce foreign investors to alter their investment-related behaviour.[26]

It is this recognition of the connection between the 'treatment' status of treaty promises and the role of such promises in altering the investment-related behaviour of investors that provides an argument that dispute resolution procedures constitute a form of 'treatment' of investors. Dispute resolution procedures are, after all, included in treaties for the same reason as other treaty promises, namely to affect the investment-related behaviour of investors. More specifically, they provide assurance to foreign investors that either the substantive promises in the treaty will be fulfilled, or investors damaged because those promises are not fulfilled will receive compensation. This parallel between the promise in a BIT of a certain type of substantive treatment and the promise in a BIT of a specific form of dispute resolution provides a prima facie reason for finding dispute resolution procedures to constitute a form of 'treatment' of investors. Both are merely attempts to influence the investment-related behaviour of foreign investors.

However, while this argument supports concluding that dispute resolution procedures constitute a form of 'treatment' of investors, in one sense of the word, it does not conclusively show that such procedures constitute 'treatment' under an MFN clause. After all, the term 'treatment' as used in the MFN context could certainly have a specialised meaning, and only include substantive treaty promises. Consequently, this argument cannot by itself overcome arguments of opponents of the application of MFN clauses to dispute resolution procedures, who insist that the 'treatment' referred to in MFN clauses should be understood as including only substantive treaty promises, not dispute resolution procedures.

Subsection 3.2, then, will accept the presumption of opponents of the application of MFN clauses to dispute resolution procedures that the term 'treatment' as used in an MFN clause refers only to substantive treaty promises. It will demonstrate, however, that this presumption has no effect on the ability of MFN clauses to alter the dispute resolution procedures available to investors, due to the impact of dispute resolution procedures on the 'favourability' of the 'treatment' delivered by substantive treaty promises.

3.2 Dispute resolution procedures and the 'favourability' of substantive treaty promises

Perhaps the most important limitation on the operation of an MFN clause in an investment treaty is that it does not give an investor the power just to decide whether it would prefer to be covered by the promise in the BIT applicable to it, or if it would prefer to be covered by a promise from a third-State BIT. Rather, the treaty promise applicable to the investor will be whichever is more 'favourable' to it.

The meaning of the 'favourability' of a treaty promise in the MFN context has, however, been little examined. As this subsection will show, however, considerations of the 'favourability' of substantive treaty promises can themselves demonstrate that dispute resolution procedures can be altered by an MFN clause, even if it is conceded that dispute resolution procedures do not themselves constitute an element of the 'treatment' received by investors.

The first point to note is that the inclusion of the 'favourability' standard means that the functioning of an MFN clause cannot simply be a matter of the individual desires of investors. If that were the case, the provision would merely allow investors to claim any treaty promise in a third-State treaty, rather than requiring that the provision be in some way 'more favourable'.

The means of identifying the applicable standard for comparing the favourability of 'treatment' of investors, then, comes from referring back to the nature of the 'treatment' covered by an MFN clause. As discussed above, what makes substantive treaty promises a form of 'treatment' of investors is that they are actions taken by the Host State, directed at investors, with the purpose of influencing the investor's investment-related behaviour. What makes a treaty promise more or less favourable *as 'treatment'*, then, must relate to the impact that promise has upon the investor's investment-related behaviour. Any other impact the promise has is simply external to the status of the promise as 'treatment' of investors from the Home State, and so is irrelevant to the MFN clause.

The investment-related behaviour of an investor, however, is directed solely at the success of the investment.[27] The 'success' of an investment can potentially be measured in many ways, but the combination of the goal of a BIT being to encourage desired forms of foreign investment, and the emphasis in an MFN clause on the comparison between the 'treatment' received by Home State investors and those from any third-State, make clear that in the MFN context the relevant standard is a comparative market-based one. That is, what makes a substantive treaty promise more or less favourable in the MFN context is the degree to which it would facilitate or impede the beneficiary investors in a competitive marketplace.[28] If the existence of the promise allows the Home State investors to undertake actions that improve their competitive position in the Host State's market, then that promise is 'more favourable' for those investors. If it does not, then it is not.

Understanding the meaning of 'more favourable' in this way, however, emphasises an important point, namely that the Home State investors subjective perceptions of the BIT promise become central. That is, the emphasis in the 'favourability' evaluation on the actions investors will take as a result of the promise being made mean that there are two aspects to the 'favourability' of a BIT promise in the MFN context: (a) the substantive content of the promise the Host State has made; and (b) the perceived likelihood that the promise will be fulfilled.

It is clearly true that the substance of a BIT promise has the ability to impact upon the competitive position of investors, and so this element is uncontroversial. After all, even if investors do not believe that a promise will be fulfilled, and so do not immediately alter their investment-related behaviour in response to the promise, so long as the promise is indeed actually fulfilled, investors will receive benefits from it. The fulfilment of the BIT promise will, therefore, place the Home State's investors in a more competitive position than they would have been in without the BIT, even if they did not themselves undertake any actions to benefit from it.

The second element of the favourability of a BIT promise in the MFN context, however, is arguably more controversial. The importance of emphasising the reasonable substantive perceptions of investors,[29] rather than concentrating solely on the objective benefits provided by the promise itself, arises from the fact that investors only value the promises included in BITs because of an expectation that they will indeed be fulfilled. For example, a promise by a State that routinely expropriates the investments of foreign investors that it will not do so in the future will receive little attention from investors, absent some independent indication of its reliability. Even if the promise is made in good faith, then, and the State will indeed avoid future expropriations, investors will keep operating their investments in a cautious way that provides them the maximum protection should an expropriation happen. They will, therefore, lose much of the benefit of the promise, until enough time has passed that the reliability of the promise increases to an acceptable level.[30] While the BIT promise, therefore, is itself a form of 'treatment' of investors, independent of the perceptions of investors, its 'favourability' is to an important extent determined by the reasonable subjective perceptions of investors of its likely fulfilment.

With respect to the likelihood of fulfilment of a promise, however, little has as clear an impact upon the perceptions of investors as the inclusion within a BIT of effective dispute resolution procedures. Whether these procedures are viewed from the perspective of the ability of investors to receive compensation for breaches of BIT promises, or because the possibility of having to pay compensation will make States less likely to breach the BIT in the first place, the effectiveness of the dispute resolution procedures in a BIT has a clear impact upon the expectation of investors that a promise in a BIT will be fulfilled.

This point, of course, is similar to the emphasis in the *Maffezini* decision and its followers on the 'essential' role of dispute resolution procedures in ensuring the 'protection of the rights envisaged' in an investment treaty.[31] However, it importantly does not rely on a conclusion that dispute resolution procedures are, on their own, a form of 'treatment' received by investors. Rather, the 'treatment' received by investors remains the substantive promise contained in the BIT, and the dispute resolution procedures to which that promise is subject have their impact in making that substantive promise more 'favourable', as appearing to investors as more likely to be fulfilled.[32]

3.3 An important qualification

It must be reiterated, however, that what is being determined by a tribunal when making a 'favourability' evaluation is not whether the dispute resolution procedures in the third-State treaty are more favourable than those in the Basic Treaty. Rather, what is in question is whether a particular substantive promise in the Basic Treaty, backed up by the dispute resolution procedures in that treaty, is more favourable than that same promise in the third-State treaty, backed up by the dispute resolution procedures in that treaty.

This emphasis on evaluating the favourability of the substantive promise, rather than the dispute resolution procedures themselves, has two important consequences. First, unless the third-State treaty includes some version of the specific promise being invoked in the Basic Treaty, its dispute resolution procedures cannot be accessed via the MFN clause in the dispute resolution procedures. After all, the existence of that promise is certainly more favourable than its absence, no matter how effective the third-State treaty dispute resolution procedures may be.

Second, since what is being evaluated is not the dispute resolution procedures of the third-State treaty, but those procedures *as applied to that specific substantive promise*, the dispute resolution procedures of the third-State treaty are only applicable to the specific substantive promises in the Basic Treaty for which there is a comparable provision in the third-State treaty. Any substantive promises in the Basic Treaty that do not have corresponding but more favourable promises in the third-State treaty remain covered by the less effective dispute resolution procedures listed in the Basic Treaty.

4 Applications

The discussion above argues that dispute resolution procedures can be understood as subject to MFN claims only through the impact of the dispute resolution procedures in a BIT on the 'favourability' of the substantive promises the BIT contains. This section will be devoted to identifying two particularly important consequences of this understanding of the operation of MFN clauses. First, it will be argued in subsection 4.1 that the understanding of 'treatment' laid out in section 3 entails that an MFN clause will not only provide investors with access to the specific dispute resolution procedures to which the Host State has consented in third-State treaties, but can also provide access to procedures to which the Host State has never consented. Second, it will be argued in subsection 4.2 that the understanding of 'favourability' advanced above entails that an MFN clause can expand the definition of 'investor' or 'investment' included in a BIT, and thereby allow investors to access the dispute resolution procedures included in third-State treaties even though they do not themselves meet the Basic Treaty's jurisdictional requirements. Finally, an important qualifier will be acknowledged regarding the practical ability of Home State investors to use an MFN clause to alter the dispute resolution procedures offered in a BIT.

4.1 The availability to an investor, through a most-favoured nation clause, of a dispute resolution forum to which a Host State has never consented

One of the most controversial issues in the ongoing discussions regarding the applicability of MFN clauses to dispute resolution provisions is whether an MFN clause can provide an investor with access to a forum not mentioned at all in the Basic Treaty, or if instead it can only serve to remove restrictions on an investor's access to a forum already mentioned in the Basic Treaty. While this factor has not played a decisive role in any decision yet handed down, it has been cited by more than one tribunal as an important consideration, and has also been used by some commentators as a means of explaining the clear split in jurisprudence regarding the applicability of MFN clauses to dispute resolution procedures.[33] This subsection will demonstrate that once one accepts that dispute resolution procedures can impact on the 'favourability' of the substantive promises made in the Basic Treaty, the existence of explicit Host State consent to a particular forum is not essential for an investor to be able to access that forum via an MFN clause.

While jurisprudence regarding MFN clauses up to the present time has focused upon the use of MFN clauses to gain access to allegedly more favourable provisions in a third-party treaty, it is important to remember that this is not the only manner in which MFN clauses operate. Rather, as the name indicates, MFN clauses give access to more favourable *treatment*, with access only being given to more favourable treaty provisions in so far as they constitute a form of treatment.

It is often recognised that this means that forms of treatment other than treaty clauses can serve to ground an MFN claim. However, a further consequence is given significantly less attention, namely that the goal of an MFN clause is to equalise the *treatment* received by the Home State's investors and those from the third-State, not to give the beneficiary State's investors access to the specific promises included in the third-State treaty.[34]

As argued above, however, 'treatment' of investors in the MFN context must be understood in terms of action taken by the Host State with the goal of altering the investment-related behaviour of investors. Importantly, though, to the extent that investors from the Home State and the third-State differ, granting precisely the same privilege to those two different groups of investors might not result in them receiving equal 'treatment'. That is, contextual factors not directly connected to the promise made by the Host State might result in the two groups of investors altering their investment-related behaviour in different ways, because those contextual factors mean that the promise will impact upon them differently.[35]

For example, consider a situation in which the Basic Treaty includes a very broad protection from expropriation, backed up by dispute resolution in the domestic courts of the Host State, while the third-State treaty includes a very limited protection from expropriation, again backed up by dispute resolution in the domestic courts of the Host State. An initial analysis of this situation would lead to the conclusion that investors from the third-State are not receiving more favourable treatment than investors from the Home State. After all, investors from the Home State are benefiting from a better substantive promise than those from the third-State, and both groups of investors have access to precisely the same dispute resolution procedure.

Focusing on the impact of these treaty promises on the investment-related behaviour of investors, however, clarifies that in some circumstances this analysis may not be correct. It may, for example, be that investors from the Home State justifiably believe that for social or political reasons they are likely to be subjected to discrimination in the courts of the Host State. By contrast, investors from the third-State have no reason for such concerns. In such a situation it is clear that investors from the Home State will be far less willing than investors from the third-State to alter their investment-related behaviour in order to benefit from the substantive treaty promise included in the applicable BIT, as they are far less certain that in their case it will actually be enforced.

In terms of the 'favourability' of that substantive treaty promise, then, as measured by the impact of the promise on the investment-related behaviour of investors, investors from the third-State are indeed receiving more favourable 'treatment' than those from the Home State, despite benefiting from a more limited substantive promise and precisely the same dispute resolution procedures.

This means, though, that merely giving Host State investors access to the relevant provisions of the third-State treaty will not equalise the 'treatment' received by the two groups of investors. After all, as already noted, the substantive promise made to third-State investors is actually less generous than that made to Home State investors, and the dispute resolution procedures in the two treaties are exactly the same. Nonetheless, the Host State has, through the MFN clause in the Basic Treaty, promised to equalise the 'treatment' it gives to the two groups of investors. This problem is resolved by acknowledging that equalising the 'treatment' received by the two groups of investors requires not just giving both groups access to the same dispute resolution procedures, but giving them both access to dispute resolution procedures of equivalent degrees of fairness and effectiveness.

Investors, after all, have little reason to care about the particular forum in which their claim is addressed beyond concerns of fairness and effectiveness. Consequently, while it is argued above that the 'favourability' of the 'treatment' received by Home State investors is influenced by the applicable dispute resolution procedure, a more nuanced analysis would clarify that it is the fairness and effectiveness of the dispute resolution procedure that influences the 'favourability' of the substantive promise, not the identity of the specific forum invoked.

This means, however, that an MFN clause in a Basic Treaty does not merely obligate a Host State to resolve any disputes with Home State investors in accordance with any 'more favourable' procedures to which the Host State has consented in any third-State treaty. Rather, the obligation imposed by the MFN clause is to resolve such disputes in a forum as fair and effective as any consented to in a third-State treaty. Moreover, this obligation exists even when the only available forum that meets this requirement is one to which the Host State has never consented in any third-State treaty. The Host State's obligation under the MFN clause, after all, is to provide equivalent 'treatment' to the Home State investor to that given to third-State investors, not merely to allow them access to the same procedures.

4.2 The impact of a most-favoured nation clause on the definition of 'investor' or 'investment' included in the Basic Treaty

Understanding 'favourability' as described in this chapter also provides helpful insight into a further contentious issue on the application of MFN clauses, namely whether an MFN clause can serve to alter the meaning of jurisdictional terms in the Basic Treaty. This issue came to the fore in *Societe Generale v Dominican Republic*[36], in which the claimant, whose claim did not fall under the definition of 'investment' in the Basic Treaty, attempted to invoke the treaty's MFN clause in order to access a broader definition of 'investment' included in other BITs signed by the Host State. The tribunal held that this could not be done because the MFN clause in a treaty 'applies only to the treatment afforded to such defined investment, but not to the definition of 'investment' itself'.[37]

The basic conception adopted by the tribunal in this decision is that when a State promises to provide MFN treatment to any 'investment', as defined in the Basic Treaty, then such treatment is simply not owed to anything that does not fall under that definition. That is, the benefits provided by an MFN clause are only promised by the Host State to those entities covered by the jurisdictional terms of the Basic treaty. Consequently, as the claimant's investment is not covered by the jurisdictional terms of the Basic treaty, it cannot receive any benefits from the MFN clause. It is, therefore, simply irrelevant whether 'more favourable' jurisdictional terms are being offered by the Host State to investors from any third-State.

This is facially attractive reasoning, but the discussion above regarding the nature of a 'favourability' analysis makes clear that it is mistaken. That is, the tribunal's argument only considers the impact of an MFN clause on enterprises that do not constitute 'investments' under the Basic Treaty, and notes that since 'more favourable' treatment was never promised to such enterprises, it simply does not matter whether an expanded definition of 'investment' would be more favourable for them. The tribunal gives no consideration at all, however, to the potential impact of an expanded definition of 'investment' on enterprises that are already covered by the definition of 'investment' in the Basic Treaty. Since MFN treatment was indeed promised to such enterprises, if an expanded definition of 'investment' would be 'more favourable' for them than the definition included in the BIT, then the Host State is obliged by the MFN clause in the Basic Treaty to provide all the 'treatment' promised in that treaty to this expanded group of enterprises.

The tribunal, then, while correct that the promise involved in an MFN clause relates only to the 'treatment' owed to 'investments' as defined in the Basic Treaty, rather than to the definition of 'investment' itself, fails to acknowledge that there may be instances in which an alteration in the definition of 'investment' will in fact result in 'more favourable' treatment being received by entities covered under the original definition. In such a case, there is simply no principled reason to deny the expansion of the definition of 'investment', as it directly affects the 'treatment' received by 'investments' as the term is defined in the Basic Treaty.

It may not be immediately obvious how an enterprise already covered by a BIT can benefit from an expansion in the jurisdictional coverage of the BIT. After all, such an expansion merely extends to other enterprises' protections already being received by the enterprise in question. Facially, then, it would seem that in such a situation a benefit is being received by those entities newly receiving coverage, but no benefit at all is received by those covered by the original jurisdictional terms of the BIT.

The discussion in subsection 3.2 of the proper analysis of 'more favourable', however, provides an answer to this question. As argued there, any 'favourability' analysis must focus on the reasonable subjective perceptions of Home State investors as to the likelihood that the promised treatment will actually be delivered.

However, as witnessed by the large number of cases in which the existence of a BIT-covered 'investment' or 'investor' is challenged by the Host State, definitions of these terms in BITs are never easy to apply. They are, after all, terms adopted in a situation in which no knowledge is available of the precise enterprises that will need coverage. Consequently, the jurisdictional terms included in a BIT are framed in a deliberately vague manner, often in the form of a non-exhaustive list of examples, as a means of avoiding a situation in which an enterprise is denied coverage simply because it had not been thought of by the Contracting States during the drafting of the BIT.

Many enterprises, then, operate in this 'grey zone' of the definition of 'investment' or 'investor', in which it is at least questionable whether or not they qualify for coverage under the BIT. Consequently, for many foreign investors/investments, there would be very 'reasonable doubts' that the rights granted under the BIT would indeed be enforced by an atribution tribunal, due solely to the risk that the tribunal may find that the definition of 'investor'/'investment' did not apply. In such a case, enforcement of the promises included in the BIT will be completely denied. As a result, an expanded definition of 'investor'/'investment' that removed the significant risk that a tribunal would find the enterprise not to be covered by the BIT would in fact be 'more favourable' to that enterprise, even if most tribunals would indeed find it to be already covered by the jurisdictional terms of the BIT.

In any situation, then, in which investors have reasonable doubts whether a tribunal will find that either they or their investment is not covered by the Basic Treaty, that investor/investment will benefit from an expanded definition of 'investor/investment' that removes the risk of a finding of no jurisdiction. The primary effect of this expanded definition, of course, will be on those enterprises now covered by the jurisdictional terms of the Basic Treaty that were not covered previously. However, it is nonetheless also the case that the expanded definition of 'investor'/'investment' will have the effect of giving certainty of BIT-coverage to some enterprises arguably already covered by the original jurisdictional terms included in the Basic Treaty. As a result, such enterprises can operate in a manner reflecting their increased certainty of coverage by the dispute resolution procedures offered in the Basic Treaty, and thereby compete more effectively in the Host State's marketplace. Consequently, an MFN clause included within that treaty can legitimately be used to expand the definition of 'investor/investment' in the treaty, despite only being applicable to investors/investments already covered by the treaty.

5 Conclusion: an important limitation on the application of most-favoured nation clauses to dispute resolution procedures

This chapter has, so far, argued for what might appear to be a very expansive interpretation of the effects of an MFN clause. There is, however, an important qualification that must be acknowledged, that limits significantly the ability of investors to use MFN clauses to access dispute resolution procedures in third-State treaties.

While this chapter has focused primarily on the jurisdictional decision in *Maffezini v Spain*, and the subsequent decisions of those tribunals that have formed Stream One, the genesis of Stream Two can also be traced to a single leading case, namely *Plama v Bulgaria*.[38] According to the *Plama* tribunal, a State is only obligated to arbitrate with an investor if it has given 'clear and unambiguous' consent to do so. Moreover, this requirement cannot be satisfied by a generalised MFN clause that makes no reference to its applicability to dispute resolution procedures.[39]

This argument has recently been endorsed and applied by the tribunal in *ICS Inspection and Control Services Ltd v Argentine Republic*, and an analysis of the arguments offered by the *ICS* tribunal is helpful in illustrating some important points about the application of MFN clauses to dispute resolution procedures.[40] The specific argument adopted by the *ICS* tribunal differs from that used in *Plama*, but nonetheless the argumentative rationale adopted by both tribunals is the same, and the *ICS* tribunal also ultimately rejects jurisdiction on the ground that, absent other supporting evidence of Contracting State intent, a generalised MFN clause cannot sufficiently manifest the 'clear and unambiguous' State consent required for international arbitration.[41]

Some commentators have questioned whether the 'clear and unambiguous' standard is properly applied to investor-State arbitration, but that is not an issue that needs to be addressed here.[42] Instead, even accepting that this standard is correct, significant problems arise from the manner in which the ICS tribunal applies that standard when evaluating the applicability of the treaty's MFN clause to dispute resolution procedures.

The central step in the tribunal's argument on this point occurs in paragraph 278 of the award, where it states that

> to be of assistance to the Claimant in the present case, the MFN clause must constitute more than a mere prohibition of discrimination between investors based on their provenance: the MFN clause must also be in itself a manifestation of consent to the arbitration of investment disputes according to the rules that the MFN provision might attract from other comparator treaties. Should the MFN provision not be found to operate in a jurisdictional manner, that is to act independently as a substitute for the consent found in the basic treaty's dispute resolution clause, it cannot have the effect advocated for by the Claimant here.[43]

Arbitration, of course, requires consent. This much is uncontroversial. As a result, it also follows that if a tribunal is to base its jurisdiction on the application of an MFN clause to dispute resolution procedures, it must be demonstrable that the State has in some way consented to those procedures. For this reason, the tribunal's holding that the MFN clause in the Basic Treaty must 'be in itself a manifestation of consent' to arbitration in accordance with the dispute resolution procedures of the third-State treaty appears, on its face, not to be unreasonable.

Nonetheless, acknowledgement that a State must have consented even to an arbitration based on an MFN clause does not dictate how that consent must be found, and it is on this point that the tribunal's reasoning becomes problematic. The tribunal would clearly have been correct to decline jurisdiction if it had concluded that the language of the dispute resolution clause in the third-State treaty to which ICS was appealing did not itself provide 'clear and unambiguous' State consent to immediate investor-State arbitration of ICS' claim. In such a case, after all, the language in question would not have manifested State consent even if it had been included in the treaty itself as part of a dispute resolution clause, rather than appealed to through the invocation of an MFN clause. That is, an MFN clause cannot create State consent to arbitration where it is otherwise lacking.

The *ICS* tribunal, however, never examines the language of the third-State treaty dispute resolution clause to which ICS is appealing. Instead, it declines jurisdiction based on a holding that the language of the MFN clause itself does not sufficiently manifest Argentina's 'clear and unambiguous' consent to investor-State arbitration.[44] That is, it holds that an MFN clause can only apply to dispute resolution procedures if it is 'clear and unambiguous' that the States party to the treaty containing the MFN clause intended it do so.

The difficulty with this argument is that MFN clauses do not apply only in the context of dispute resolution procedures. Instead, they apply to any 'treatment' delivered to investors by the Host State. This means, however, that a 'clear and unambiguous' standard can only be appropriate when an MFN clause is being applied to dispute resolution procedures if either: (a) MFN clauses only ever apply when there is 'clear and unambiguous' evidence that the Home and Host States intended them to apply in that context; or (b) MFN clauses function differently in the context of dispute resolution procedures than they do in any other context.

Option (a) can clearly be rejected, as there is absolutely no support in either case law or commentary for such a narrow reading of the applicability of MFN clauses. Indeed, a 'clear and unambiguous' standard would largely undermine the purpose of an MFN clause, which is to ensure that investors from the Home State remain on an equal competitive footing with all other foreign participants in the marketplace. A 'clear and unambiguous' standard, however, would result in an MFN clause only being applicable if it was demonstrable both that the Home and Host States had actively considered the specific factual benefit being claimed, and that they had explicitly agreed that the benefit was covered by the MFN clause. Facts of this specificity would, of course, rarely be available, and Host States would be left almost unrestrained in their ability to privilege particular investors to the detriment of investors from the Home State, despite the existence of an MFN clause.

Option (b), similarly, while more facially plausible than option (a), is ultimately also inconsistent with the manner in which MFN clauses operate. An MFN clause is a promise from one State to another that no 'more favourable treatment' will be provided to investors from any third-State than is provided to those from the beneficiary State. This promise, however, it is important to note, is substance-neutral. That is, as explained in secton 4.1, it is a promise to provide a certain level of 'treatment', not a promise to provide certain types of benefits. Consequently, if an action by the Host State results in investors from a third-State receiving 'more favourable treatment' than investors from the Home State, then investors from the Home State are entitled to equivalent treatment themselves. The factual mechanism through which that 'more favourable treatment' was provided is simply irrelevant to determining whether the right to equivalent treatment exists.

MFN clauses, then, simply do not operate in a way that allows a 'clear and unambiguous' standard to be used when determining the applicability of an MFN clause to dispute resolution procedures. 'Clear and unambiguous' may indeed be the correct standard to apply when addressing the factual question of a State's consent to particular dispute resolution procedures. However, this is a factual evaluation regarding the 'favourability' of the dispute resolution procedures being claimed by the investor, and cannot justify a broader claim that the MFN clause in question *never* applies to dispute resolution procedures. A general conclusion of this nature can only be reached through standard techniques of treaty interpretation, applying conventional levels of proof, rather than the heightened 'clear and unambiguous' standard used in the context of State consent to dispute resolution procedures.

Even accepting this analysis of the operation of MFN clauses, however, there remains one further justification that might be offered for the adoption of a 'clear and unambiguous' standard in determinations of the applicability of MFN clauses to dispute resolution procedures. Indeed, there are indications in the *ICS* award that it was this final argument that was most influential in the *ICS* tribunal's own reasoning.[45] The argument in question focuses not on the manner in which MFN clauses operate, but rather on the substantive outcome of the interpretative process. That is, a teleological argument might be made that whatever standard is appropriate when determining the operation of an MFN clause, a State can nonetheless only be obligated to arbitrate if there is 'clear and unambiguous' evidence that it has consented to do so. Consequently, since application of an MFN clause to dispute resolution procedures may result in a State being obligated to arbitrate, MFN clauses can only be found to apply to dispute resolution procedures where there is 'clear and unambiguous' evidence that they were intended to do so.

The problem with this argument is that it misunderstands the nature of the obligation that an MFN clause imposes, which is to provide investors from the beneficiary State with any 'more favourable treatment' than the Host State provides to investors from any third-State. An obligation to provide treatment, however, is not the same as the actual provision of that treatment. That is, while an MFN clause creates a legal obligation for the Host State to take certain actions, it does not thereby also create the facts required for the Host State to have lived up to its obligation. By way of illustration, if a Host State has granted tax-free status to investors from a third-State, an MFN clause obligates it to grant the same tax-free status to investors from the beneficiary State. Nonetheless, despite the existence of the obligation, the tax-free status has indisputably not been granted. It is, after all, this failure to grant the tax-free status that underlies the claim being brought to arbitration by the investor. The MFN clause, then, merely serves as a mechanism through which an arbitral tribunal can craft a remedy to compensate the investor for the Host State's failure to take the actions that it was legally obligated to take.

This distinction between fact and obligation, however, plays a particularly important role in the application of MFN clauses to dispute resolution procedures. As the *ICS* tribunal notes, after all, a State is only obligated to arbitrate when it has actually consented to do so.[46] Whether a State has consented to arbitration, however, is a question of fact, not of obligation. As a result, when an MFN clause imposes on the Host State an obligation to consent to investor-State arbitration, it does not thereby also provide the Host State's actual consent. That consent must be given separately. An MFN clause, even when it is applied to dispute resolution procedures, does not constitute a standing offer to arbitrate. The MFN clause merely obligates the State to make such a standing offer, it does not create the fact of an offer where an offer has not actually been made.[47]

Proponents of the consent-focused approach to the application of MFN clauses to dispute resolution procedures, then, cannot rely on the teleological argument being considered here as a means of justifying the use of a 'clear and unambiguous' standard for determining the applicability of an MFN clause to dispute resolution procedures. Such a standard is only appropriate in the identification of State consent to dispute resolution, and an MFN clause does not provide that consent. Consequently, to the extent that intent is determinative in the interpretation of an MFN clause, that intent must be identified in accordance with the ordinary standards used in treaty interpretation, and not in accordance with the heightened standard argued to be applicable in the context of State consent to arbitration.

Nonetheless, even though the *ICS* tribunal's reliance on a consent-based standard for determining the applicability of an MFN clause to dispute resolution procedures was mistaken, it does not follow that the tribunal was wrong to decline jurisdiction over ICS' claim. After all, the fact that an MFN clause only obligates a State to consent to arbitration, and does not provide the State's consent, entails that the *ICS* tribunal would have lacked jurisdiction over ICS' claim even if it had concluded that the MFN clause in the treaty did apply to dispute resolution procedures. This is because of a very important limitation on the ability of investors to use an MFN clause to access dispute resolution procedures other than those listed in the Basic Treaty itself.

A Host State violates an MFN clause whenever it refuses to arbitrate in accordance with 'more favourable' third-State treaty dispute resolution procedures. However, the only tribunal with jurisdiction to remedy that wrong is one constituted in accordance with procedures to which the State has actually consented, namely those in the Basic Treaty. Consequently, while an investor would ultimately be able to claim damages from the Host State for any additional losses it incurred because of the Host State's violation of the MFN clause, it would nonetheless have to obey the jurisdictional prerequisites included in the Basic Treaty prior to being allowed to bring its claim to arbitration. The arbitral tribunal, after all, would lack jurisdiction until that point, and a tribunal without jurisdiction cannot craft a remedy, no matter how clear a treaty violation may be.

Notes

Introduction

1 The phrase 'bounded anarchy' is one that some commentators have used to refer to public international law, but describing public international law in this way involves a fundamental misunderstanding of the nature of anarchism as a theory of social organisation. Public international law, after all, is a much more straightforward example of an anarchic system, in which no rules are imposed from above, and rules are only imposed by the system itself to a degree consistent with the consent of participants. Moreover, the manner of the development of public international law rules centres on consent, whether in the form of treaties or customary international law, unilateral acts, general principles of law, etc. rather than on the coercive imposition of rules from one entity or group onto another entity or group. Those who argue for the 'bounded' nature of the anarchy involved in public international law tend to focus on the existence of institutions, but institutions are simply not inconsistent with anarchy. The issue, rather, is the coerciveness of those institutions.

1 The meaning of 'investment' in the ICSID Convention

1 This chapter is based on an article originally co-authored with Anuj Kumar Vaksha.
2 Convention on the Settlement of Investment Disputes between States and Nationals of Other States (ICSID Convention), Art. 25(1).
3 See, e.g., J. D. Mortenson, 'The Meaning of "Investment": ICSID's *Travaux* and the Domain of International Investment Law', (2010) 51 Harvard J Int'l L 257; M. E. Hiscock, 'The Emerging Legal Concept of Investment', (2008) 27 Penn State International Law Review 765; M. Jezewski, 'There Is No Freedom Without Solidarity: Towards a New Definition of Investment in International Economic Law', Soc Int'l Econ L, Working Paper No. 51/08, 2008; D. Krishan, 'A Notion of Investment', in T. Grierson (ed.), *Investment Treaty Arbitration: A Debate and Discussion*, 2008, Huntington, NY: Juris Publishing; N. Rubins, 'The Notion of "Investment" in International Investment Arbitration', in N. Horn and S. Kröll (eds), *Arbitrating Foreign Investment Disputes*, 2004, Alphen aan den Rijn: Kluwer Law International, p. 283.
4 See, e.g., Mortenson, op. cit., n 3.
5 See, e.g., Krishan, op. cit., n 3.
6 See, e.g., Y. Andreeva, 'The Tribunal in Malaysian Historical Salvors v. Malaysia Adopts a Restrictive Interpretation of the Term "Investment"', (2008) 25 J Int'l Arb 503.
7 By way of analogy, one could argue that the Contracting States of a power-conferring treaty are better understood as 'parents' than as 'engineers'. That is, engineers create a machine to achieve a particular purpose; as a result, a mechanic working on that machine can use the intentions of the engineers as a guide to how it is designed to function.

A parent, on the other hand, creates a child, and may be full of intentions as to what the child will go on to be and to do. Ultimately, however, the parent's only control is over the child's initial creation, and the child will go on to develop its own identity, often quite radically inconsistent with the one the parent hoped it would have.

8 See, e.g., J. Brunnée, 'Consent', in *Max Planck Encyclopedia of Public International Law*, 2010, Oxford: Oxford University Press, 'a review of the main international law-making processes reveals that the consent of individual States often plays only an indirect role in creating the rules that bind them, and sometimes none at all'; M. Lister, 'The Legitimating Role of Consent in International Law', (2011) 11 Chicago J Int'l L 663, 'state consent has an important, though limited, role in establishing the legitimacy of some parts of international law', p. 664.

9 See, e.g., A. N. Pronto, 'Some Thoughts on the Making of International Law', (2008) 19 Eur J Int'l L 601, p. 613, explaining the International Law Commission's reticence to encourage negotiation of a treaty based on its draft Articles on the responsibility of States for internationally wrongful acts as 'amount[ing] to a sort of post-modernist take on the codification of international law, which minimized the importance of treaties while preferring the development of the law through the continuing development of customary international law'.

10 A. Bianchi, 'Human Rights and the Magic of Jus Cogens', (2008) 19 Eur J Int'l L 491, p. 491, noting that '[t]here is an almost intrinsic relationship between peremptory norms and human rights'.

11 This is still fundamentally true, even though it is now recognised that international organisations can also enter into treaties. See the Vienna Convention on the Law of Treaties between States and International Organizations or between International Organizations (VCLT).

12 Brunnée, op. cit., n 8, para. 5, 'States must consent to be legally bound by a treaty'.

13 See generally D. Hollis, 'Why State Consent Still Matters: Non-State Actors, Treaties, and the Changing Sources of International Law', (2005) 2 Berkeley J Int'l L 1.

14 See, e.g., the 1226 treaty in which Emperor Frederick II of the Holy Roman Empire secured concessions for the citizens of Marseille that had previously only been available to the citizens of Pisa and Genoa. S. K. Hornbeck, 'The Most-Favored-Nation Clause', (1909) 3 Am J Int'l L 395, p. 398.

15 See generally J. Braithwaite and P. Drahos, *Global Business Regulation*, 2000, Cambridge: Cambridge University Press.

16 These rules are, of course, contained in the VCLT.

17 See, e.g., F. G. Jacobs, 'Varieties of Approach to Treaty Interpretation: With Special Reference to the Draft Convention on the Law of Treaties before the Vienna Diplomatic Conference', (1969) 18 Int'l & Comp LQ 318, p. 319, 'The teleological approach seeks to interpret the treaty in the light of its objects and purposes'. This approach has, for example, famously been adopted by the European Court of Justice. H. G. Schermers and D. F. Waelbroeck, *Judicial Protection in the European Union*, 2001, Alphen aan den Rijn: Kluwer Law International, para. 40, 'In several cases the Court had to … choose the Interpretation which best serves the purpose for which the provision was made'.

18 Ibid.

19 VCLT, Art. 31(1).

20 I. Sinclair, *The Vienna Convention on the Law of Treaties*, 2nd edn, 1984, Manchester: Manchester University Press, p. 19, noting that 'there is now strong judicial support for the view that the rules of treaty interpretation incorporated in the Convention are declaratory of customary law'.

21 *Malaysian Historical Salvors, SDN, BHD v Malaysia*, ICSID Case No. ARB/05/10, Decision on the Application for Annulment, 16 April 2009, para. 57.

22 C. Schreuer, 'Investment Disputes', in *Max Planck Encyclopedia of Public International Law*, 2010, Oxford: Oxford University Press, para. 15, 'Action in the domestic courts of the Host State is the traditional way in which investment claims are pursued, at least initially'.

23 As throughout this book, 'Home State' refers to the State in which the investment in question originated.
24 See generally C. F. Amerasinghe, *Diplomatic Protection*, 2008, Oxford: Oxford University Press.
25 As throughout this book, 'Host State' refers to the State into which the investment in question has been made.
26 J. Dugard, 'Diplomatic Protection', in *Max Planck Encyclopedia of Public International Law*, 2010, Oxford: Oxford University Press, para. 2, 'Today it is accepted that diplomatic protection may only be enforced by peaceful means, such as negotiation, arbitration, or judicial proceedings, and not by forcible means'.
27 Schreuer, op. cit., n 22, para. 3, noting that diplomatic protection 'carries serious disadvantages for the protected investor'.
28 Schreuer, op. cit., n 22, para. 13, 'A State has the right to exercise diplomatic protection on behalf of a national. It is under no duty or obligation to do so'.
29 *Case Concerning the Barcelona Traction, Light and Power Company, Limited (Belgium v Spain)*, 5 February 1970, para. 78, quoted in R. D. Bishop, J. Crawford and M. Reisman (eds), *Foreign Investment Disputes*, 2005, Alphen aan den Rijn: Kluwer Law International, p. 768,

> [A] State may exercise diplomatic protection by whatever means and to whatever extent it thinks fit, for it is its own right that the State is asserting. Should the national or legal person on whose behalf it is acting consider that their rights are not adequately protected, they have no remedy in international law.

30 Schreuer, op. cit., n 22, para. 3, 'Under international law the investor's State of nationality may refuse to pursue the claim or may abandon it at any stage'.
31 A. Newcombe and L. Paradell, *Law and Practice of Investment Treaties: Standards of Treatment*, 2009, Alphen aan den Rijn: Kluwer Law International, section 1.1, 'In the late nineteenth and early twentieth centuries, as the world economy became increasingly internationalized, the limits of the diplomatic protection model became apparent'.
32 Ibid., section 1.14, 'Disputes over the treatment of foreign investment increased and intensified after WWII as the process of decolonization resulted in colonial territories becoming states'.
33 The most authoritative overview of ICSID and the ICSID Convention is provided in Schreuer, op. cit., n 22.
34 Indeed, if an arbitration is commenced at ICSID, the investor's Home State is precluded from exercising diplomatic protection or bringing any sort of international claim. ICSID Convention, Art. 27.
35 Newcombe and Paradell, op. cit., n 31, section 1.4, 'After the First World War (WWI), it became more common for agreements to provide that individual claimants could make claims directly'.
36 This is not to say that the Home State cannot be allowed to intervene into an ICSID arbitration, but only that it lacks any inherent right to do so.
37 ICSID Convention, Art. 27.
38 Newcombe and Paradell, op. cit., n 31, section 1.3, 'The theory underlying the principle of diplomatic protection is that an injury to a state's national is an injury to the state itself, for which it may claim reparation from any responsible state'.
39 On the lack of Home State involvement in the investment arbitration process, see generally A. Roberts, 'Power and Persuasion in Investment Treaty Interpretation: The Dual Role of States', (2010) 104 Am J Int'l L 179.
40 A treaty may, of course, also grant the Home and Host States the right to resolve disputes over the interpretation of the treaty. However, the Home State usually retains no power to intervene in any dispute resolution process between the Host State and the investor.
41 ICSID Convention, Art. 55.
42 ICSID Convention, Art. 25(1).

43 See generally A. Rau, 'Arbitral Jurisdiction and the Dimensions of Consent', University of Texas School of Law, Law and Economics Research Paper, No. 103, 2008.

44 See, e.g., *Southern Pacific Properties (Middle East) Ltd v Egypt*, Decision on Jurisdiction, 27 November 1985, Egypt found to have consented to arbitrate with Southern Pacific Properties (SPP) as a result of a clause in its own foreign investment law, with no additional consent to arbitrate specifically with SPP being necessary.

45 See, e.g., S. Greenberg, C. Kee and J. R. Weeramantry, *International Commercial Arbitration*, 2011, Port Melbourne: Cambridge University Press, section 3.4.1, 'Without an arbitration agreement there can be no arbitration'; N. Blackaby and C. Partasides, *Redfern and Hunter on International Arbitration*, 2009, New York, NY: Oxford University Press, section 1.52, '[C]onsent is essential. Without it there can be no valid arbitration'.

46 ICSID Convention, Art. 25(1). The Convention also includes other jurisdictional constraints, but these are not addressed here.

47 See, e.g., *Malaysian Historical Salvors, SDN, BHD v Malaysia*, ICSID Case No. ARB/05/10, Decision on Jurisdiction, 17 May 2007, declining jurisdiction for lack of an investment under ICSID Convention, Art. 25; *Patrick Mitchell v The Democratic Republic of Congo*, Case No. ARB/99/7, Decision on the Application for Annulment of the Award, 1 November 2006 (same).

48 Namely, those specific injuries covered by the treaty in question.

49 See, e.g., the sources cited op. cit., n 3.

50 Schreuer, op. cit., n 22, para. 33.

51 See, e.g., *Joy Mining Machinery Ltd v Egypt*, Award on Jurisdiction, ICSID Case No. ARB/03/11, 6 August 2004 (bank guarantees); *Fedax NV v Venezuela*, ICSID Case No. ARB/96/3, IIC 101, Decision on Jurisdiction (debt instruments), 1997.

52 See, e.g., *Joy Mining*, ibid.; *Salini Costruttori, SpA v Kingdom of Morocco*, ICSID Case No. ARB/00/4, Decision on Jurisdiction, 23 July 2001; *Fedax v Republic of Venezuela*, ICSID Case No. ARB/96/3, Decision of the Tribunal on Objections to Jurisdiction, 11 July 1997.

53 In reference to the *Salini* case, ibid.

54 B. Legum and C. Mouawad, 'The Meaning of "Investment" in the ICSID Convention', in P. H. F. Bekker, R. Dolzer and M. Waibel (eds), *Making Transnational Law Work in the Global Economy*, 2010, Cambridge: Cambridge University Press, p. 326, at p. 330, noting that under the objective approach, 'any transaction falling outside the scope of these limits would not be deemed an ICSID investment (and thus would not fall within ICSID jurisdiction, irrespective of any agreement between the parties)'.

55 C. Schreuer (ed.), *The ICSID Convention: A Commentary*, 2001, Cambridge: Cambridge University Press, para. 122.

56 Ibid. See also ibid., para. 119, relying upon 'a perusal of the cases that have come before ICSID tribunals'.

57 Ibid., para. 122.

58 O. K. Fauchald, 'The Legal Reasoning of ICSID Tribunals: An Empirical Analysis', (2008) 19 Eur J Int'l L 301; C. Schreuer and M. Weiniger, 'Conversations across Cases: Is There a Doctrine of Precedent in Investment Arbitration?', 5 January 2007 (draft on file with author).

59 On the issue of precedent in investment arbitration generally, see G. Kaufmann-Kohler, 'Arbitral Precedent: Dream, Necessity or Excuse?', (2007) 23 Arb Int'l 357.

60 Schreuer, op. cit., n 55, para. 122.

61 See, e.g. Mortenson, op. cit., n 3, p. 272, arguing that '[t]ribunals following Schreuer's lead, however, have been far more aggressive, converting his descriptive reflections into a prescriptive set of requirements'.

62 Schreuer, op. cit., n 55, para. 122, 'These features should not necessarily be understood as jurisdictional requirements but merely as typical characteristics of investments under the Convention'.

63 Schreuer, op. cit., n 22, para. 153, 'These features should not necessarily be understood as jurisdictional requirements but merely as typical characteristics of investments under the Convention'.

64 See, e.g., Andreeva, op. cit., n 6, p. 506,

> [G]iven that the term "investment" is not defined in the Convention and is instead set out in great detail in the BIT. Is it not the will of the States that submit themselves to ICSID jurisdiction that matters most? Is it not the way they choose to define covered investments that sets the boundaries for that jurisdiction?.

65 See, e.g., *Biwater Gauff (Tanzania) Ltd v Tanzania*, ICSID Case No. ARB/05/22, Award, 24 July 2008, para. 317, 'over the years, many tribunals have approached the issue of the meaning of "investment" by reference to the parties' agreement, rather than imposing a strict autonomous definition'.

66 See, e.g., P. Reuter, *Introduction to the Law of Treaties*, 1989, London: Pinter Publishers, para. 142, 'The primacy of the text, especially in international law, is the cardinal rule for any interpretation'; I. Sinclair, *The Vienna Convention on the Law of Treaties*, 1984, Manchester: Manchester University Press, p. 115, 'The Commission accordingly came down in favour of the view that the starting point of interpretation is the elucidation of the meaning of the text, not an investigation ab initio into the intentions of the parties'.

67 See generally J. Klabbers, 'International Legal Histories: The Declining Importance of *Travaux Préparatoires* in Treaty Interpretation', (2003) 50 Neth Int'l L Rev 267.

68 VCLT, Art. 32.

69 Mortenson, op. cit., n 3, p. 260, 'The term "investment" is a quintessentially "ambiguous" term justifying "[r]ecourse [to] ... the preparatory work of the treaty and the circumstances of its conclusion"'.

70 See, e.g., *Malaysian Historical Salvors, SDN, BHD*, above, n 21,

> In any event, courts and tribunals interpreting treaties regularly review the *travaux préparatoires* whenever they are brought to their attention; it is mythological to pretend that they do so only when they first conclude that the term requiring interpretation is ambiguous or obscure;

Biwater Gauff (Tanzania) Ltd, above, n 65, 'On the contrary, it is clear from the *travaux préparatoires* of the Convention that several attempts to incorporate a definition of "investment" were made, but ultimately did not succeed'.

71 Report of the Executive Directors, para. 27.

72 ICSID Convention, Preamble, 'Declaring that no Contracting State shall by the mere fact of its ratification, acceptance or approval of this Convention and without its consent be deemed to be under any obligation to submit any particular dispute to conciliation or arbitration'; C. F. Amerasinghe, 'The International Center for Settlement of Investment Disputes and Development through the Multinational Corporation', (1976) 9 Vand J Transnat'l L 793, p. 800, 'both parties to the dispute must have consented to have recourse to ICSID'; P. C. Szasz, 'The Investment Disputes Convention – Opportunities and Pitfalls: How to Submit Disputes to ICSID', (1970) 5 J Law Econ Dev 23, p. 26, 'The most important jurisdictional requirement is that of consent, by both parties, to the submission of a dispute to the Centre'.

73 See, e.g., Mortenson, op. cit., n 3, p. 292, noting 'the startling inaccuracy of the suggestion that there was no attempt to define "investment"'.

74 Schreuer, op. cit., n 22, para. 152, noting that 'all attempts to reach agreement on a definition to be inserted into the Convention failed'.

75 Schreuer, op. cit., n 22, paras 121–2.

76 In the words of Christoph Schreuer, op. cit., n 22, paras 121–2, '[t]he subsequent discussions showed a widely held opinion that a definition of the term "investment" was necessary'.

77 Mortenson, op. cit., n 3, pp. 289–91.

78 See similarly J. M. Boddicker, 'Whose Dictionary Controls? Recent Challenges to the Term "Investment" in ICSID Arbitration', (2010) 25 Am U Int'l L Rev 1031, p. 1045,

'BIT and FTA definitions may narrow but not expand the scope of jurisdiction granted by [ICSID Convention, Art. 25(1)]. Therefore, a BIT or an FTA alone cannot confer jurisdiction' (footnotes omitted); Rubins, op. cit., n 3, p. 289, 'In the end, however, a textual analysis of the Convention and Institution Rules reveals, and commentators now agree, that there is an objective boundary to the definition of investment for purposes of ICSID jurisdiction' (footnotes omitted).

79 Under the recently adopted ICSID Arbitration Rules, Rule 37, a State may now make a submission in an arbitration in which it is not a party, but only as an amicus, at the same level as any other amicus submission.

80 ICSID Convention, Art. 64,

> Any dispute arising between Contracting States concerning the interpretation or application of this Convention which is not settled by negotiation shall be referred to the International Court of Justice by the application of any party to such dispute, unless the States concerned agree to another method of settlement.

81 See, e.g., G. Vannieuwenhuyse, 'Bringing a Dispute Concerning ICSID Cases and the ICSID Convention before the International Court of Justice', (2009) 8 L & Prac Int'l Cts & Tribs 115; Schreuer, op. cit., n 22, paras 1259–64.

82 See, e.g., North American Free Trade Agreement, Art. 1131(2).

83 ICSID Convention, Art. 64, referring to 'the States concerned'.

84 ICSID Convention, Art. 64, referring to '[a]ny dispute arising between Contracting States concerning the interpretation or application of this Convention'.

85 *The ICSID Caseload – Statistics (Issue 2013–1)*, p. 10: in 63 per cent of ICSID cases jurisdiction was based on a BIT; in 11 per cent of ICSID cases jurisdiction was based on another form of treaty; in 20 per cent of ICSID cases jurisdiction was based on an investment contract between the investor and the Host State, https://icsid.worldbank.org/ICSID/FrontServlet?requestType=ICSIDDocRH&actionVal=ShowDocument&CaseLoadStatistics=True&language=English41 (accessed 22 February 2013).

86 ICSID Convention, Art. 64 relates to '[a]ny dispute arising between Contracting States concerning the *interpretation or application* of this Convention' (emphasis added).

87 Ibid., '[a]ny dispute arising between Contracting States concerning the interpretation or application of this Convention *which is not settled by negotiation*' (emphasis added).

88 This situation has not served as the basis of an ICSID dispute yet, but with the enormous number of BITs now in effect, it will plausibly arise in the future.

89 See, e.g., Mortenson, op. cit., n 3, p. 300, suggesting as a limit that the dispute must arise from a 'plausibly economic activity or asset'; *Malaysian Historical Salvors, SDN, BHD*, above, n 21, acknowledging the 'fundamental assumption that the term "investment" does not mean "sale"'.

90 *Malaysian Historical Salvors, SDN, BHD*, above, n 21,

> [I]n the debate over the draft of that Report, Mr. Broches recalled that none of the suggested definitions for the word "investment" had proved acceptable. He suggested that while it might be difficult to define the term, an investment in fact was readily recognizable.

91 P. Vargiu, 'Beyond Hallmarks and Formal Requirements: A "Jurisprudence Constante" on the Notion of Investment in the ICSID Convention', (2009) 10 J World Invest & Trade 753, p. 767, 'ICSID tribunals constituted after the Joy Mining decision have usually provided their own interpretation of the notion of investment, comprised of a variable number of elements treated sometimes as mere hallmarks, sometimes as formal requirements'.

92 ICSID Convention, Art. 37(2)(b),

> Where the parties do not agree upon the number of arbitrators and the method of their appointment, the Tribunal shall consist of three arbitrators, one arbitrator

appointed by each party and the third, who shall be the president of the Tribunal, appointed by agreement of the parties.

93 ICSID Convention, Art. 54, 'Each Contracting State shall recognize an award rendered pursuant to this Convention as binding and enforce the pecuniary obligations imposed by that award within its territories as if it were a final judgment of a court in that State'.

94 While this expansive view of the power of parties to a dispute over Art. 25(1)'s definition of 'investment' has not been adopted by a tribunal, it can be seen in commentary. See, e.g., Mortenson, op. cit., n 3, p. 299, 'There is a good case that the historical agreement was for the requirement [of an investment] to have no administrable effect – that it is a nonjusticiable norm whose enforcement depends solely on the give and take among political entities'; Andreeva, op. cit., n 6, p. 506,

> [G]iven that the term "investment" is not defined in the Convention and is instead set out in great detail in the BIT. Is it not the will of the States that submit themselves to ICSID jurisdiction that matters most? Is it not the way they choose to define covered investments that sets the boundaries for that jurisdiction?.

95 Cf., e.g., Krishan, op. cit., n 3, proposing the adoption of the International Monetary Fund's definition of 'investment'.

96 It should be emphasised that the relevant issue is consent to investor-State arbitration, not merely ICSID arbitration.

97 See generally M. Malik, 'Recent Developments in the Definition of Investment in International Investment Agreements, Second Annual Forum of Developing Country Investment Negotiators', 2008, http://www.iisd.org/pdf/2008/dci_recent_dev.pdf (accessed 22 February 2013).

98 The idea that treaty terms can have an evolutionary meaning has recently been endorsed by the ICJ in *Dispute Regarding Navigational and Related Rights (Costa Rica v Nicaragua)*, 13 July 2009, para. 66,

> [W]here the parties have used generic terms in a treaty, the parties necessarily having been aware that the meaning of the terms was likely to evolve over time, and where the treaty has been entered into for a very long period or is "of continuing duration", the parties must be presumed, as a general rule, to have intended those terms to have an evolving meaning.

99 A finding of customary international law also requires a finding of *opinio juris*; however, this element is not relevant in the present context.

2 The legal impact of notifications under Article 25(4) of the ICSID Convention

1 The use of the word 'connected' refers to the fact that Home States are also involved, under ICSID Convention, Art. 64.

2 See *PSEG Global, Inc, The North American Coal Corporation, and Konya Ingin Electrik Uretim ve Ticaret Limited Sirketi v Turkey*, ICSID Case No. ARB/02/5, Decision on Jurisdiction, 4 June 2004, pp. 135–47 (including a discussion of case law).

3 See e.g., Antonio R. Parra *The History of ICSID*, 2012, p. 31, (noting that 'Scant use was made of the mechanism of Article 25(4) of the Convention ... oddly, perhaps, after the attention lavished on the mechanism in the preparation of the Convention').

4 See, e.g., ICSID Convention, Art. 54.

5 Kenneth S. Jacob, 'Reinvigorating ICSID with a New Mission and with Renewed Respect for Party Autonomy', 33 *Virginia Journal of International Law*, 123, (1992), p. 128. ('ICSID

establishes a system of double consent ... A Host State wishing to use the Centre must first assent to the Convention by ratifying the treaty. This step does not entail any particular obligation to use ICSID arbitration').

6 Report of the Executive Directors, para. 22.

7 See generally the historical discussion in Julian Davis Mortenson, 'The Meaning of "Investment": ICSID's *Travaux* and the Domain of International Investment Law', (2010), 51, Harvard J Int'l L 257.

8 Convention on the Recognition and Enforcement of Foreign Arbitral Awards, Art. 2.

9 L. Reed, J. Paulsson and N. Blackaby, *Guide to ICSID Arbitration*, 2011, p. 35 ('The only requirement of form is that consent must be in writing').

10 Or appeal to the investor's Home State for diplomatic protection.

11 See Jacob, supra note 5.

12 See Mortenson, supra note 7, at 283–89.

13 *PSEG Global, Inc*, above, n 2, pp. 135–47 (including a discussion of case law).

14 C. H. Schreuer, et al., *The ICSID Convention: A Commentary*, 2009, at ¶ 930, (noting that a State 'may even give consent in respect of a dispute that belongs to a class that was listed as one it would not consider submitting').

15 For this interpretation of ICSID Convention, Art. 25(4), see J. Mortenson, 'The Meaning of "Investment": ICSID's *Travaux* and the Domain of International Investment Law', (2010) 51 Harvard J Int'l L 257.

16 ICSID Convention, Art. 25(4), 'The Secretary-General shall forthwith transmit such notification to all Contracting States'.

17 See, e.g. Mortenson, op. cit., n 15.

18 See, e.g., L. T. Wells, Jr., 'Multinationals and the Developing Countries', in T. L. Brewer, S. Young and S. E. Guisinger (eds), *The New Economic Analysis Multinationals*, 2003, at p. 106, p. 110–11 ('In earlier days domestic enterprises were often protected from competition with foreign investors by a number of barriers. Elaborate government procedures were required to approve the entry of foreign firms').

19 C. Schreuer (ed.), *The ICSID Convention: A Commentary*, 2001, Cambridge: Cambridge University Press, para. 626.

20 Ibid., para. 632.

21 Note that the Spanish text does not use 'consider'. However, both the English and French versions use this term, and the proposed text was originally discussed in an English version that included the term 'consider'. Consequently, the Spanish version should be taken as inaccurate on this point.

22 Report of the Executive Directors, para 31. Emphasis added.

23 See Schreuer, supra note 14 at ¶ 924.

24 Schreuer, op. cit., n 19, para. 632.

25 *History of the Convention on the Settlement of Investment Disputes Between States and Nationals of Other States*, Vol. 2, (1968), p. 824.

26 *Travaux*, vol. 2, p. 824.

27 Ibid.

28 A. Broches, 'The Convention on the Settlement of Investment Disputes: Some Observations on Jurisprudence', in *Selected Essays*, 1994.

29 BITs and other treaties are not discussed by Broches, but the issues parallel those with domestic legislation, so the same analysis can be applied in that context.

30 A. Broches, *Selected Essays*, 1994, Dordrecht: Martinus Nijhoff, p. 169 (original emphasis).

31 ICSID Convention, at art. 25(1) ('when the parties have given their consent, no party may withdraw its consent unilaterally').

32 See Broches, supra note 28, at p. 169.

33 Ibid at p. 169–70.

34 Broches, op. cit., n. 30, p. 170.

35 Ibid., p. 169.

3 The role of an investment arbitrator and the use of non-binding documents and literature in investment arbitration

1 R. Tuck and M. Silverthorne (eds), *Hobbes: On the Citizen*, 1998, Cambridge: Cambridge University Press, p. 154: '[S]ince laws are obeyed not for their content, but because of the will of the instructor, law is not advice but command'.

2 See, e.g., M. Greenberg, 'The Standard Picture and Its Discontents', in L. Green and B. Leiter (eds), *Oxford Studies in Philosophy of Law*, Vol 1, 2011, Oxford: Oxford University Press, p. 85: 'An intuitive way of putting the point is that the law is supposed to be binding, where that means generally binding all things considered – not just legally binding (which the law trivially is)'; M. A. Fitzmaurice, *International Protection of the Environment*, 2002, The Hague: Kluwer Law International, p. 125: 'Some outstanding authors reject the concept of "soft law" altogether and claim that either law is binding or it is not law at all'; J.-R. Sieckmann, 'Basic Rights in the Model of Principles', in R. Martin and G. Sprenger (eds), *Challenges to Law at the End of the 20th Century*, 1997, Stuttgart: Franz Steiner Verlag, p. 32: 'Legal systems claim the validity and bindingness of their norms for the norm addressees'.

3 Statute of the International Court of Justice, 26 June 1945, 59 Stat 1055, 33 UNTS 993 (ICJ Statute). Article 38 does not itself refer to the 'sources' of international law, listing instead only those instruments that the ICJ 'shall apply' in determining the law. It is, therefore, only directly binding on the ICJ itself. However, it has come to be recognised as the authoritative, although not exhaustive, guide to the sources of international law. See, e.g., V. D. Degan, *Sources of International Law*, 1997, The Hague: Kluwer, p. 5: 'It can therefore be presumed that Article 38 determines sources of that international law which is generally accepted by States'; G. M. Danilenko, *Law-Making in the International Community*, 1993, Dordrecht: Martinus Nijhoff, p. 36, referring to 'the widespread recognition that sources of law listed in Art. 38 of the I.C.J. Statute are at the same time sources of international law in general'.

4 See generally M. Shaw, *International Law*, 6th edn, 2008, Cambridge: Cambridge University Press, Ch 3.

5 It should be emphasised that ICJ Statute, Art. 38 is no longer considered to be a complete statement of the sources of international law, but only of the most important sources. See, e.g., J. d'Aspremont, *Formalism and the Sources of International Law*, 2011, Oxford: Oxford University Press, p. 71, noting that Art. 38 'has never purported to exhaust the list of sources of international law'; J. Pauwelyn, *Conflict of Norms in Public International Law*, 2003, Cambridge: Cambridge University Press, p. 89, noting as sources of law in addition to those listed in Art. 38, 'unilateral acts of states' and 'acts of international organisations'. Nonetheless, this expansion has not altered the connection Art. 38 embodies between law and bindingness, as under the classical conception of international law these additional 'sources' also only generate law in so far as they are binding.

6 See, e.g., *Gabčíkovo-Nagymaros Project (Hungary/Slovakia)*, Judgment, [1997] ICJ Reports 7, paras 49–58.

7 See, e.g., C. M. Chinkin, 'The Challenge of Soft Law: Development and Change in International Law', (1989) 38 Int'l & Comp LQ 850; G. J. H. Hoof, *Rethinking the Sources of International Law*, 1983, Deventer: Kluwer Law and Taxation Publishers, p. 188.

8 W. M. Reisman, 'A Hard Look at Soft Law', (1988) 82 Am Soc'y Int'l L Proc 373, p. 374, noting that 'scholars in many weak and small states view some very "hard" law ... as naked power'.

9 In this respect it relies upon a similar approach to the analysis of the work of international investment arbitration (IIA) tribunals as that advocated in W. M. Reisman, 'Soft Law and Law Jobs', (2011) 2 J Int'l Disp Settlement 25. However, while Reisman's article and this

chapter are both based upon a recognition of the importance of 'law jobs', the analysis and conclusions of the two pieces differ greatly.

10 A survey of the historical development of international investment law is available in A. Newcombe and L. Paradell, *Law and Practice of Investment Treaties: Standards of Treatment*, 2009, Alphen aan den Rijn: Kluwer Law International, Ch 1.

11 H. Thirlway, 'The Sources of International Law', in M. D. Evans (ed.), *International Law*, 2nd edn, 2006, Oxford: Oxford University Press, p. 118:

> The Permanent Court was to be the first standing international tribunal to decide disputes between States; if States were to be willing to accept it, one of the matters that had to be defined in advance was the nature of the law that the Court would apply

(referring to Statute of the Permanent Court of International Justice, Art. 38, which subsequently became ICJ Statute, Art. 38).

12 That is, 'international treaties', 'international custom' and 'the general principles of law recognized by civilized nations'.

13 ICJ Statute, Art. 38 also recognises 'judicial decisions' as non-binding 'means for the determination of rules of law', but as case law is addressed in a separate chapter of this book, it is not addressed here.

14 R. J. Gardiner, *International Law*, 2003, Harlow: Pearson Education, p. 27,

> [T]he task of identifying propositions of general international law ... is not as open-ended a process as it may sound; but it does require a willingness to undertake what may sometimes amount to considerable academic research. Sub-paragraph (d) recognises that where such work has already been done it may be of value to the Court.

15 Thirlway, op. cit., n 11, p. 139,

> The definition given in Article 38 of the Statute of the Court has proved to embody a workable structure of recognized law-making processes, and despite the criticisms made of it, and the multiplicity of new approaches to international law, that definition seems likely to continue to guide the international community and the international judge

(citations omitted).

16 On the 'fair and equitable treatment standard', see generally I. Tudor, *The Fair and Equitable Treatment Standard in International Foreign Investment Law*, 2008, New York, NY: Oxford University Press; S. Fietta, 'Expropriation and the "Fair and Equitable" Standard: The Developing Role of Investors' "Expectations" in International Investment Arbitration', (2006) 23 J Int'l Arb 375; R. Dolzer, 'Fair and Equitable Treatment: A Key Standard in Investment Treaties', (2005) 39 Int'l Law 87.

17 Newcombe and Paradell, op. cit., n 10, pp. 5–8.

18 On the historical background to the development of these two courts, see M. S. M. Amr, *The Role of the International Court of Justice as the Principal Judicial Organ of the United Nations*, 2003, The Hague: Kluwer Law International, pp. 6–22.

19 See generally J. G. Merrills, *International Dispute Settlement*, 5th edn, 2011, Cambridge: Cambridge University Press (discussing the broad range of contemporary international dispute mechanisms).

20 A 'norm-adopting' legal tribunal is one with the authority to develop and pronounce legal norms that are then followed by other tribunals within the same legal structure, either due to formal obligation or merely because of the authority of the norm-adopting tribunal.

21 See, e.g., O. Schachter, *International Law and Theory in Practice*, 1991, Dordrecht: Martinus Nijhoff, noting that 'international lawyers have a strong tendency to welcome the

decisions of judicial tribunals, especially those of the International Court of Justice, as authoritative law, even as the touchstone of law', p. 39. See also M. M. Aljaghoub, *The Advisory Function of the International Court of Justice 1946–2005*, 2006, Berlin: Springer Verlag, p. 6, noting 'the authority of [the ICJ's] opinions as authoritative statements of law'; M. N. S. Sellers, 'The Authority of the International Court of Justice', (2002) 8 Int'l Legal Theory 41, p. 41, noting that '[r]ecently some lawyers and statesmen have begun to cite judgments of the International Court of Justice as if they were decisive evidence of the content of international law'; R. Szafarz, 'Introduction', in R. Szafarz (ed.), *The Compulsory Jurisdiction of the International Court of Justice*, 1993, Dordrecht: Martinus Nijhoff, p. ix, referring to the ICJ as 'the most authoritative organ to voice opinions on matters of international law'.

22 S. Subedi, *International Investment Law: Reconciling Policy and Principle*, 2008, Oxford: Hart Publishing, p. 81, noting that 'the idea of granting access to foreign investors to treaty-based bodies operating under international law is a novelty and a post-Second World War innovation'.

23 L. Reed, J. Paulsson and N. Blackaby, *Guide to ICSID Arbitration*, 2011, Alphen aan den Rijn: Kluwer Law International, pp. xi–xii, 'ICSID arbitration was little used for the first 20 years of its existence ... The situation changed dramatically beginning in the mid-1990s as a consequence of the proliferation of bilateral treaties for the promotion and protection of investment'.

24 As of 12 December 2011, 192 States were entitled to appear before the ICJ, http://www.icj-cij.org/jurisdiction/index.php?p1=5&p2=1&p3=1&sp3=a (accessed 21 January 2013).

25 In investor-State arbitration, of course, only one of these parties will be a State. However, ultimately two States are involved in the dispute, as the investor must operate within the legal framework established by the State-State agreement(s) under which it is bringing its claim.

26 See generally R. Mackenzie, K. Malleson, P. Martin and P. Sands QC, *Selecting International Judges: Principle, Process, and Politics*, 2010, Oxford: Oxford University Press, pp. 187–91.

27 See, e.g., Reed, et al., op. cit., n 23, pp. 130–3 (discussing the appointment procedure for ICSID arbitrators).

28 See, e.g., *Urbaser SA and Consorcio de Aguas Bilbao Bizkaia, Bilbao Biskaia Ur Partzuergoa v Argentine Republic*, ICSID Case No. ARB/07/26 (appointment by Argentina of an individual who had previously written on the interpretation that should be given to a clause of the treaty at stake in the arbitration). On the rejection of the claimant's challenge to this arbitrator, see T. Cole, 'Arbitrator Appointments in Investment Arbitration: Why Expressed Views on Points of Law Should be Challengeable', *Investment Treaty News Quarterly*, 23 September 2010 (as the claimants argued, McLachlan had basically already stated how he would rule on at least one central issue in the case), http://www.iisd.org/itn/2010/09/23/arbitrator-appointments-in-investment-arbitration-why-expressed-views-on-points-of-law-should-be-challengeable-2/ (accessed 2 January 2011).

29 See, e.g., T. Begic, *Applicable Law in International Investment Disputes*, 2005, The Hague: Eleven International Publishing, pp. 169–87, discussing cases in which ICSID annulment committees have addressed applications for annulment of ICSID awards for failure to apply the proper law.

30 Ibid., 'Substantive interpretation', then, is not the same as deciding *ex aequo et bono*.

31 But see *contra* G. Kaufmann-Kohler, 'Arbitral Precedent: Dream, Necessity or Excuse?', (2007) 23 Arb Int'l 357, arguing that 'arbitral precedent' should be regarded as a necessity for certain types of disputes.

32 This is not, of course, to state that all judges are subject to doctrines of binding precedent, but only to acknowledge the existence of an obligation of conformity, even within jurisdictions that do not recognise binding precedent. See, e.g., V. Fon and F. Parisi, 'Judicial Precedents in Civil Law Systems: A Dynamic Analysis', (2006) 26 Int'l Rev Law Econ 519, examining the persuasive impact of precedent in civil law systems.

33 See generally O. Spiermann, '"Who Attempts Too Much Does Nothing Well": The 1920 Advisory Committee of Jurists and the Statute of the Permanent Court of International Justice', (2002) 73 Brit YB Int'l L 187.

34 ICJ Statute, Art. 38 is, for example, recommended as non-binding guidance for ICSID tribunals in the Report of the Executive Directors, para. 40:

> Under the Convention an Arbitral Tribunal is required to apply the law agreed by the parties. Failing such agreement, the Tribunal must apply the law of the State party to the dispute (unless that law calls for the application of some other law), as well as such rules of international law as may be applicable. The term "international law" as used in this context should be understood in the sense given to it by Article 38(1) of the Statute of the International Court of Justice, allowance being made for the fact that Article 38 was designed to apply to inter-State disputes.

35 See, e.g., Chinkin, op. cit., n 7, p. 851, '[s]oft law instruments range from treaties, but which include only soft obligations ... to non-binding or voluntary resolutions and codes of conduct ... to statements prepared by individuals in a non-governmental capacity, but which purport to lay down international principles'.

36 See, e.g., I. F. I. Shihata, *The Legal Treatment of Foreign Investment*, 1993, Washington, DC: World Bank, p. 43, on the development of the World Bank Guidelines on the Treatment of Foreign Direct Investment:

> This purpose [i.e. promoting foreign direct investment], it was thought, would be better served if part descriptive, part normative principles were developed, which, given their preparation by international organizations of near universal membership and the broad consultations we intended to undertake, could receive broad acceptance in practice.

37 See generally G. C. Shaffer and M. A. Pollack, 'Hard vs. Soft Law: Alternatives, Complements, and Antagonists in International Governance', (2010) 94 Minn L Rev 706, discussing the means by which States use soft law instruments to alter their international legal obligations.

38 See, e.g., *Malaysian Historical Salvors, SDN, BHD v Malaysia*, ICSID Case No. ARB/05/10, Decision on the Application for Annulment, 16 April 2009, para. 78 (rejecting prior case law and giving 'precedence to awards and analyses that are consistent' with the tribunal's own views); *SGS Société Générale de Surveillance SA v Republic of the Philippines*, ICSID Case No. ARB/02/6, Decision on Jurisdiction, 29 January 2004, para. 125 (rejecting the conclusions of an earlier tribunal involving the same claimant and parallel legal issues as 'unconvincing').

39 See, e.g., ICSID Convention, Art. 52(1)(e), allowing annulment of an ICSID award that has 'failed to state the reasons on which it is based'.

40 K. E. W. Mitchell, 'Arbitrator Selection and Appointment Under the North American Free Trade Agreement', in T. Weiler (ed.), *NAFTA Investment Law and Arbitration: Past Issues, Current Practice, Future Prospects*, 2004, Leiden: Transnational Publishers, p. 313, 'Generally, a party attempts to select an arbitrator predisposed to a favorable consideration of their case, but not legally biased such as to result in disqualification'. On the impact of the structure of arbitrator selection on the arbitral process, see generally T. Cole, 'Authority and Contemporary International Arbitration', (2010) 70 La L Rev 801.

41 The study was undertaken by Madhu Agrawal, an undergraduate research assistant, based on the collection of publicly available investment arbitration awards collected at http://italaw.com. Madhu's work was completed in mid-2011. The subsequent categorisation and analysis of the results of the study was undertaken by the author of this chapter.

42 'Citation' as used here refers to citation in a single decision. That is, if a single writing is cited many times in a single decision, this nonetheless counts as a single citation.

Alternatively, if a single writing is cited by a single tribunal in two separate decisions, this counts as two citations.

43 http://www.unidroit.org/english/principles/contracts/main.htm (accessed 11 January 2012).

44 http://vvv.oecd.org/dataoecd/32/21/1954854.pdf (accessed 5 April 2012).

45 Given the low number of citations of the writings highlighted, it is worth emphasising that no empirical study is methodologically flawless. Consequently, it is certainly possible that there may be one or more additional State-generated authoritative writings that have been cited more than once by IIA tribunals. It would, after all, only require that a single citation has been missed for a writing to drop below the 'two or more citations' threshold being used here. Nonetheless, small possible variations of this nature do not affect the truth of the broader point being made regarding the rate of citation of State-generated authoritative writings.

46 This statement is true whether the standard is the number of different writings cited or the number of citations received by individual writings.

47 Tribunals may, of course, cite instead to non-authoritative writings, but such citations cannot perform the same role as citations to authoritative writings.

48 See generally N. Rubins and B. Lauterberg, 'Independence, Impartiality and Duty of Disclosure in Investment Arbitration', in C. Knahr, et al. (eds), *Investment and Commercial Arbitration*, 2010, The Hague: Eleven International Publishing, p. 153.

49 Ibid.

50 It is worth emphasising that this analysis has been restricted to investment treaty arbitration. It cannot be applied directly to investment arbitrations conducted under an investment contract directly between an investor and the Host State.

51 See, e.g., citations above, n 38.

52 See, e.g., the wide diversity of opinions on the meaning of 'investment' expressed in T. Cole, 'Power-Conferring Treaties: The Meaning of "Investment" in the ICSID Convention', (2011) 24 Leiden J Int'l L 305; D. Krishan, 'A Notion of ICSID Investment', in T. J. Grierson Weiler (ed.), *Investment Treaty Arbitration and International Law*, 2008, Huntington, NY: Juris Publishing, Inc; J. D. Mortenson, 'The Meaning of "Investment": ICSID's *Travaux* and the Domain of International Investment Law', (2010) 51 Harvard J Int'l L 257.

53 Although it should be emphasised that this qualification only applies to the use of allegedly authoritative writings as a guide to the content of international investment law. It does not apply to the use of authoritative writings as a guide to the content of public international law, even if done by IIA tribunals.

54 W. J. Aceves, 'Symposium Introduction: Scholarship as Evidence of International Law', (2003) 26 Loy LA Int'l & Comp L Rev 1, p. 1, 'International law has long-recognized the role of scholarship as a subsidiary means for the determination of rules of law' (quotation marks omitted).

55 Thirlway, op. cit., n 11, p. 129,

> Now that there exists a much greater body of judicial and arbitral decisions enunciating rules of law, the emphasis in practice has shifted to the contribution made by such decisions, and away from the views of "the most highly qualified publicists of the various nations".

56 I. Brownlie, *Principles of Public International Law*, 7th edn, 2008, Oxford: Oxford University Press, p. 25, 'Whatever the need for caution, the opinions of publicists are used widely'.

57 Thirlway, op. cit., n 11, p. 129.

58 Thirlway, op. cit., n 11, p. 129.

59 ICJ Statute, Art. 38 was, of course, originally developed for the Permanent Court of International Justice, not the ICJ. Aceves, op. cit., n 54, p. 4, 'The use of international legal scholarship as evidence of international law was codified in the Statutes of both the

Permanent Court of International Justice and the International Court of Justice'. However, that distinction makes no difference to the point being made here.

60 See, e.g., J. W. Salacuse, *The Law of Investment Treaties*, 2010, New York, NY: Oxford University Press, pp. 156–7, 'Both counsel and tribunals in investor-state arbitrations routinely refer to such works in analysing the meaning of treaty terms in specific cases'; C. Schreuer (ed.), *The ICSID Convention: A Commentary*, 2001, Cambridge: Cambridge University Press, para. 617, 'As would be expected, ICSID tribunals and *ad hoc* committees have frequently relied on academic writings on various points of international law'.

61 Thirlway, op. cit., n 11, p. 129, 'The Court itself does not quote teachings'.

62 See, e.g., the annulment committee in *Malaysian Historical Salvors, SDN, BHD*, above, n 38. Of the three members of the committee, one was the serving Vice President of the International Court of Justice, while another was a former President.

63 See, e.g., the majority decision by the annulment committee in *Malaysian Historical Salvors, SDN, BHD*, above, n 38, which cited to academic writings despite being authored by a current Vice President and a past President of the International Court of Justice.

64 This is not to say, of course, that norm-adopting tribunals are completely immune to any form of criticism. However, the acknowledged right they have to adopt legal norms insulates them from a significant amount of the criticism directed at IIA tribunals that do not possess this right.

4 The minimum standard of treatment and the protection of foreign investors during an armed conflict

1 See, e.g., R. A. Arnold, *Macroeconomics*, 9th edn, 2010, Mason, OH: South-Western Cengage Learning, p. 436, 'Some economists go on to suggest that our trading inclination is a good thing in that, when we trade with people, we not only tolerate them but we have much less reason to fight with them'; T. Friedman, *The Lexus and the Olive Tree: Understanding Globalization*, 1999, New York, NY: Picador, p. 195, 'No two countries that both had McDonald's had fought a war against each other since each got its McDonald's'. But see M. T. Berger, *The Battle for Asia: From Decolonization to Globalization*, 2004, Abingdon and New York, NY: RoutledgeCurzon, p. 136, '[G]lobalization has exacerbated conflict within nation-states and these latter struggles are far more of a problem than conflict between nation-states in many parts of the world in the post-Cold War era'.

2 The only international investment arbitration case directly addressing damage allegedly caused to an investor by a State's involvement in an armed conflict is *Asian Agricultural Products Ltd v Republic of Sri Lanka*, ICSID Case No. ARB/87/3 (shrimp farm destroyed during military action undertaken as part of a counter-insurgency operation). Other cases have also had some connection to armed conflict, but did not directly focus on damage directly attributable to a conflict. See, e.g., *Toto Costruzioni Generali SpA v The Republic of Lebanon*, ICSID Case No. ARB/07/12 (failure to remove foreign troops assisting the government maintain order, thereby preventing work being performed); *American Manufacturing & Trading, Inc v Republic of Zaire*, ICSID Case No. ARB/93/1 (domestic looting by members of the military).

3 While many commentaries on international investment law will touch on issues relevant to the treatment of foreign investors during an armed conflict, the only detailed contemporary discussion available is C. Schreuer, 'The Protection of Investments in Armed Conflicts', (2012) 9 Transnat'l Oisp Man. Schreuer, however, focuses exclusively on the application of common investment treaty clauses in the context of an armed conflict, and gives little attention to the issues discussed in the present chapter.

4 I. A. Moosa, *Foreign Direct Investment*, 2002, Basingstoke: Palgrave Macmillan, pp. 16–18, discussing changes in patterns of foreign direct investment through the course of the twentieth century.

5 See, e.g., S. Page and D. Willem te Velde, *Foreign Direct Investment by African Countries*, 2004, http://www.odi.org.uk/resources/docs/5739.pdf (accessed 21 January 2013), discussing foreign direct investment outflows from several African countries; D. Aykut and D. Ratha, 'South-South FDI Flows: How Big Are They?', (2003) 13 Transnat'l Corp 149, p. 150, 'The 1990s were also marked by a surge in FDI outflows from developing countries, from $12 billion in 1991 to $99 billion in 2000, as a result of a rapid growth of income and wealth in many developing countries' (citations omitted).

6 The terms 'Home State' and 'Host State' are used throughout this chapter to refer, respectively, to the State from which an investor comes, and the State in which the investment is made.

7 For a general survey of potentially applicable investment treaty provisions, see Schreuer, op. cit., n 3.

8 *LFH Neer and Pauline Neer (USA) v United Mexican States*, US-Mexico Claims Commission, 1926, http://untreaty.un.org/cod/riaa/cases/vol_IV/60-66.pdf (accessed 21 January 2013).

9 B. Sabahi, *Compensation and Restitution in Investor-State Arbitration: Principles and Practice*, 2011, Oxford: Oxford University Press, p. 1, 'The modern law of international investment is dominated by a network of bilateral and multilateral investment treaties'; R. Geiger, 'The Multifaceted Nature of International Investment Law', in K. P. Sauvant (ed.), *Appeals Mechanism in International Investment Disputes*, 2008, New York, NY: Oxford University Press, p. 18, 'The present landscape of international investment law is dominated by treaty provisions, contained in either bilateral, regional, plurilateral or multilateral instruments on various aspects of investment relations'.

10 R. Dolzer and C. Schreuer, *Principles of International Investment Law*, 2008, Oxford: Oxford University Press, p. 17,

> [G]iven the vagaries of international economic relations, the reference to customary law in some treaties and the patchwork of the current net of treaties with its remaining gaps, it would also be entirely premature to declare that the ongoing controversies on the state of customary law will not occupy foreign offices, judges, and arbitrators in the future.

11 Ibid.

12 See, e.g., A. Newcombe and L. Paradell, *Law and Practice of Investment Treaties: Standards of Treatment*, 2009, Alphen aan den Rijn: Kluwer Law International, section 6.3, 'In the absence of an IIA, the minimum standard of treatment remains the relevant treatment standard in diplomatic protection claims'.

13 L. B. Ederington, 'Property as a Natural Institution: The Separation of Property from Sovereignty in International Law', (1997) 13 Am U Int'l L Rev 263, p. 266, 'As the epigraph from Emmerich Vattel's classic treatise, *The Law of Nations*, illustrates, international law historically has been inclined to this notion of private property as a fundamental, primeval institution that exists independent of state sovereignty' (citations omitted).

14 J.-M. Henckaerts and L. Doswald-Beck, *Customary International Humanitarian Law*, 2005, Cambridge: Cambridge University Press, p. 178, 'In occupied territory ... movable public property that can be used for military operations may be confiscated; ... private property must be respected and may not be confiscated'; E. M. Borchard, 'Enemy Private Property', (1924) 18 Am J Int'l L 523, p. 523, referring to 'a sound development in political and legal theory which was deemed natural and incidental to the evolution of modern civilization, namely, a conviction as to the essential distinction between private property and public property'.

15 P. H. F. Bekker, 'The Legal Status of Foreign Economic Interests in Occupied Iraq', (2003) Am Soc'y Int'l L In, July, n 9,

> With regard to enemy private property within the other belligerent state's territory, general state practice today is to sequester such property (i.e., to seize it temporarily)

rather than to confiscate it, leaving its subsequent disposal to be dealt with by subsequent arrangements.

16 R. J. Hunter, 'Property Risks in International Business', (2006) 15 Currents: Int'l Trade L J 23, p. 28, 'Generally speaking, the property of the subjects of an enemy found within a country may be taken or appropriated by the government without notice unless there has been a treaty entered into that specifically deals with this subject'; Bekker, op. cit., n 15.

17 See, e.g., Sabahi, op. cit., n 9, p. 66, referring to the appointment by Germany during the Second World War of a sequestrator to run sequestrated investments; R. A. Picciotti, 'Legal Problems of Occupied Nations after the Termination of Occupation', (1966) 33 Mil L Rev 25, p. 38,

> During World War II both Axis countries and Allied nations sequestered foreign assets. The Allied countries appointed property custodians to administer enemy assets within their borders. Alien property custodians in Germany were empowered to collect debts owed to residents of Allied nations.

On the unacceptability of a generalised expropriation of enemy-owned private property, see E. Borchard, 'Are We Entitled to Confiscate Enemy Private Property?', (1923) 23 Col L Rev 383, p. 387,

> If the theory be advanced that each member of the defeated nation must bear the burden of confiscation merely because he is a member, the answer is that the same theory would justify killing or enslaving all civilians, including women and children, whereas advancing civilization had established it as a definite rule, for sound reasons of humanity, policy, and common sense, that individual responsibility for group action would no longer be carried so far as to impose on the civilian the confiscation of his private property.

18 Bekker, op. cit., n 15.

19 R. A. Picciotti, 'Legal Problems of Occupied Nations after the Termination of Occupation', (1966) 33 Mil L Rev 25, p. 39, noting that 'sequestrations do not involve transfer of ownership'; S. J. Rubin, '"Inviolability" of Enemy Property', (1945) 11 Law Contemp Probl 166, p. 181, referring to 'an international law obligation to return enemy private property'.

20 *Re Rizzo and Others (No 3)*, 1955, Franco-Italian Conciliation Commission, (1958) International Law Reports 322,

> In the present instance, the act contrary to international law is not the measure of sequestration, but an alleged lack of diligence on the part of the French State – or, more precisely, of him who was acting on its behalf – in the execution of the said measure.

21 Ibid.

22 See, e.g., G. J. H. van Hoof, *Rethinking the Sources of International Law*, 1983, Deventer: Kluwer Law and Taxation Publishers, p. 36, discussing the distinction drawn by positivist theorists between legal rules and 'other sorts of social rules ... that the community follows but does not enforce through public power'.

23 See, e.g., M. Payandeh, 'The Concept of International Law in the Jurisprudence of H.L.A. Hart', (2010) 21 Eur J Int'l L 967, p. 978, 'In Hart's conception international law is on a par with the social rules of a primitive society, not with the more sophisticated municipal legal system'; F. Parisi, 'Spontaneous Emergence of Law: Customary Law', in B. Bouckaert and G. de Geest (eds), *Encyclopedia of Law & Economics*, 2000, Cheltenham: Edward Elgar and Ghent: University of Ghent, p. 603,

> Judicial recognition of spontaneous norms amounts to a declaratory (rather than constitutive) function that treats custom as a legal fact. The legal system "finds" the law

by recognizing social norms, but does not "create" the law. The most notable illustration is the system of international law, where, absent a central legislative authority, custom stands next to treaties as a primary source of law.

24 Treaties, of course, also constitute a source of international law, and so some formal deliberation can indeed be involved in the creation of international law. However, the creation of treaty obligations still does not resemble the creation of domestic law through legislative bodies, so this does not undermine the point being made. Indeed, treaty obligations more closely resemble contract obligations, themselves intimately connected to social relations, than they do obligations legislated into domestic law.

25 Not all sanctions applied to enforce international law, of course, are developed and applied 'individually', as nothing prevents States acting collectively, including through the United Nations Security Council. However, collective actions of this type are ultimately merely co-ordinated actions of individual States, rather than the actions of a formally distinct enforcement body applying pre-decided sanctions. Enforcement actions by the Security Council might be argued to bear some resemblance to enforcement actions taken under domestic law, however enforcement by the Security Council is a very rare exception to the standard manner of enforcement of public international law, so cannot undermine the general claim being made here.

26 Good treatments of the opposing sides to this debate can be found in J. R. Bolton, 'Is There Really "Law" in International Affairs?', (2000) 10 Transnat'l Law Contemp Probl 1, and A. D'Amato, 'Is International Law Really "Law"?', (1985) 79 Northwest U L Rev 1293.

27 It is, of course, important that the parallel between human social relations and international relations between States is not pushed too far. After all, States rarely grab coffee with a friend or sleep with another State's spouse. States, that is, do not have the independent consciousness necessary for any real social group to exist. However, while the relations between States may not be genuine social relations, this does not mean that they cannot structurally resemble real social relations, and it is on this structural resemblance that the argument advanced here is based.

28 However, for an opposing view, see F. V. García Amador, 'Document A/CN.4/96, International Responsibility: Report by F. V. García Amador, Special Rapporteur', *Yearbook of the International Law Commission 1956*, Vol II, New York, NY: United Nations, pp. 173–231, paras 151–9, arguing that the MST has been replaced by human rights law due to their intimate connection.

29 J. Crawford, *Third Report on State Responsibility*, 2000, New York, NY: United Nations General Assembly, para. 349, 'Evidently, human rights obligations are not owed to States as the primary beneficiaries'.

30 It is, however, important to distinguish the MST from *erga omnes* obligations. An *erga omnes* obligation is owed to all States due to an individual interest of every State in the subject matter of the obligation. Consequently, each State can complain of its violation. The MST, on the other hand, is owed to the community of States, but solely as a social obligation. The same universal right to complain of its violation does not, therefore, arise.

31 A. Broches, *Selected Essays*, 1994, Dordrecht: Martinus Nijhoff, p. 15, 'international law imposes a duty on States to observe a minimum standard of treatment of aliens. But this duty is owed to the alien's national State, not to him personally'.

32 But see *contra* N. Gallus, 'The "Fair and Equitable Treatment" Standard and the Circumstances of the Host State', in C. Brown and K. Miles (eds), *Evolution in Investment Treaty Law and Arbitration*, 2011, Cambridge: Cambridge University Press, p. 241, 'The customary international law minimum standard of treatment is just that, a minimum standard'; *Glamis Gold, Ltd v The United States of America*, Award, 2009, para. 615,

> The customary international law minimum standard of treatment is just that, a minimum standard. It is meant to serve as a floor, an absolute bottom, below which

conduct is not accepted by the international community. Although the circumstances of the case are of course relevant, the standard is not meant to vary from state to state or investor to investor.

33 R. McCorquodale, 'The Individual and the International Legal System', in M. D. Evans (ed.), *International Law*, 2006, Oxford: Oxford University Press, p. 307, '[Traditionally] the dominant view has been that individuals had no effective independent role in the international legal system. Their role was wholly determined by States and was entirely subject to States' consent'.

34 Ibid., pp. 307–8,

> The development of international law, particularly international human rights law, in the second half of the twentieth century has been the main reason why the issue of the role of individuals in the international legal system has again come to prominence.

35 A. Alvarez Jiménez, 'Minimum Standard of Treatment of Aliens, Fair and Equitable Treatment of Foreign Investors, Customary International Law and the Diallo Case Before the International Court of Justice', (2010) 84 Revista Académica e Institucional de la UCPR 5, p. 6, 'contrary to what some States have contemplated in bilateral and regional treaties, the minimum standard of treatment of aliens is an elusive concept in public international law, whose nature and content, or contents, remain to be determined'; García Amador, op. cit., n 28, para. 154, 'None of the international bodies which have accepted and applied the principle has been able to define it: either no attempt to do so has been made, or, in the few cases where it has been made, it has been with little success'.

36 Newcombe and Paradell, op. cit., n 12, pp. 235–6, noting that 'respondent states in a series of early [international investment arbitration] cases have cited the 1926 *Neer* case ... as reflecting the minimum standard of treatment'.

37 *Neer*, above, n 8, pp. 60–1.

38 *Neer*, above, n 8, pp. 61–2.

39 *Neer*, above, n 8, p. 61.

40 Although it might initially appear that 'wilful neglect of duty' refers to something more than merely socially inappropriate behaviour (i.e. a 'duty'), note that it is not the violation of the duty itself that results in the violation of the MST, but 'wilful' nature of the violation.

41 See, e.g., the definition of 'outrage' provided in the *Oxford English Dictionary*, which includes references to a 'gross or malicious wrong or injury done to feelings, principles, etc ... Fierce and overwhelming indignation, anger, etc., experienced in response to some injustice or affront'.

42 Newcombe and Paradell, op. cit., n 12, p. 237, '[International investment arbitration] tribunals have confirmed that the minimum standard of treatment is constantly in the process of development and has continued to evolve since 1926' (citations and quotation marks omitted).

43 See, e.g., García Amador, op. cit., n 28, paras 151–9, arguing that the recent development of international human rights law has rendered the MST obsolete.

44 McCorquodale, op. cit., n 33, p. 329, 'the role of the individual in [the international legal system] is continuing to expand, often despite the wishes of States'.

45 M. Haas, *International Human Rights: A Comprehensive Introduction*, 2008, Abingdon and New York, NY: Routledge, p. 9,

> A book on international human rights would have been very short indeed *before* the formation of the United Nations in 1945. Today, a textbook on the subject can only provide a foundation or introduction to a vast realm of contemporary reality.

46 See, e.g., Office of the United Nations High Commissioner for Human Rights, *The Core International Human Rights Treaties*, 2006, New York, NY: United Nations.

47 See generally G. Robertson, *Crimes Against Humanity: The Struggle for Global Justice*, 3rd edn, 2006, New York, NY: New Press.
48 See, e.g., C. McLachlan, L. Shore and M. Weiniger, *International Investment Arbitration: Substantive Principles*, 2007, Oxford: Oxford University Press, pp. 45–76; Evans, op. cit., n 33, pp. 315–21.
49 D. J. Bederman, *International Law Frameworks*, 3rd edn, New York, NY: Thomson Reuters/ Foundation Press 2010, p. 81, 'One thing is clear: people certainly do not have the same sets of rights as States do under a classic formulation of international law'.
50 McCorquodale, op. cit., n 33, p. 317, 'Thus, in principle, there is no independent ability for individuals to bring claims before international human rights bodies'.
51 Importantly for present purposes, this clearly includes all international investment treaties.
52 See, e.g., International Covenant on Civil and Political Rights, 1966, Preamble, 'Recognizing that these rights derive from the inherent dignity of the human person'; International Covenant on Economic, Social and Cultural Rights, 1966, 'Recognizing that these rights derive from the inherent dignity of the human person'; Universal Declaration of Human Rights, 1948, Preamble, referring to 'recognition of the inherent dignity and of the equal and inalienable rights of all members of the human family'. I am indebted on this point to discussions with Allen Buchanan.
53 The word 'serious' is, of course, essential here, as only serious violations of international standards constitute violations of the MST. Consequently, the mere fact that a human right has been violated does not entail that the MST has been violated. Nonetheless, the importance of human rights to the international community justifies a conclusion that an act need fall less far below the conduct required by human rights to constitute a violation of the MST, than would be the case for other international standards.
54 *Glamis Gold*, above, n 32, para. 616, 'It therefore appears that, although situations may be more varied and complicated today than in the 1920s, the level of scrutiny is the same. The fundamentals of the Neer standard thus still apply today'; *Cargill, Incorporated v United Mexican States*, ICSID Case No. ARB(AF)/05/2, Award, 2009, para. 286, 'The Tribunal holds that the current customary international law standard ... at least reflects the adaptation of the agreed Neer standard to current conditions'. But see *Merrill & Ring Forestry LP v The Government of Canada*, Award, 2010, para. 213,

> In conclusion, the Tribunal finds that the applicable minimum standard of treatment of investors is found in customary international law and that, except for cases of safety and due process, today's minimum standard is broader than that defined in the *Neer* case and its progeny.

55 See, e.g., Agreement Between the Federal Republic of Germany and the Republic of India for the Promotion and Protection of Investments, 1995, Preamble, 'Recognising the reciprocal protection of such investments under an agreement ... will be conducive to the stimulation of individual business initiative and will increase prosperity in both States'; Treaty Between the United States of America and the People's Republic of Bangladesh Concerning the Reciprocal Encouragement and Protection of Investment, 1989, Preamble, 'Recognizing that agreement upon the treatment to be accorded such investment will stimulate the flow of private capital and the economic development of the Parties'.
56 See subsection 2.2.
57 *Neer*, above, n 8, p. 62.
58 *Merrill & Ring Forestry*, above, n 54, para. 209,

> State practice, with respect to the standard for the treatment of aliens in relation to business, trade and investments, has generally endorsed an open and non-restricted approach to the applicable standard to the treatment of aliens under international law.

59 Convention (IV) relative to the Protection of Civilian Persons in Time of War, 1949.

60 Ibid., Art. 27. See also International Law Commission, *Draft Articles on the Law of Treaties with Commentaries*, 1966, New York, NY: United Nations, p. 267,

> [The International Law Commission] considered that in the international law of to-day the outbreak of hostilities between States must be considered as an entirely abnormal condition, and that the rules governing its legal consequences should not be regarded as forming part of the general rules of international law applicable in the normal relations between States.

61 See subsection 2.2.

62 See generally International Law Commission, *Articles on the Effects of Armed Conflicts on Treaties, with Commentaries*, 2011, New York, NY: United Nations.

63 A. Aust, *Modern Treaty Law and Practice*, 2nd edn, 2007, Cambridge: Cambridge University Press, p. 309, 'historically, treaties were assumed to be abrogated by the outbreak of an armed conflict between the parties'. See also B. A. Boczek, *International Law: A Dictionary*, 2005, Lanham, MD: Scarecrow Press, pp. 345–6; O. Dörr and K. Schmalenbach (eds), *Vienna Convention on the Law of Treaties: A Commentary*, 2012, Berlin: Springer, pp. 1257–8. But see *Society for Propagation of Gospel in Foreign Parts v Town of New Haven*, 21 US 464 (1823),

> We think, therefore, that treaties stipulating for permanent rights, and general arrangements, and professing to aim at perpetuity, and to deal with the case of war as well as of peace, do not cease on the occurrence of war, but are, at most, only suspended while it lasts; and unless they are waived by the parties, or new and repugnant stipulations are made, they revive in their operation at the return of peace.

64 See, e.g., A. Redfern and M. Hunter, *Law and Practice of International Commercial Arbitration*, 4th edn, 2004, London: Sweet & Maxwell, § 1–147, 'It was again the [International Chamber of Commerce] that, in 1953, promoted a new treaty to govern international commercial arbitration'.

65 A. McNair, *Law of Treaties*, 2nd edn, 1961, Oxford: Oxford University Press.

66 Aust, op. cit., n 63, p. 309, 'McNair saw the issue as turning upon the nature and purpose of each treaty, since that was a good indication of the presumed intention of the parties'.

67 Aust, op. cit., n 63, p. 310, 'It should, therefore, be clear that there is no presumption that hostilities, however intensive or prolonged, will necessarily have the effect of terminating or suspending the operation of treaties between the parties to the conflict'.

68 Ibid., p. 309.

69 Ibid., pp. 309–10.

70 Ibid., pp. 309–10.

71 Ibid., p. 309.

72 See, subsection 2.4.

73 International Law Commission, op. cit., n 62.

74 International Law Commission, op. cit., n 62, Art. 5, Commentary, para. 3, 'The Commission rejected the inclusion of a reference to the intention of the parties to the treaty'. Notably, there is also no presumption that treaties *do not* terminate upon commencement of an armed conflict, *contra* Schreuer, op. cit., n 3, p. 2, 'The Draft Articles contain a presumption of continuity of treaties'.

75 International Law Commission, op. cit., n 62, Art. 6, Commentary, para. 1.

76 International Law Commission, op. cit., n 62, Annex, Indicative list of treaties referred to in Art. 7.

77 It might be argued that investment treaties are treaties 'concerning private rights'. See, e.g., International Law Commission, op. cit., n 62, Art. 7, Commentary 48, referring to bilateral investment treaties as 'concerning private rights'. However, while investment treaty provisions granting investors access to investor-State arbitration clearly thereby

incorporate a 'private right', it is far from clear that the substantive treaty provisions investor-State arbitration is intended to enforce are also 'private rights'. They are, rather, the rights of the Home State, even though enforced by the investor. But see Z. Douglas, 'The Hybrid Foundations of Investment Treaty Arbitration', (2003) 74 Brit YB Int'l L 151, p. 191, 'the new rights arising upon the breach of the treaty vest directly in the investor'. Consequently, simply categorising investment treaties as treaties 'concerning private rights' is too simplistic.

78 For a discussion of this type, see Schreuer, op. cit., n 3.

79 On 'indirect expropriation', see generally A. K. Hoffmann, 'Indirect Expropriation', in A. Reinisch (ed.), *Standards of Investment Protection*, 2008, Oxford: Oxford University Press, p. 151; W. M. Reisman and R. D. Sloane, 'Indirect Expropriation and Its Valuation in the BIT Generation', (2003) Brit YB Int'l L 115.

80 United Nations Conference on Trade and Development, *Bilateral Investment Treaties in the Mid-1990s,* 1988, Geneva: UNCTAD, p. 66, 'Indirect expropriation occurs when the country takes an action that substantially impairs the value of an investment without necessarily assuming ownership of the investment'.

81 Hoffmann, op. cit., n 79, p. 151.

82 Reisman and Sloane, op. cit., n 79, pp. 118–19.

83 For a discussion of other requirements, see generally Hoffmann, op. cit., n 79.

84 *Pope & Talbot Inc v The Government of Canada*, Interim Award, 2000, para. 102.

85 Hoffmann, op. cit., n 79, pp. 158–9.

86 *Middle East Cement Shipping and Handling Co SA v Arab Republic of Egypt*, ICSID Case No. ARB/99/6, Award, 2002, para. 107.

87 See also R. Dolzer and M. Stevens, *Bilateral Investment Treaties*, 1995, Leiden: Brill, n 268, stating that 'indirect takings' can occur as a result of sequestration.

5 The history and development of the most-favoured nation clause

1 See A. van Aaken, 'Fragmentation of International Law: The Case of International Investment Protection', (2008) 17 Finnish YB Int'l L 91. On the issue of fragmentation in international law more generally, see particularly the contributions to the Symposium, 'Diversity or Cacophony? New Sources of Norms in International Law?', (2004) 25 Mich J Int'l L 845. See also *Fragmentation of International Law: Difficulties Arising from the Diversification and Expansion of International Law*, Report of the Study Group of the International Law Commission, 58th Session, 1 May–9 June, 3 July–11 August 2006, paras 4–8, UN Doc A/CN.4/L.702, 18 July 2006.

2 F. Spoorenberg and J. Viñuales, 'Conflicting Decisions in International Arbitration', (2009) 8 L & Prac Int'l Cts & Tribs 91; R. Teitel and R. Howse, 'Cross-Judging: Tribunalization in a Fragmented but Interconnected Global Order', (2009) 41 NYU J Int'l L & Pol 959, pp. 977–81.

3 A. K. Bjorklund, 'Private Rights and Public International Law: Why Competition Among International Economic Tribunals Is Not Working', (2007) 59 Hastings LJ 241, pp. 246–7.

4 International Centre for Settlement of Investment Disputes, *The ICSID Caseload – Statistics 10 (2010)*, http://icsid.worldbank.org/ICSID/FrontServlet?requestType=ICSIDDocRH&actionVal=CaseLoadStatistics (accessed 5 February 2012), noting that multilateral treaties have served as the basis for only 11 per cent of all cases brought to ICSID.

5 For example, in the 2010 'OGEMID of the Year' Awards (a survey of international investment arbitration specialists), four of the six decisions nominated for 'Arbitration Decision of the Year' were also nominated for 'Most Surprising or Controversial Arbitration Decision of the Year', OGEMID Awards, Transnational Dispute Management, http://www.transnational-dispute-management.com/ogemidawards/ (accessed 15 March 2012). Similarly, in 2008, the same decision won both categories. Ibid.

6 S. K. Hornbeck, 'The Most-Favored-Nation Clause', (1909) 3 Am J Int'l L 395, p. 395, describing the MFN clause as the 'cornerstone of all modern commercial treaties'; M.-F. Houde, 'Most-Favoured-Nation Treatment in International Investment Law', in Organisation for Economic Co-operation and Development, *International Investment Law: A Changing Landscape*, 2005, Paris: OECD, pp. 127, 129, 'MFN treatment has been a central pillar of trade policy for centuries'; G. Schwarzenberger, 'The Most-Favoured Nation Standard in British State Practice', (1945) 22 Brit YB Int'l L 96, p. 97, 'The m.f.n. standard forms one of the basic standards of international law, and it is not surprising that it can be traced back to the dawn of international law'; J. Viner, 'The Most-Favored-Nation Clause in American Commercial Treaties', (1924) 32 J Pol Econ 101, p. 101, describing the use of MFN clauses as 'a common practice of most nations since the beginning of the seventeenth century'.

7 An MFN clause in an investment treaty may refer to 'investors'. However, it may refer instead to 'investments', or even to both investors and investments. For purposes of simplicity, this chapter refers simply to investors unless the difference between investors and investments is important to the analysis.

8 S. Fietta, 'Most Favoured Nation Treatment and Dispute Resolution Under Bilateral Investment Treaties: A Turning Point?', (2005) 8 Int'l Arb L Rev 131, p. 131, '[S]uch provisions require each contracting State to accord to investors of the other contracting state treatment that is no less favourable than that accorded to the investors of third-states'; see also Schwarzenberger, op. cit., n 6, p. 96, 'Used in its technical sense, the m.f.n. standard may be defined as treatment on a footing not inferior to that of the most favoured third-State'; S. D. Sutton, '*Emilio Augustin Maffezini v Kingdom of Spain* and the ICSID Secretary-General's Screening Power', (2005) 21 Arb Int'l 113, p. 120, 'The principles that apply are that any basic treaty containing the clause could attract provisions of another treaty signed by one of the parties containing elements that are more favourable to the beneficiary. … ' (quoting international investment arbitrator Francisco Orrego Vicuna).

9 S. W. Schill, 'Multilateralizing Investment Treaties Through Most-Favored-Nation Clauses', (2009) 27 Berkeley J Int'l L 496, p. 502,

> MFN clauses oblige the State granting MFN treatment to extend to the beneficiary State the treatment accorded to third-States in case this treatment is more favourable than the treatment under the treaty between the granting State and the beneficiary State.

10 B. Coutain, 'The Unconditional Most-Favored-Nation Clause and the Maintenance of the Liberal Trade Regime in the Postwar 1870s', (2009) 63 Int'l Org 139, p. 146, '[A] bilateral treaty is to a certain extent converted into a multilateral treaty by the unconditional most-favored-nation principle' (internal quotation marks omitted); Houde, op. cit., n 6, p. 129, describing the MFN clause as 'the multilateralisation instrument par excellence of the benefits accorded to foreign investors and their investments' (internal quotation marks and italics omitted).

11 It has occasionally been argued that equality of commercial treatment is a basic principle of international law and so does not need to be secured via a treaty clause. As the early twentieth-century diplomat Culbertson stated:

> [A]s a diplomatic representative of the United States I took the position that … equality of commercial treatment, as it is applied in the most-favored-nation principle … is a right of international common law and that a government has the obligation to grant that equality,

W. S. Culbertson, 'Most-Favored-Nation Treatment', (1937) 31 Proc Am Soc'y Int'l L 73, p. 74; see also A. Mertens, 'A Defense of the Most-Favored-Nation Clause', (1931) 156

Annals Am Acad Pol & Soc Sci 107, p. 109, 'Most-favored-nation treatment is not only a condition of economic equilibrium; it is more and more coming to be identified with the regime of rights'. However, while a useful political stance, this view is ultimately inconsistent with international legal practice. United Nations Conference on Trade and Development, *Most-Favoured-Nation Treatment*, UN Doc UNCTAD/ITE/IIT/10 (Vol. III), UN Sales No. E.99.II.D.11, 1999, Geneva: UNCTAD, p. 2, noting that 'MFN is generally more than the minimum standard required under customary international law'; Houde, op. cit., n 6, p. 129, 'While MFN is a standard of treatment which has been linked by some to the principle of the equality of States, the prevailing view is that a MFN obligation exists only when a treaty clause creates it'; Schwarzenberger, op. cit., n 6, p. 103, '[T]hough widely recognized in treaties by which States grant to each other reciprocal free-dom of commerce, it cannot be admitted that that principle has as yet developed into a rule of customary international law'.

12 As one commentator has noted:

> Thus, if MFN clauses are viewed as having the primary objective of promoting non-discrimination and harmonisation, then an adjudicator may consider that the very purpose of the clause is to permit, indeed encourage, a comparison to other {BITs} to ensure that the most favourable rights, including procedural rights, are available,

E. Whitsitt, 'Application of Most-Favoured-Nation Clauses to the Dispute Settlement Provisions of Bilateral Investment Treaties: An Assessment of the Jurisprudence', (2009) 27 J Energy & Nat Resources L 527, p. 530.

13 See, e.g., UNCTAD, op. cit., n 11, p. 4, 'In other words, the MFN standard seeks to prevent discrimination against investors from foreign countries on grounds of their nationality'; Coutain, op. cit., n 10, p. 146, 'The MFN clause was devised to reduce uncertainty by automatically preventing discrimination against treaty-powers and repetitive treaty renegotiations every time conditions are altered by a new commercial treaty' (internal quotation marks omitted); Hornbeck, op. cit., n 6, p. 398, 'The object sought is uniform treatment without discrimination'; S. W. Schill, 'Most-Favored-Nation Clauses as a Basis of Jurisdiction in Investment Treaty Arbitration: Arbitral Jurisprudence at a Crossroads', (2009) 10 J World Invest & Trade 189, p. 210, '[T]he rationale of MFN clauses consists in creating a level playing field for foreign investors independent of their nationality'.

14 For the purposes of this chapter, teleological interpretation means an interpretation of an MFN clause that is based upon the policy goals the interpreting body believes motivated the clause's adoption.

15 Moreover, portraying MFN clauses as a mechanism for eliminating discrimination ignores the fact that an MFN clause does not prevent discrimination in favour of the beneficiary of the clause, just against it. See, e.g., Schwarzenberger, op. cit., n 6, p. 96, 'M.f.n. treatment does not exclude the grant by the promisor of additional advantages beyond those conceded to the most favored third-State. M.f.n. treatment is compatible with preferential treatment of the beneficiary by the promisor'. Yet surely if the purpose of MFN clauses was to eliminate market discrimination, they would eliminate all discrimination, not just discrimination unfavourable to the beneficiary of the clause.

16 See, e.g., *Siemens AG v Argentine Republic*, ICSID Case No. ARB/02/8, Decision on Jurisdiction, 3 August 2004, paras 108–9, allowing the claimant access to the more favourable aspects of a dispute resolution clause in a third-State treaty, but excluding the less favourable aspects of that clause, on the ground that MFN clauses relate only to more favourable treatment; *Emilio Agustín Maffezini v The Kingdom of Spain*, ICSID Case No. ARB/97/7, Objections to Jurisdiction, 25 January 2000, paras 54–7, holding that MFN clauses apply to dispute resolution procedures on the ground that '[i]nternational arbitration and other dispute settlement arrangements … are essential … to the protection of the rights envisaged under the pertinent treaties'; Schill, op. cit., n 9, pp. 568–9,

'MFN clauses therefore form part of the ongoing process of multilateralizing international investment relations and constitute one of the explicit normative bases of this development'.

17 It is, of course, not being maintained that no previous work has been done on the operation of MFN clauses in international investment law. However, such work as has been done has been focused upon specific issues relating to MFN clauses, rather than addressing the operation of MFN clauses themselves. See, e.g., A. F. Rodriguez, 'The Most-Favored-Nation Clause in International Investment Agreements: A Tool for Treaty Shopping', (2008) 25 J Int'l Arb 89; Schill, op. cit., n 13; R. Teitelbaum, 'Who's Afraid of Maffezini? Recent Developments in the Interpretation of Most Favored Nation Clauses', (2005) 22 J Int'l Arb 225; M. Valenti, 'The Most Favored Nation Clause in BITs as a Basis for Jurisdiction in Foreign Investor-Host State Arbitration', (2008) 24 Arb Int'l 447; S. Vesel, 'Clearing a Path Through a Tangled Jurisprudence: Most-Favored-Nation Clauses and Dispute Settlement Provisions in Bilateral Investment Treaties', (2007) 32 Yale J Int'l L 125.

18 UNCTAD, op. cit., n 11, p. 39, noting that MFN treatment 'is a core principle in international investment agreements'; Fietta, op. cit., n 8, p. 131, 'The vast majority of BITs in force around the world today contain some form of MFN provision'.

19 N. Eliasson, 'Investor-State Arbitration and Chinese Investors: Recent Developments in Light of the Decision on Jurisdiction in the Case *Mr. Tza Yap Shum v The Republic of Peru*', (2009) 2 Contemp Asia Arb J 347, p. 361; see also Houde, op. cit., n 6, p. 158, 'The proper application and interpretation of a particular MFN clause in a particular case requires a careful examination of the text of that provision undertaken in accordance with the treaty interpretation rules as set out in the Vienna Convention'; Schwarzenberger, op. cit., n 6, p. 103, 'It is well to keep in mind the warning voiced by Judge Anzilotti, and more recently by Sir Arnold McNair, that speaking strictly, there is no such thing as the most-favoured-nation clause: every treaty requires independent examination' (footnotes and quotation marks omitted).

20 As noted by one early commentator,

> [t]he parties concerned should clearly express their intention; but it might happen, and indeed it would often happen, that they did not do so. Provision must be made in international law, as in municipal law, for cases in which there was no stipulation in the text, and for cases in which the text was not clear and precise,

Q. Wright, 'The Most-Favored-Nation Clause', (1927) 21 Am J Int'l L 760, p. 762; see also UNCTAD, op. cit., n 11, p. 6, 'There is no evidence that, by using different wording, the parties to these various agreements intended to give the MFN clauses a different scope. Whatever the specific terminology used, it does not change the basic thrust of MFN'; Schwarzenberger, op. cit., n 6, p. 104, 'Though there is no such thing as the m.f.n. clause, it is equally necessary to emphasize that there is such a thing as the m.f.n. standard'. Another commentator emphasises that MFN has become a term of art:

> "MFN" is a term of art in international law and treaty obligations employing this term of art have an ancient pedigree. When state parties enter into modern investment treaties with an MFN clause, they surely do not intend to relegate the received wisdom on the nature, scope and effect of such clauses to the dustbin of history.

Z. Douglas, 'The MFN Clause in Investment Arbitration: Treaty Interpretation Off the Rails', (2011) 2 J Int'l Disp Settlement 97, p. 99.

21 On the relationship between international investment law and public international law, see generally J. Bering, et al., Sub-Committee on Investment Law, International Law Association German Branch, *General Public International Law and International Investment Law – A Research Sketch on Selected Issues*, 2009, Frankfurt: International Law Association German Branch.

22 As throughout the book, Home State is used in this chapter to refer to the State of which a foreign investor is a national.

23 Basic Treaty is used in this chapter to refer to the treaty containing the MFN clause.
24 See, e.g., Schill, op. cit., n 9, p. 512, arguing that the adoption of the MFN clause 'was closely connected to the free trade movement in the Nineteenth and early Twentieth Centuries'.
25 Schwarzenberger, op. cit., n 6, p. 97, referring to '[i]mperial grants of customs privileges to cities within the Holy Roman Empire on the basis of favours obtained "by whatsoever other town"'; see also E. J. Conroy, 'The American Interpretation of the Most Favored Nation Clause', (1926) 12 Cornell LQ 327, p. 338. Conroy notes:

> There had been occasional crude quasi-most favored nation clauses in antiquity, and a few among the commercial cities of the Mediterranean during the Middle Ages, but the clause did not come into any sort of regular use until the seventeenth century, with the rise of the mercantile system, and the bitter competition for trade and colonies that it brought in,

ibid., citations omitted.
26 See, e.g., UNCTAD, op. cit., n 11, p. 14, 'The first example of an MFN clause was when King Henry V of England signed a treaty (Treaty for Mercantile Intercourse with Flanders on 17 August 1417) with Duke John of Burgundy in Amiens. …'; Hornbeck, op. cit., n 6, p. 398, arguing that the use of MFN clauses can be traced to as early as 1226, when Emperor Frederick II of the Holy Roman Empire signed a treaty granting concessions to the citizens of Marseille that had previously only been available to citizens of Pisa and Genoa; Houde, op. cit., n 6, p. 129, claiming the MFN clause 'can be traced back to the twelfth century, although the phrase seems to have first appeared in the seventeenth century'; Schwarzenberger, op. cit., n 6, p. 97, '[T]he principles of m.f.n. and national treatment make their first appearance in international law proper in the commercial treaties concluded during the twelfth century between England and the Continental powers and cities'.
27 See Coutain, op. cit., n 10, p. 139, asserting that by the nineteenth century use of the MFN clause was central enough to international commerce that it can be viewed as having had a primary role in 'the maintenance of a liberal world economy in the turbulent 1870s'.
28 Hornbeck, op. cit., n 6, p. 395, 'The phrase "most-favoured-nation" first appeared in commercial treaties toward the close of the seventeenth century'; J. M. Kline and R. D. Ludema, 'Building a Multilateral Framework for Investment: Comparing the Development of Trade and Investment Accords', (1997) 6 Transnat'l Corp 1, p. 6, 'The term "most favoured nation" appears to have originated with the 1692 treaty between Denmark and the Hanse cities'.
29 'Draft Articles on Most-Favoured-Nation Clauses', *Yearbook of the International Law Commission 1978*, Vol II, Pt Two, New York, NY: United Nations, pp. 16, 30, UN Doc A/CN.4/SER.A/1978/Add.1, http://untreaty.un.org/ilc/publications/yearbooks/Ybkvolumes(e)/ILC_1978_v2_p2_e.pdf (accessed 5 February 2012) (hereinafter Draft Articles).
30 Ibid., p. 53, 'A most-favoured-nation clause, unless otherwise agreed, obviously attracts benefits extended to a third-State both before and after the entry into force of the treaty containing the clause'; Committee of Experts for the Progressive Codification of International Law, Report of the Sub-Committee, *The Most-Favoured-Nation Clause*, League of Nations Doc C.205.M.79 1927 V (1927), reprinted in (1928) 22 Am J Int'l L (Special Supplement) 133, p. 134 (hereinafter Committee of Experts), '"[T]he provision known as the most-favoured-nation clause was devised to ensure to the contracting States not only the benefit of concessions previously made but also of those subsequently to be made by either of the contracting States"' (quoting W. S. Culbertson, (1925) Int'l Econ Pol 56).
31 Hornbeck, op. cit., n 6, pp. 399–400,

> In the beginning, this extension of favors was made but to one or two specified states. … The next step was to extend the advantages to include such favors as should be granted to certain other specified nations; then to include advantages granted to any nation whatsoever.

32 Hornbeck, op. cit., n 6, p. 401, 'During the nineteenth century, the use of the clause increased and became so common, in one or another of its various forms, that its appearance came to be looked upon almost as a matter of course'; Houde, op. cit., n 6, p. 129, 'MFN treaty clauses spread with the growth of commerce in the fifteenth and sixteenth centuries'; Schill, op. cit., n 9, p. 509, '[T]he function of MFN clauses changed under the influence of mercantilist ideology in the course of the Seventeenth and Eighteenth Centuries'.

33 Conroy, op. cit., n 25, p. 330, 'The [bilateral clause] is the regular form; the unilateral clause is exceptional, and its presence indicates a position of hopeless inferiority in the promisor nation'.

34 UNCTAD, op. cit., n 11, p. 13, 'It was only in the seventeenth century that the point of reference for MFN was no longer a limited number of named countries, but any third-state'; Schwarzenberger, op. cit., n 6, p. 97, 'The privileges granted to the beneficiary are no longer necessarily defined with reference to one or several specifically named countries. … '.

35 Committee of Experts, op. cit., n 30, p. 134, '"[T]he provision known as the most-favoured-nation clause was devised to ensure to the contracting States not only the benefit of concessions previously made but also those subsequently to be made by either of the contracting States"' (quoting Culbertson, op. cit., n 30, p. 56); R. Pomfret, *The Economics of Regional Trading Arrangements*, 1997, Oxford: Clarendon Press, p. 17, 'The instrument for ensuring that tariff reduction was accomplished by diminishing discrimination among trading partners was the inclusion of the most-favoured-nation clause in commercial treaties'.

36 Pomfret, ibid., p. 33,

> Between 1860 and 1930 the principle of non-discrimination governed the commercial policies of the major trading nations. … At the same time, there were frequent deviations from non-discriminatory policies [that] … provided evidence of governments viewing discriminatory trade policies as serving national purposes;

R. Pahre, 'Most-Favored-Nation Clauses and Clustered Negotiations', (2001) 55 Int'l Org 859,p. 873, arguing that 'MFN must be understood as a regime norm chosen for political reasons independent of the tariff bargaining problem'.

37 Tactical use of MFN clauses can, of course, also be seen in later periods and in the treaty practices of other States. Moreover, MFN clauses have at times even been used as a tactical tool for exerting purely political pressure, rather than merely gaining economic advantage. See, e.g., T. C. Sorensen, 'Most-Favored-Nation and Less Favorite Nations', (1974) 52 Foreign Aff 273, p. 273, discussing a bill proposed to the US Congress that would

> deny to any "nonmarket economy country" eligibility for most-favored-nation tariff treatment … during any period in which that country denies to its citizens the right or opportunity to emigrate, specifically by imposing more than a nominal tax or other charge.

38 Conroy, op. cit., n 25, pp. 337–8,

> The introduction and rise of the conditional form of the clause was due to … an attempt by the United States to break down the impossible tariffs and ironclad monopolies which the mercantile system, then at its height, had established in Europe.

39 Conroy, op. cit., n 25, p. 339.

40 Conroy, op. cit., n 25, p. 339.

41 That the United States' approach to the MFN clause arose from its concern with control over its negotiating positions, rather than a protectionist opposition to low tariffs, is indicated by the fact that even while insisting on the use of conditional MFN clauses,

the United States was quite liberal in its voluntary reductions in tariffs. C. Kreider, 'The Most-Favored-Nation Clause', (1949) 39 Am Econ Rev 1039, p. 1041 (book review).

42 The earliest known conditional MFN clause appeared in a treaty concluded between the United States and France in 1778. Pomfret, op. cit., n 35, p. 18, 'From its first commercial treaty, with France in 1778, until 1923 the USA maintained that MFN pledges must be interpreted as conditional, even when the precise wording of a treaty was unclear'; R. Snyder, 'The MFN Clause and Recent Trade Practices', (1940) 55 Pol Sci Q 77, p. 79.

43 M. Hilf and R. Geiß, 'Most Favoured Nation Clause', in *Max Planck Encyclopedia of Public International Law*, 2010, Oxford: Oxford University Press, Online Edition, para. 13, http://www.mpepil.com (accessed at September 2009 website update) (search for 'Most Favoured-Nation Clause' in the search box) (subscribers only),

> Until the late 18th century the clause was exclusively drafted in an unconditional manner, [i.e.] the right to most-favoured-nation treatment would inure automatically as soon as a third-State was more favourably treated than the beneficiary State with regard to the subject matter comprised by the clause.

44 Committee of Experts, op. cit., n 30, pp. 135–6.

45 C. L. Jones, 'The American Interpretation of the "Most Favored Nation" Clause', (1908) 32 Annals Am Acad Pol & Soc Sci 119, p. 123, 'Even when the second nation offers the same nominal concessions as given by the first it cannot secure identical treatment under the clause unless the treaty-making power considers the second sacrifice actually equal to the first'; Hilf and Geiß, op. cit., n 43, para. 14.

46 Conroy, op. cit., n 25, p. 336, 'The claiming of a favour under the conditional clause necessitates a great deal of negotiation'; Jones, op. cit., n 45, p. 122, 'What is the character of the concessions which will be considered an equivalent is to be left entirely to the treaty-making powers of the respective states. The mutual concessions are "to be honorably determined by the governments concerned"'; Viner, op. cit., n 6, p. 122,

> The grantor of concession to one country for compensation is itself the judge of the equivalent compensation offered for the same concessions by other countries. If it does not wish to extend its concession to third countries, it need only deny the equivalence of the compensation offered.

47 See, e.g., the statement made by John Jay to Congress in 1787, that

> [w]here a privilege is gratuitously granted, the nation to whom it is granted becomes in respect to that privilege a favored nation ... but where the privilege is not gratuitous, but rests on compact, in such case the favor, if any there be, does not consist in the privilege yielded, but in the consent to make the contract by which it is yielded. ... The favor, therefore, of being admitted to make a similar bargain, is all that in such cases can reasonably be demanded under the article.

Viner, op. cit., n 6, p. 104, citing S. B. Crandall, *Treaties, Their Making and Enforcement*, 2nd edn, 1916, Washington, DC: John Byrne & Co, pp. 404–5; see also Hornbeck, op. cit., n 6, p. 408, 'The United States argued for a more specific equivalent, saying that if they were to give France freely that for which England had paid, France would be enjoying a treatment more favored that [sic] that of the most-favored nation'.

48 In the words of the US Minister to Argentina in 1897:

> It is clearly evident that the object sought in all the varying forms of expression [of MFN clauses] is equality of international treatment, protection against the wilful preference of the commercial interests of one nation over another. But the allowance of

> the same privileges and the same sacrifice of revenue duties to a nation which makes no compensation that had been conceded to another nation for an adequate compensation instead of maintaining destroys that equality, which the "most favored nation" clause was intended to secure.

Jones, op. cit., n 45, p. 123, citing J. B. Moore, *A Digest of International Law*, Vol 5, 1906, Washington, DC: US Government Printing Office, p. 278.

49 See, e.g., H. Hauser, 'The Most-Favored-Nation Clause: A Menace to World Peace', (1931) 156 Annals Am Acad Pol & Soc Sci 101, p. 103,

> [T]he United States maintains that the rule of reciprocity does not preclude the granting of special favors to contiguous states, i.e. to Canada and Mexico, nor does it prevent the United States from granting whatever privileges it desires to its "protectorates" in the Caribbean.

50 See Schill, op. cit., n 9, p. 511, noting that conditional MFN clauses 'prevailed in Europe until 1860'. This is not to say, however, that the Europeans did not have objections to the way in which they were used by the United States. One commentator, for instance, notes that:

> European countries, irritated by the repeated refusals of the United States to acknowledge obligations under its most-favored-nation pledges and by the extraordinary heights to which American protectionism was carrying import duties on European products, began to denounce their most-favored-nation treaties with the United States, to consent to new tariff arrangements only on a temporary basis, and openly and otherwise to discriminate in their customs legislation against American products,

Viner, op. cit., n 6, pp. 126–7.

51 See Pomfret, op. cit., n 35, p. 18, 'The sole important practitioner of conditional MFN treatment was the United States'; Hornbeck, op. cit., n 6, pp. 405–6, 'This form appears in most of the treaties of the United States. ... [T]he special limiting clause which expresses the American idea and forms the basis of the American interpretation was first inserted in treaties made by the United States'. Other countries have also made significant use of the conditional MFN clause. See, e.g., Committee of Experts, op. cit., n 30, p. 37, noting the use of the conditional MFN clause in Latin America. For excellent coverage of Japan's practice with regard to the MFN clause, see generally S. Murase, 'The Most-Favored-Nation Treatment in Japan's Treaty Practice During the Period 1854–1905', (1976) 70 Am J Int'l L 273.

52 See generally V. G. Setser, 'Did Americans Originate the Conditional Most-Favored-Nation Clause?', (1933) 5 J Mod Hist 319, presenting the evidence supporting the view that the conditional MFN clause in the treaty was originally proposed by France, not the United States; Pahre, op. cit., n 36, p. 873, noting that France wanted a conditional MFN clause in the Franco-American commercial convention in order 'to keep Britain isolated from the rest of Europe' and 'avoid the suggestion that it was fighting a war of aggrandizement'.

53 Schill, op. cit., n 9, p. 511, noting that the conditional MFN clause 'also prevailed in Europe until 1860'.

54 Pomfret, op. cit., n 35, p. 17, 'In Europe the conditional form was often used between 1820 and 1860, but was similar in effect to unconditional MFN treatment because of the prevalence of single-schedule tariffs and rarity of special concessions'.

55 Pomfret, op. cit., n 35, p. 17, noting that 'a single treaty with an unconditional clause rendered inoperative any conditionality in MFN clauses of treaties involving the same countries'; see also Schwarzenberger, op. cit., n 6, p. 102; Viner, op. cit., n 6, p. 119.

56 Notably, it was not just the treaty-making powers of the United States that underwrote the consistency of the US adoption of the conditional MFN clause. The US Supreme

Court also interpreted ambiguously drafted MFN clauses in treaties as constituting conditional forms of the clause. See, e.g., *Whitney v Robertson*, 124 US 190, 192–3 (1888).

57 Pomfret, op. cit., n 35, p. 18.

58 See, e.g., O. Accominotti and M. Flandreau, 'Bilateral Treaties and the Most-Favored-Nation Clause: The Myth of Trade Liberalization in the Nineteenth Century', (2008) 60 World Pol 147, p. 150, 'British negotiators felt that MFN would enable Britain to rely on France to make concessions to third parties; and Britain in turn would benefit without making further concessions itself'; Hauser, op. cit., n 49, p. 101, describing the incorporation of an MFN clause into a Franco-German treaty as having 'a purely protectionist origin'; Jones, op. cit., n 45, p. 126, noting England's endorsement of the view that imposing higher tariffs on imports subsidised by a foreign government did not violate MFN clauses, as it merely eliminated a form of competitive discrimination introduced by the foreign government in question; Pahre, op. cit., n 36, p. 867, noting that in 1881 Britain terminated renegotiation of a treaty with France because France had refused to give Britain the tariff reductions it sought, and Britain hoped to gain the same reductions automatically through the application of an MFN clause in the British-French treaty to a French-Belgian treaty that was under negotiation.

59 See, e.g., the 'Swiss Cow' case, in which Germany granted a tariff reduction for cows raised above a certain elevation, even if there was no other difference between the cows in question, discussed in the Draft Articles, op. cit., n 29, pp. 31–2. This allowed Germany to provide benefits to Switzerland while not extending them to Denmark. Ibid.

60 Committee of Experts, op. cit., n 30, pp. 143–4,

> In order to be able to confer a favour upon certain selected districts or persons, or respecting particular objects, without extending it to all States with which the favouring nation has treaties containing most-favoured-nation clauses, resort is sometimes had to conditions or limitations imposed upon the favour, which those whom it is designed to benefit will meet but which will exclude all others;

Viner, op. cit., n 6, p. 109, noting the use of 'specialization', or 'the fine classification of commodities and rates in tariff schedules' as a means of avoiding the impact of MFN clauses.

61 Pahre, op. cit., n 36, p. 886, noting an instance in 1891 in which Austria and Germany kept tariff concessions secret until negotiations with Italy, Switzerland and Belgium were completed.

62 Pahre, op. cit., n 36, pp. 867, 883–4.

63 Pomfret, op. cit., n 35, p. 20, 25, 'Between 1870 and 1914 trade became less free and discrimination became more common. … On the whole the decade after Versailles continued the post-1870 trend of increasing tolerance for discriminatory trade policies'; see also Hauser, op. cit., n 49, p. 102, 'From about 1880 to 1914, this clause embittered the relations of France with practically every foreign power. … '.

64 Pomfret, op. cit., n 35, p. 27; Hauser, op. cit., n 49, p. 102.

65 Hilf and Geiß, op. cit., n 43, para. 17, noting that despite a decline in the use of MFN clauses in the immediate aftermath of the First World War, the clause soon became a common feature again in commercial treaties. But see L. M. Sears, 'The Most-Favored-Nation Clause', (1949) 262 Annals Am Acad Pol & Soc Sci 196, p. 196 (book review), noting that as of 1949 'the importance of the clause has diminished'.

66 Culbertson, op. cit., n 11, p. 77.

67 Pomfret, op. cit., n 35, p. 23, 'The United States, with the conditional MFN bargaining tool, received less favourable treatment for exports to continental Europe than did free trade Britain, which had nothing to offer in return for MFN treatment'; Viner, op. cit., n 6, p. 125, noting the United States' failure to secure favourable tariff treatment through the use of conditional MFN clauses.

68 See Committee of Experts, op. cit., n 30, p. 137, asserting that '[t]he unconditional form is practically universal now'.

69 Conroy, op. cit., n 25, p. 329, '[T]he most favored nation clause is a sort of residual clause covering all favors not otherwise provided for; but the chief purpose in practice, and the only purpose of any importance, is to govern tariff relations'.

70 Conroy, op. cit., n 25, p. 329, noting that 95 per cent of claims made under MFN clauses are for tariff reductions. However, there was some early recognition that MFN clauses would ultimately come to have importance within the field of foreign investment. See, e. g., Wright, op. cit., n 20, p. 761, 'It thus seems probable that as opportunities for foreign investment by their nationals become a more important interest of states, they will make efforts to assure most-favored-nation treatment in this regard'.

71 UNCTAD, op. cit., n 11, p. 1, 'The most-favoured-nation treatment (MFN) standard is a core element of international investment agreements'; G. Egli, 'Don't Get Bit: Addressing ICSID's Inconsistent Application of Most-Favored-Nation Clauses to Dispute Resolution Provisions', (2007) 34 Pepp L Rev 1045, p. 1065, noting that MFN clauses have increasingly become a common feature of international investment policy; Houde, op. cit., n 6, p. 158, referring to the prevalent use of MFN clauses in investment treaties; E. Kunstek, 'Procedural Effects of BITs' Most Favoured Nation Clauses on ICSID Arbitration', (2008) 15 Croatian Arb YB 97, p. 98, noting that almost all BITs contain MFN clauses.

72 See Houde, op. cit., n 6, p. 142, n 36, '"[The MFN clause] contributes greatly to the rationalization of the treaty-making process and leads to the automatic self-revision of treaties which are based on the most-favoured-nation standard"' (quoting G. Schwarzenberger, *International Law as Applied by International Courts and Tribunals*, Vol 1, 1957, London: Sweet & Maxwell, p. 243).

73 As throughout this book, Host State is used in this chapter to refer to the State in which a foreign investment is made.

74 A. Newcombe and L. Paradell, *Law and Practice of Investment Treaties: Standards of Treatment*, 2009, Alphen aan den Rijn: Kluwer Law International, p. 11, 'By the early 1900s, there was general agreement amongst international lawyers in Europe and the US that there existed a minimum standard of justice in the treatment of foreigners'.

75 Sutton, op. cit., n 8, p. 119,

> Many states entered into treaties (sometimes called "capitulations") with Asian and African states as the result of which subjects, when entering into the territory of Asian and African states, remained wholly under the jurisdiction of their Home states, and their consuls exercised jurisdiction over their fellow subjects.

76 A. T. Guzman, 'Why LDCs Sign Treaties that Hurt Them: Explaining the Popularity of Bilateral Investment Treaties', (1998) 38 Va J Int'l L 639, p. 641,

> In the years that followed World War II, however, developing countries questioned the Hull Rule, claiming the right to determine how they would treat investors and the standard of compensation that should apply if that treatment was sufficiently harmful. This challenge to the Hull Rule proved successful, and by the mid 1970s (and perhaps sooner), the Hull Rule had ceased to be a rule of customary international law.

77 Newcombe and Paradell, op. cit., n 74, pp. 18–19,

> Disputes over the treatment of foreign investment increased and intensified after WWII as the process of decolonization resulted in colonial territories becoming states. Many of these newly independent states, along with the Eastern European communist states, adopted socialist economic policies, including large scale nationalizations of key sectors of their economies.

78 R. Dolzer and M. Stevens, *Bilateral Investment Treaties*, 1995, Leiden: Brill, pp. 10–11. The first ever BIT was concluded between Germany and Pakistan on 25 November 1959.

United Nations Conference on Trade and Development, *The Entry into Force of Bilateral Investment Treaties (BITs), IIA Monitor, no 3*, 2006, Geneva: UNCTAD, p. 3, UN Doc UNCTAD/WEB/ITE/IIA/2006/9. For a short but useful account of the historical development of the contemporary BIT regime, see Egli, op. cit., n 71, pp. 1048–53.

79 A. R. Parra, 'Applicable Law in Investor-State Arbitration', in A. W. Rovine (ed.), *Contemporary Issues in International Arbitration and Mediation*, 2008, Leiden: Brill, p. 7,

> Nowadays, almost all of the ICSID Convention cases that are being initiated concern such treaty claims. The tribunals have, in these newer cases, all applied to the merits of the disputes the provisions of the underlying treaties, as well as general international law rules.

80 J. Boone, 'How Developing Countries Can Adapt Current Bilateral Investment Treaties to Provide Benefits to Their Domestic Economies', (2011) 1 Global Bus L Rev 187, p. 190,

> [A]lmost all of these treaties provide ADR provisions that allow states to bring claims regarding the interpretation or application of a treaty provision as well as allow investors to bring claims against states for treaty violations, often referred to as investor-State Arbitration;

S. D. Franck, 'The Nature and Enforcement of Investor Rights Under In-vestment Treaties: Do Investment Treaties Have a Bright Future?', (2005) 12 UC Davis J Int'l L & Pol'y 47, pp. 53–4,

> BITs also provide procedural rights that permit the enforcement of the substantive rights. ... [I]nvestors can directly bring a claim against a Sovereign for violation of a treaty, functioning in a manner similar to private attorneys general in the protection of the public interest.

81 J. W. Salacuse and N. P. Sullivan, 'Do BITs Really Work? An Evaluation of Bilateral Investment Treaties and Their Grand Bargain', (2005) 46 Harv Int'l LJ 67, p. 67.

82 It should be emphasised, however, that this statement does not mean that encouraging foreign investment is the only purpose of BITs, or that it means the purpose of a BIT is to encourage foreign investment of any type under any circumstances. Such an expansive interpretation of the object and purpose of BITs would lead to precisely the type of teleological reasoning criticised in this chapter with respect to the interpretation of MFN clauses.

83 UNCTAD collects an extensive index of investment treaties, many available in full text and in more than one language: United Nations Conference on Trade and Development, Investment Instruments Online, http://www.unctadxi.org/templates/DocSearch____779.aspx (accessed 16 March 2012).

84 Of course, it is always possible that a particularly incompetent treaty-negotiating team will not be aware of the investment treaties already signed by the State with which they are negotiating. But given the easy accessibility of such information, it would be unreasonable to presume such ignorance absent clear evidence.

85 This does not mean, of course, that there will be no natural limits on the favourability of treatment included in a BIT. After all, if the BIT imposes equivalent obligations on both States party to it, then one State may be willing to accept less favourable treatment than is already being received by another State, simply because it is itself unwilling to grant that more favourable treatment.

86 See UNCTAD, op. cit., n 11, p. 13, 'With regard to investment, the development of MFN became common in the 1950s with the conclusion of international investment agreements, including BITs. The MFN standard was included in such treaties from the beginning. ... '; Houde, op. cit., n 6, p. 130, 'The inclusion of MFN clauses became a

general practice in the numerous bilateral, regional and multilateral investment-related agreements which were concluded after the [Havana] Charter failed to come into force in 1950'.

87 UNCTAD, op. cit., n 11, p. 2, noting that exceptions in MFN clauses in international investment agreements are usually only applied in 'explicitly-recognized' policy areas such as taxation and intellectual property; P. Acconci, 'Most-Favoured-Nation Treatment', in P. Muchlinski, et al. (eds), *The Oxford Handbook of International Investment Law*, 2008, Oxford: Oxford University Press, pp. 368–9, noting that generally, MFNs in investment treaties are 'unrestricted' and 'un-limited *ratione materiae*, *ratione personae*, and *ratione temporis*', but that in some treaties there are exceptions and reservations.

88 See UNCTAD, op. cit., n 11, p. 4, 'MFN applies both in the trade and the investment fields. However, contrary to trade, where the MFN standard only applies to measures at the border, there are many more possibilities to discriminate against foreign investment'.

89 G. Van Harten and M. Loughlin, 'Investment Treaty Arbitration as a Species of Global Administrative Law', (2006) 17 Eur J Int'l L 121, p. 146, arguing that the substantive impact of BITs on a State's traditional regulatory activities is so broad that investment arbitration can properly be characterised as a form of administrative review of State action.

90 Moreover, there is clear empirical evidence that widespread application of MFN clauses to tariff schedules provides benefits to countries of all sizes and economic power. See, e.g., K. Saggi, 'The MFN Clause, Welfare, and Multilateral Cooperation Between Countries of Unequal Size', (2009) 88 J Dev Econ 132, pp. 132–3; see also M. Ghosh, et al., 'Developing-Country Benefits from MFN Relative to Regional / Bilateral Trade Arrangements', (2003) 11 Rev Int'l Econ 712, p. 726, '[S]mall countries are better off under the MFN as it does not allow bilateral bargaining'; K. Saggi and F. Sengul, 'On the Emergence of an MFN Club: Equal Treatment in an Unequal World', (2009) 42 Can J Econ 267, p. 269, 'We find that the formation of an MFN club enhances aggregate world welfare, and the larger the club, the more desirable it is from a welfare perspective'. Similar evidence has yet to be generated with respect to MFN clauses in investment treaties.

91 See generally UNCTAD, op. cit., n 11, p. 1, 'The MFN standard may also have implications for Host countries' room for manoeuvre in respect of future investment agreements, because it can create a so-called "free rider" situation'; E. Chalamish, 'The Future of Bilateral Investment Treaties: A De Facto Multilateral Agreement?', (2009) 34 Brook J Int'l L 303, p. 305, 'Through their inclusion of most-favored-nation ("MFN") clauses, these agreements form a complex network that resembles a de facto multilateral agreement'; Van Harten and Loughlin, op. cit., n 89, p. 146, noting that because of the broad scope of BITs, 'arbitrators rule on the legality of state conduct, evaluate the fairness of governmental decision-making, determine the appropriate scope and content of property rights, and allocate risks and costs between business and society'.

92 Committee of Experts, op. cit., n 30, p. 133.

93 Ibid.

94 E. Ustor, 'First Report on the Most-Favoured Nation Clause', *Yearbook of the International Law Commission 1969*, New York, NY: United Nations, pp. 157, 159, UN Doc A/CN.4/213.

95 Draft Articles, op. cit., n 29, p. 16; see also Houde, op. cit., n 6, p. 139, 'In 1978, the ILC adopted the Draft Articles on Most-Favoured-Nation Clauses and recommended to the General Assembly of the United Nations that they be used for a Convention on the subject'.

96 Houde, op. cit., n 6, p. 139, 'The General Assembly did not act upon this recommendation and took no substantive action on the draft articles'; see also S. Zamora, 'International Relations and Development', in C. C. Joyner (ed.), *The United Nations and International Law*, 1997, Cambridge: Cambridge University Press, pp. 232, 239.

97 Houde, op. cit., n 6, p. 139, 'In determining to proceed with the project, the ILC acknowledged the importance of the role of the most-favoured-nation treatment obligation in the sphere of international trade'.

98 See Newcombe and Paradell, op. cit., n 74, p. 47, 'The end of the 1980s and the 1990s witnessed an exponential growth in the conclusion of international investment and trade treaties. BITs quintupled during the 1990s'.
99 Report of the International Law Commission, 61st Session, 4 May–5 June, 7 July–7 August 2009, paras 208, 211–12, 216, UN Doc A/64/10; GAOR, 64th Session, Supp No. 10 (2009). The centrality of the impact of MFN clauses on dispute resolution in investment arbitration is made clear through the ILC's research programme's incorporation of the topic of 'The Maffezini Problem under Investment Treaties', under the supervision of co-rapporteur Rohan Perera, ibid., para. 216.
100 *Anglo-Iranian Oil Co (UK v Iran)*, Judgment on Jurisdiction, 22 July 1952, [1952] ICJ 93.
101 Ibid., p. 97.
102 Ibid., pp. 97–8.
103 Ibid., pp. 95–6.
104 ICJ Statute, Art. 36. For a useful short account of ICJ jurisdiction, see R. Szafarz, *The Compulsory Jurisdiction of the International Court of Justice*, 1993, Dordrecht: Martinus Nijhoff, pp. 3–14.
105 ICJ Statute, Art. 36(1).
106 *Anglo-Iranian Oil Co*, above, n 100, pp. 98–101.
107 Ibid., p. 95; see also Szafarz, op. cit., n 104, discussing compulsory jurisdiction of the ICJ in both case law and treaty law.
108 ICJ Statute, Art. 36(2), (4).
109 *Anglo-Iranian Oil Co*, above, n 100, pp. 103–4. Ibid.
110 *Anglo-Iranian Oil Co*, above, n 100, pp. 103–4.
111 Ibid., pp. 108–10.
112 Ibid., p. 108.
113 Ibid., p. 110.
114 Ibid., p. 110.
115 Ibid., pp. 108–10.
116 G. M. Danilenko, *Law-Making in the International Community*, 1993, Dordrecht: Martinus Nijhoff, p. 58, 'According to the prevailing opinion, the sovereign equality of states excludes any automatic effect of treaties on third-States which remain for them *res inter alios acta*'. Indeed, the doctrine was explicitly cited by the Court in its decision in *Anglo-Iranian Oil Co*, above, n 100, pp. 103–10.
117 *Anglo-Iranian Oil Co*, above, n 100, pp. 108–10.
118 Ibid., pp. 108–10.
119 See, e.g., Douglas, op. cit., n 20, p. 101.
120 One final important point regarding this case is worth noting, as it is far from clear that the ICJ did not actually have jurisdiction over the United Kingdom's claim through the operation of the MFN clauses in the Basic Treaties. Fatally for its claim, the United Kingdom had attempted to rely upon Iran's consent to the compulsory jurisdiction of the ICJ. Had the United Kingdom attempted instead to bring its claim under the consensual jurisdiction of the ICJ, alleging that the MFN clauses in the Basic Treaties incorporated Iranian consent to the jurisdiction of the ICJ, the Court's argument rejecting jurisdiction would not have been applicable. The ICJ may, as a result, have upheld its jurisdiction over the United Kingdom's claim.
121 *Rights of Nationals of the United States of America in Morocco (US v France)*, Judgment, 27 August 1952, [1952] ICJ 176.
122 Ibid., pp. 178–81; see also K. H. Nadelmann, 'American Consular Jurisdiction in Morocco and the Tangier International Jurisdiction', (1955) 49 Am J Int'l L 506, providing an informative account of US law on consular jurisdiction, with a particular focus on Morocco.
123 *Rights of Nationals of the United States*, above, n 121, p. 184.
124 Ibid., p. 180.
125 Ibid., pp. 190–1.
126 Ibid., p. 190.

127 Ibid., p. 191. Even today, it is indeed quite common for MFN clauses to be described as functioning via a form of 'incorporation by reference'. See, e.g., *Plama Consortium Limited v Republic of Bulgaria*, ICSID Case No. ARB/03/24, Decision on Jurisdiction, 8 February 2005, para. 229. However, contemporary uses of this phrase do not contradict the ICJ's view that incorporation ends once the more favourable treatment is no longer provided to the third-State, but instead merely express the view that MFN clauses incorporate by reference presently existing treatment. Nonetheless, as Douglas has argued, even contemporary uses of the phrase 'incorporation by reference' are troubled, as they simply do not accurately describe the manner in which MFN clauses work. Douglas, op. cit., n 20, pp. 105–8.

128 In 1928, the Committee of Experts for the Progressive Codification of International Law noted that there was 'a difference of opinion' as to whether a benefit gained via an MFN clause terminates once the more favourable treatment is no longer provided to the third-State. Committee of Experts, op. cit., n 30, p. 140. However, in line with the ICJ's decision in this case, the rapporteur concluded that the benefit should indeed be understood to terminate when the treatment on which it is based terminates. Ibid.

129 *Rights of Nationals of the United States*, above, n 121, p. 192.

130 *Ambatielos Claim (Greece v UK)* [1956] 12 RIAA 83. The *Ambatielos* decision was not an ICJ decision or a decision of any other regularly constituted international tribunal, but rather the result of a State-State arbitration between the United Kingdom and Greece. Nonetheless, the reasoning of the tribunal has proven persuasive to subsequent tribunals, and its holding has been uniformly adopted by international investment tribunals as reflecting a reality of the operation of MFN clauses. See, e.g., *Siemens*, above, n 16, paras 100–2; *Maffezini*, above, n 16, Award on Jurisdiction, paras 48–53; *National Grid PLC v Argentine Republic*, UN Commission on International Trade Law, Decision on Jurisdiction, 20 June 2006, paras 83–9, http://italaw.com/documents/NationalGrid-Jurisdiction-En.pdf (accessed 5 February 2013).

131 It should be emphasised that the *Ambatielos* tribunal did not invent the *ejusdem generis* principle, which was already recognised as applicable to the operation of MFN clauses. See, e.g., Schwarzenberger, op. cit., n 6, p. 108, 'For practical purposes it is essen-tial to bear in mind the exact scope of each particular m.f.n. clause; for m.f.n. treatment can only be claimed with respect to favours *ejusdem generis* granted by the promisor to third-States'. However, the tribunal's use of the principle has come to be a standard reference for understanding its operation in international law.

132 *Ambatielos*, above, n 130, p. 107.

133 Ibid., p. 91. For excellent overviews of the facts behind the *Ambatielos* award and the reasoning of the award itself, see, e.g., K. Lipstein, 'The Ambatielos Case. Last Phase', (1957) 6 Int'l & Comp LQ 643; S. E. K. Hulme, 'The Ambatielos Case', (1957) 1 Melb U L Rev 64; D. H. N. Johnson, 'The Ambatielos Case', (1956) 19 Mod L Rev 510.

134 *Ambatielos*, above, n 130, pp. 91–3.

135 Ibid., pp. 93–4, 100.

136 Ibid., p. 94.

137 Ibid., p. 94.

138 Ibid., p. 94.

139 Ibid., p. 94, stating that the diplomatic negotiations were commenced in 1925 and were unsuccessfully resumed in 1949 after being interrupted by the Second World War.

140 *Ambatielos*, above, n 130, p. 94, stating that Greece finally brought the claim before the ICJ on 9 April 1951.

141 *Ambatielos Case (Greece v UK)*, Judgment, 19 May 1953, [1953] ICJ 10, p. 17.

142 *Ambatielos*, above, n 130, p. 106.

143 Ibid., pp. 105–6.

144 Ibid., p. 106, quoting the Treaty of Commerce and Navigation, Great Britain-Greece, Art. X, 10 November 1886, [1886] UKTS 08252.

145 Ibid., pp. 106–7; see also Houde, op. cit., n 6, p. 127, 'The *ejusdem generis* principle provides that an MFN clause can attract the more favourable treatment available in other

treaties only in regard to the "same subject matter," the "same category of matter," or the "same class of matter"'.

146 *Ambatielos*, above, n 130, p. 107.

147 Ibid., pp. 109–10.

148 This constraint can be seen as a development of the holding in *Anglo-Iranian Oil Co*, above, n 100. See subsection 4.1.

149 *Contra* Schill, op. cit., n 9, p. 502, arguing that MFN clauses 'ensure equal treatment between the State benefiting from MFN treatment and any third-State'.

150 It should, however, be emphasised that the constraint placed by the *ejusdem generis* principle actually relates not to the subject matter of the treaty, but to that of the clause. However, where the clause itself provides no clear *ejusdem generis* limitation, the nature of the treaty in which it is contained can do so, as it provides the context in which the clause must be interpreted. Houde, op. cit., n 6, pp. 142–3.

151 R. Howse and E. Chalamish, 'The Use and Abuse of WTO Law in Investor-State Arbitration: A Reply to Jürgen Kurtz', (2009) 20 Eur J Int'l L 1087, p. 1088, '[A]ny attempt to merge trade and investment jurisprudence should not ignore the unique characteristics of the investment law regime'.

6 The operation of the most-favoured nation clause in international investment law

1 The word 'generally' is important here. As the discussion shows, there can be cases in which an MFN clause should be seen as applying to a specific example of pre-existing treatment.

2 It should be emphasised that the effect of an MFN clause is only unidirectional. That is, since only State B has provided more favourable treatment to a third-State, only the obligations of State B are altered. The obligations of State A remain unchanged.

3 See, e.g., *Bayindir Insaat Turizm Ticaret Ve Sanayi AS v Islamic Republic of Pakistan*, ICSID Case No. ARB/03/29, Decision on Jurisdiction, paras 163–5, 14 November 2005, allowing the claimant to claim damages for violation of a BIT provision incorporated via an MFN clause, even where the claimant invoked the third-State provision after commencement of proceedings; Z. Douglas, 'The MFN Clause in Investment Arbitration: Treaty Interpretation Off the Rails', (2011) 2 J Int'l Disp Settlement 97, p. 108, stating that 'investment treaty tribunals have attempted to convert the fiction of automatic incorporation into a reality'; M.-F. Houde, 'Most-Favoured-Nation Treatment in International Investment Law', in Organisation for Economic Co-operation and Development, *International Investment Law: A Changing Landscape*, 2005, Paris: OECD, p. 142, referring to MFN clauses as 'ingenious legal shorthand to treaty process'; G. Schwarzenberger, 'The Most-Favoured Nation Standard in British State Practice', (1945) 22 Brit YB Int'l L 96, p. 104, 'The object of any attempt to give legal expression to the m.f.n. standard is to enable the beneficiary automatically to acquire the rights, present and future, granted by the promisor to any third-State'.

4 The 'right to claim' understanding of MFN obligations in international investment law has received recent support in academic commentary. See, e.g., Douglas, op. cit., n 3, p. 105, arguing that an MFN clause has no effect until a claim is made under it and 'does not, in truth, operate automatically to "incorporate" provisions of a third treaty so that all that remains for a tribunal to do is to interpret the amended text of the basic treaty'. Unfortunately, Douglas consistently confuses the 'instantaneous obligation' understanding of MFN clauses with the view that MFN clauses serve as a form of 'incorporation by reference'. Consequently, his argument does not really address the justifications behind adopting the 'instantaneous obligation' interpretation.

5 B. Kingsbury and S. Schill, 'Investor-State Arbitration as Governance: Fair and Equitable Treatment, Proportionality and the Emerging Global Administrative Law', New York

University School of Law, Public Law and Legal Theory Research Paper Series, Working Paper No. 09–46, 2009, p. 19, http://papers.ssrn.com/sol3/papers.cfm?abstract_id=1466980 (accessed 5 February 2013), noting that predictability is 'essential for Host States and foreign investors alike who need to know beforehand what kind of measures entail the international responsibility of the State'.

6 See, e.g., *Asian Agric Prods Ltd v Sri Lanka*, ICSID Case No. ARB/87/3, Final Award, para. 54, 27 June 1990, rejecting application of an MFN clause where it was unclear whether the treatment appealed to by the claimant was indeed more favourable than that delivered under the treaty containing the MFN clause.

7 It is worth emphasising that since the 'treatment' to which an MFN clause is applicable includes informal benefits provided by any level of government, rather than just benefits delivered via treaty, the current accessibility of information on treaty obligations does not mean that the monitoring costs involved would be relatively low.

8 For an interpretation of the operation of MFN clauses in accordance with the 'instantaneous obligation' understanding, see B. Coutain, 'The Unconditional Most-Favored-Nation Clause and the Maintenance of the Liberal Trade Regime in the Postwar 1870s', (2009) 63 Int'l Org 139, p. 147.

9 See, e.g., *MTD Equity Sdn Bhd & MTD Chile SA v Republic of Chile*, ICSID Case No. ARB/01/7, Award, paras 100–4, 197–206, 25 May 2004, (2005) 44 ILM 91, applying an MFN clause to expand the meaning of 'fair and equitable treatment' without requiring a claim by the claimant's Home State; *Bayindir Insaat Turizm Ticaret Ve Sanayi AS v Islamic Republic of Pakistan*, ICSID Case No. ARB/03/29, Decision on Jurisdiction, 14 November 2005, applying an MFN clause to incorporate a 'fair and equitable treatment' obligation into a treaty without requiring a claim by the claimant's Home State.

10 See, e.g., the statement by Ibrahim Shihata, Secretary-General of ICSID from 1983 to 1998, that ICSID was created 'to provide a forum for conflict resolution in a framework which carefully balances the interests and requirements of all the parties in-volved, and attempts in particular to "depoliticize" the settlement of investment disputes', I. Shihata, 'Towards a Greater Depoliticization of Investment Disputes: The Roles of ICSID and MIGA', (1986) 1 ICSID Rev Foreign Inv LJ 1, p. 4.

11 Indeed, in the early twentieth century the controversy concerned whether MFN clauses applied to future treatment, not pre-existing treatment. Committee of Experts for the Progressive Codification of International Law, Report of the Sub-Committee, *The Most-Favoured-Nation Clause*, League of Nations Doc C.205.M.79 1927 V (1927), reprinted in (1928) 22 Am J Int'l L (Special Supplement) 133, p. 140, 'Whether or not the clause applies to future as well as to past favours is much discussed by writers, although no actual case has been found in which the question was raised'; T. Barclay, 'Effect of "Most-Favored-Nation" Clause in Commercial Treaties', (1907) 17 Yale LJ 26, p. 31, noting the view of a prominent French commentator that an MFN clause 'must be considered as implying everything that existed at the moment when signed, but that it could not be considered to extend to anything later in date'.

12 VCLT, Arts 31–32, opened for signature 23 May 1969, 1155 UNTS 331, setting forth the rules of treaty interpretation, including the basic rule that a treaty must be interpreted according to the 'ordinary meaning to be given to the terms of the treaty in their context and in the light of its object and purpose'.

13 See, e.g., J. P. Sasse, *An Economic Analysis of Bilateral Investment Treaties*, 2011, Wiesbaden: Gabler Verlag, p. 47, 'Starting point for most tribunals is Article 31 of the Vienna Convention on the Law of Treaties'; S. W. Schill, 'Most-Favored-Nation Clauses as a Basis of Jurisdiction in Investment Treaty Arbitration: Arbitral Jurisprudence at a Crossroads', (2009) 10 J World Invest & Trade 189, pp. 205–6, criticising the interpretation of MFN clauses in accordance with the intentions of the Contracting Parties as inconsistent with the VCLT.

14 In support of a broad interpretation, see, for instance, E. Gaillard, 'International Arbitration Law: Establishing Jurisdiction Through a Most-Favored-Nation Clause', (2005) 233 NY LJ 1, p. 3. In support of a narrow interpretation, see, for instance, S. Vesel, 'Clearing

a Path Through a Tangled Jurisprudence: Most-Favored-Nation Clauses and Dispute Settlement Provisions in Bilateral Investment Treaties', (2007) 32 Yale J Int'l L 125, p. 175.

15 VCLT, Art. 31.

16 Ibid., Art. 32.

17 Ibid.

18 Ibid.

19 S. M. Schwebel, 'May Preparatory Work Be Used to Correct Rather than Confirm the "Clear" Meaning of a Treaty Provision?', in J. Makarczyk (ed.), *Theory of International Law at the Threshold of the 21st Century*, 1996, Leiden: Brill, pp. 541, 546; see also A. Aust, *Modern Treaty Law and Practice*, 2000, Cambridge: Cambridge University Press, p. 197. For the opposing view, see M. H. Arsanjani and W. M. Reisman, 'Interpreting Treaties for the Benefit of Third Parties: The "Salvors' Doctrine" and the Use of Legislative History in Investment Treaties', (2010) 104 Am J Int'l L 597, p. 597; U. Linderfalk, 'Is the Hierarchical Structure of Articles 31 and 32 of the Vienna Convention Real or Not? Interpreting the Rules of Interpretation', (2007) 54 Neth Int'l L Rev 133, p. 138.

20 *Contra* Report of the International Law Commission, 30th Session, 8 May–28 July 1978, UN Doc A/33/10 (1978), reprinted in [1978] 2 YB Int'l L Comm'n, pt 2, p. 8, UN Doc A/CN.4/SER.A/1978/Add.1, describing as 'obviously' true that MFN clauses apply to 'benefits extended to a third-State both before and after the entry into force of the treaty containing the clause'.

21 On the meaning of 'fair and equitable treatment' in international investment law, see C. Schreuer, 'Fair and Equitable Treatment in Arbitral Practice', (2005) 6 J World Invest & Trade 357, p. 357.

22 See also *ICS Inspection and Control Services Ltd (UK) v Republic of Argentina*, UNCITRAL, PCA Case No. 2010–19, Award on Jurisdiction, 10 February 2012, para. 317, http://italaw.com/documents/ICS_v_Argentina_AwardJurisdiction_10Feb2012_En.pdf (accessed 5 February 2013), rejecting application of an MFN clause to dispute resolution provisions as 'the 18-month litigation prerequisite would have been void *ab initio* – immediately superseded by means of the treaties' MFN clauses'. Unfortunately, the tribunal failed to address the complexities discussed in the remainder of this section, relying instead simply on the presumed understanding of the extent of the MFN clause on the part of one State party to the BIT. Such an approach, though, is inconsistent with basic rules of treaty interpretation, in which the subjective understanding of a single party cannot determine the meaning of a treaty provision. See, e.g., U. Linderfalk, *On the Interpretation of Treaties: The Modern International Law as Expressed in the 1969 Vienna Convention on the Law of Treaties*, 2007, Dordrecht: Springer, p. 205, '"[T]he object and purpose" of a treaty can hardly be anything other than the object and purpose, which the parties to the treaty intended it to have—or rather, more specifically, mutually intended it to have'.

23 See Chapter 6, section 3.1.

24 See Chapter 5, section 2.

25 Schwarzenberger, op. cit., n 3, p. 99, 'It is clear the m.f.n. clauses serve as an insurance against incompetent draftsmanship and lack of imagination on the part of those who are responsible for the conclusion of international treaties'.

26 United Nations Conference on Trade and Development, *The Role of International Investment Agreements in Attracting Foreign Direct Investment to Developing Countries*, UN Doc UNCTAD/DIAE/IA/2009/5, UN Sales No. E.09.II.D.20, 2009, Geneva: UNCTAD, p. xi, noting that international investment agreements are 'a key instrument in the strategies of most countries, in particular developing countries, to attract foreign investment'.

27 See, e.g., United Nations Conference on Trade and Development, Investment Instruments Online, http://www.unctadxi.org/templates/DocSearch____779.aspx (accessed 16 March 2012).

28 Importantly, though, this rationale only applies to BIT-based treatment, as information on other types of treatment of investors may be less easily accessed. See Chapter 6, n 7 and accompanying text.

29 The knowledge need only be attributed to the beneficiary, not to those who negotiated the treaty on its behalf.

30 See, e.g., *MTD Equity Sdn Bhd & MTD Chile SA v Chile*, ICSID Case No. ARB/01/7, Final Award, 25 May 2004, comparing the relevant provisions of the applicable Malaysia-Chile BIT with those of the Denmark-Chile and Croatia-Chile BITs.

31 J. W. Salacuse, 'Towards a Global Treaty on Foreign Investment: The Search for a Grand Bargain', in N. Horn and S. M. Kröll (eds), *Arbitrating Foreign Investment Disputes*, 2004, Alphen aan den Rijn: Kluwer Law International, pp. 51, 87,

> [F]rom the point of view of negotiation theory, the more issues that can be addressed in a multilateral negotiation the more trade-offs that the parties can devise. And the greater possible trade-offs that negotiating parties have, the more likely they are to find a basis for agreement.

32 That is, the package constituting only those provisions with which the dispute resolution provided was connected during negotiations, rather than the broader 'package' constituted by the entire treaty.

33 Of course, this argument only applies to subsequent adoptions of already-existing treatment, and the MFN clause would remain fully applicable to all subsequently adopted treaty provisions that did not mirror already-existing treatment.

34 An MFN clause may refer to 'investments' rather than 'investors,' or indeed may refer to both. However, to simplify the explanation being made here, only 'investors' will be used. Nonetheless, precisely the same argument as made in this section with respect to investors can be made with respect to investments.

35 See Chapter 6, sections 2.1–2.2.

36 The MFN clause may, for example, serve to preclude an investor's claim, if the investor is uncharacteristic of investors from its Home State, and the MFN clause has altered the terms of the Basic Treaty in a way that will benefit that larger class of investors.

37 See Chapter 5, n 48 and the accompanying text; see also *Rights of Nationals of the United States of America in Morocco (US v France)*, Judgment, 27 August 1952, [1952] ICJ 176, p. 192, and text accompanying Chapter 5, n 129.

7 Dispute resolution procedures and the favourability of treatment under a most-favoured nation clause

1 The original version of this chapter was co-authored with Madhu Agrawal.

2 *Emilio Agustín Maffezini v The Kingdom of Spain*, ICSID Case No. ARB/97/7.

3 See generally, supra pp. 82–87.

4 See, e.g. *Siemens v Argentina* (2004); *Gas Natural v Argentina* (2005); *Suez and Vivendi v Argentina* (2006).

5 *Salini v Jordan* (2004); *Plama v Bulgaria* (2005); *Berschader v Russian Federation* (2006); *Telenor v Hungary* (2006).

6 See *Anglo Iranian Oil Co (UK v Iran)*, Judgment on Jurisdiction, 22 July 1952, [1952] ICJ 93; *Rights of Nationals of the United States of America in Morocco (US v France)*, Judgment, 27 August 1952, [1952] ICJ 176; *Ambatielos Claim (Greece v UK)* [1956] 12 RIAA 83.

7 See *Anglo-Iranian Oil Co*, ibid. (case resolved on the ground that an MFN clause cannot change the terms of a treaty other than the one in which it is included); *Rights of Nationals of the United States of America in Morocco*, ibid. (case resolved on the ground that the third-State treatment claimed was no longer being delivered by the Host State); *Ambatielos*, ibid. (MFN clauses can apply to issues regarding 'the administration of justice', but in so far as this concerns substantive promises relating to the standards of justice to be applied in dispute resolution proceedings).

8 *Maffezini*, above, n 2, Award on the Merits, 13 November 2000, para. 39.

9 Ibid., paras 44–6.
10 *Maffezini*, above, n 2, Decision of the Tribunal on Objections to Jurisdiction, 25 January 2000, para. 19.
11 Ibid., paras 20, 26.
12 Ibid., para. 39.
13 Ibid., para. 40.
14 L. Reed, J. Paulsson and N. Blackaby, *Guide to ICSID Arbitration*, 2011, p. 85 ('*Maffezini v Spain* was the first ICSID treaty case to consider the question of MFN treatment for procedural rights').
15 *Maffezini v Spain*, (Decision on Objections to Jurisdiction 2000), at ¶38.
16 Ibid., para. 42.
17 Ibid., paras 43–50.
18 *Maffezini v Spain*, (Decision on Objections to Jurisdiction 2000), at ¶55.
19 To take the final step necessary to reach its conclusion, then, the tribunal invoked what it argued to be the centrality of dispute resolution procedures to the protection of the substantive rights included in investment treaties. *Maffezini*, above, n 2, Decision of the Tribunal on Objections to Jurisdiction, 25 January 2000, para. 54. That is, because '[i]nternational arbitration and other dispute settlement arrangements ... are essential ... to the protection of the rights envisaged under [investment] treaties', an MFN clause that includes an unrestricted promise not to provide more favourable treatment to investors from any third-State must be understood as applying to dispute resolution procedures as well as to the substantive treaty provisions those procedures are designed to protect.
20 *Siemens AG v The Argentine Republic*, ICSID case No. ARB/02/8. Decision on Jurisdiction, (3 August 2001), para. 102:

> the Tribunal finds that the Treaty itself, together with so many other treaties of investment protection, has as a distinctive feature special dispute settlement mechanisms not normally open to investors. Access to these mechanisms is part of the protection offered under the Treaty. It is part of the treatment of foreign investors and investments and of the advantages accessible through a MFN clause;

Gas Natural SDG, S. A. v Argentina, ICSID case No. ARB/03/10, Decision of the Tribunal on Preliminary Questions on Jurisdiction (17 June 2005), para. 31:

> The Tribunal holds that provision for international investor-state arbitration in bilateral investment treaties is a significant substantive incentive and protection for foreign investors; further, that access to such arbitration only after resort to national courts and an eighteen-month waiting period is a less favorable degree of protection than access to arbitration immediately upon expiration of the negotiation period;

Suez Sociedad General de Aguas de Barcelona, S. A. and Vivendi Universal S. A. v The Argentine Republic and *Anglian Water Group Ltd. v The Argentine Republic*, ICSID case No. ARB/03/19, Decision on Jurisdiction (3 August 2006), para. 57:

> From the point of view of the promotion and protection of investments, the stated purposes of the Argentina-Spain BIT, dispute settlement is as important as other matters governed by the BIT and is an integral part of the investment protection regime that two sovereign states, Argentina and Spain, have agreed upon;

National Grid Plc. v The Argentine Republic, Decision on Jurisdiction (20 June 2006), para. 70: 'International arbitration and other dispute settlement arrangements ... are essential, however, to the protection of the rights envisaged under the pertinent treaties; they are also closely linked to the material aspects of the treatment accorded' (quoting *Maffezini*, above, n 2, Decision of the Tribunal on Objections to Jurisdiction, 25 January 2000, para. 19).

21 *Siemens*, ibid., para. 102 (dispute resolution procedures constitute part of the 'treatment' provided to investors by the Host State); *Gas Natural*, ibid., para. 31 (dispute resolution procedures are part of the 'bundle of protections' granted to investors by Host States); *Suez*, ibid., para. 55 (dispute resolution procedures constitute part of the 'treatment' provided to investors by the Host State); *National Grid*, ibid., para. 93 (dispute resolution procedures constitute part of the 'treatment' provided to investors by the Host State).

22 *Maffezini v Spain*, (Decision on Objections to Jurisdiction 2000), at ¶62–63.

23 Vienna Convention on the Law of Treaties, Art. 31(1).

24 See, e.g. *Oxford English Dictionary*: 'Conduct, behaviour; action or behaviour towards a person'.

25 Importantly, this is different to saying that the treaty actually creates rights in the investor.

26 That is, either to invest, or to alter the manner in which they invest.

27 Importantly, this is not to say that it is directed at maximising the profitability of an investment, as profitability is merely one possible measure of the success of an investment. Long-term viability might, for example, be regarded as more important than short-term profitability where the investment is being approached as an initial 'beachhead' for further projects in the Host State.

28 There may be no competitors benefiting from the third-State treaty, so this is a theoretical investigation, rather than an empirical one.

29 The use of the term'reasonable' is important here, as it emphasises that what is in question is the views that a reasonable Home State investor would have, not the views that the specific investor bringing the claim happened to have.

30 This increase occuring because of the State's consistent behaviour in accordance with its promise.

31 As outlined above, n 20, the *Maffezini* stream of cases depended upon an unanalysed assumption that international investment arbitration was more favourable than domestic courts. However, once it is recognised that the central consideration in determining the 'favourability' of substantive treatment is the likelihood that the substantive promise will be fulfilled, it is clear that such a presumption is simply unwarranted. After all, an effective domestic court system will have the same effect on the competitive position of a foreign investor as would international investment arbitration. However, mere equality does not suffice to ground the operation of an MFN clause. The treatment provided to the third-State must be *better* than that promised under the Basic Treaty. If both procedures would effectively enforce the rights granted in the treaty, then the original procedure listed in the Basic Treaty must remain in effect. Consequently, any evaluation of substantive treaty promises is an inherently fact-intensive one, requiring a factual investigation of the ability of the procedures in the Basic Treaty to guarantee the substantive rights promised in the BIT, and a comparison with the effectiveness of investor-State arbitration to do the same. Tribunals cannot simply rely upon a blunt assertion that investor-State arbitration will effectively enforce the substantive promises made in the treaty.

32 The mere inclusion in a treaty of, for example, a promise not to expropriate without appropriate compensation is certainly more favourable than the absence of such a promise. However, the inclusion of such a promise backed up by effective dispute resolution procedures is clearly more favourable than the inclusion of that promise backed up by less effective dispute resolution procedures.

33 For the classical statement of this view see *Plama v Bulgaria*, (Decision on Jurisdiction 2005), at ¶209.

34 See, e.g. *Canada – Certain Measures Affecting the Automotive Industry*, WT/DS139/R, WT/DS142/R, 11 February 2000.

35 For example, if there is currently discrimination against investors from one State but not the other.

36 *Societe Generale v Dominican Republic*, (Objections to Jurisdiction 2008).

37 *Societe Generale v Dominican Republic*, (Objections to Jurisdiction 2008), at ¶¶40–41.

38 *Plama Consortium Limited v Republic of Bulgaria*, ICSID Case No. ARB/03/24.
39 Ibid., paras 198, 227.
40 *ICS Inspection and Control Services Limited (United Kingdom) v The Republic of Argentina*, UNCITRAL, PCA Case No. 2010–19.
41 While the *ICS* tribunal never uses the phrase 'clear and unambiguous' in its own reasoning, it both holds that 'a State's consent to arbitration shall not be presumed in the face of ambiguity' (ibid., para. 280) and explicitly embraces the reasoning adopted by the *Plama* tribunal (ibid., para. 282).
42 See e.g. S.W. Schill, 'Multilateralizing Investment Treaties Through Most-Favoured Nation Clauses', 2009 27 Berkeley J Int'l L, 496, 558–600.
43 Ibid., para. 278.
44 Ibid., paras 326–7.
45 Ibid., para. 278.
46 Ibid., para. 279.
47 For similar reasoning see *Anglo-Iranian Oil Co*, above, n 6 (rejecting the relevance of an MFN clause in a treaty that was not the document that included Iran's consent to the Court's jurisdiction).

For Product Safety Concerns and Information please contact our EU representative GPSR@taylorandfrancis.com
Taylor & Francis Verlag GmbH, Kaufingerstraße 24, 80331 München, Germany

www.ingramcontent.com/pod-product-compliance
Ingram Content Group UK Ltd.
Pitfield, Milton Keynes, MK11 3LW, UK
UKHW020138200926
475702UK00005B/811
9780415579858